Orlando and Disney World
A TravelVenture Guide
Third Edition

Other books by Bob Martin
Fly There For Less: How to Save Money Flying Worldwide

Orlando and Disney World
A TravelVenture Guide
Third Edition

Bob Martin

TeakWood Press

Copyright © 1991 by Bob Martin

All rights reserved. No part of this book may be reproduced or utilized in any form by any means, electronic, or mechanical, including photocopying, recording or by any information storage and retrieval system, without permission in writing from the publisher, except by a reviewer, who may quote brief passages in a review.

Walt Disney World is a registered trademark of The Walt Disney Co. The use of this and any other trademarked names is only in an editorial fashion with no intention of infringement of the trademark.

TravelVenture is a trademark of TeakWood Press.

Published by
TeakWood Press
160 Fiesta Drive
Kissimmee, Florida 34743
407-348-7330
Order Desk: 800-654-0403

Cover design by Paul LiCalsi, L&L Graphics
Printed in the United States of America

Library of Congress Cataloging-in-Publication Data
Martin, Bob, 1939-
   Orlando and Disney World : a travelVenture guide / Bob Martin. -- 3rd ed.
     p.   cm.
   Includes index.
   ISBN 0-937281-05-0 (pbk.) : $9.95
   1. Orlando Region (Fla.)--Description and travel--Guide-books.
2. Family recreation--Florida--Orlando Region--Guide-books. 3. Walt Disney World (Fla.)--Guide-books. I. Title.
F319.07M37 1991   90-25767
917.59'24--dc20   CIP

*To Bev,
without you it would still be just a dream*

Contents

Introduction 1
    Background 3
    How to use this guidebook 4
    Prices and changes 5

Before you go 6
    Weather 6
    What to wear 6
    When to go 7
    Getting there 7
    Additional information 10

TravelPlanner: attractions 12
    Attractions by location 12
    Attractions by type and interest 13
    Attractions by time to see 15

Attractions 17
    Albin Polasek Galleries 17
    Charles Hosmer Morse Museum of American Art 18
    Cornell Fine Arts Center 20
    Discovery Island 21
    Disney Learning Adventures 22
    Disney-MGM Studios Theme Park 23

Downtown Orlando Walking Tour 38
Elvis Presley Museums 47
Epcot Center 49
Flying Tigers Warbird Air Museum 73
Gatorland Zoo 75
Kissimmee Livestock Market 77
Leu Gardens and Leu House Museum 78
Magic Kingdom 81
Medieval Life 97
Mystery Fun House 98
Orange County Historical Museum 99
Orlando Museum of Art 101
Orlando Science Center 102
The Potter Train Museum 103
River Country 104
Scenic Boat Tour 105
Sea World 107
The Sinkhole 114
Tupperware International Headquarters 117
Typhoon Lagoon 118
Universal Studios Florida 120
Water Mania 127
Wet 'n Wild 128
Wonders of Walt Disney World 130
Xanadu 131

TravelPlanner: nightlife 133
Nightlife by location 133
Nightlife by type 134

Nightlife 135
Arabian Nights 135
Broadway at the Top 136
Church Street Station 137
Fort Liberty Wild West Dinner Show & Trading Post 138
Hoop-Dee-Doo Musical Revue 140
King Henry's Feast 140
Little Darlin's Rock 'n' Roll Palace 141

 Mardi Gras 143
 Mark Two Dinner Theater 143
 Medieval Times 144
 The Plantation Dinner Theater 145
 Pleasure Island 146
 Polynesian Luau Review 148

TravelPlanner: shopping 149
 Shopping by location 149
 Shopping by type 150

Shopping 151

TravelPlanner: dining 163
 Restaurants by location 163
 Restaurants by cuisine 165

Dining 168

TravelPlanner: lodging 215
 Lodging by location 215
 Lodging by cost 216

Lodging 219

Index 249

Introduction

So, you're going to Disney World. Good choice. Orlando and Disney World make up one of the most popular travel destinations in the United States. When Walt Disney chose a site near Orlando on which to build Disney World, this once-rural area shot up into a destination Goliath. And not without reason. Orlando and Disney World provide wholesome fun that has wide appeal. Of course the kids enjoy themselves, but so do grown ups. Adult visitors outnumber children four to one. And if you're honeymoon bound, Disney World has become the world's leading honeymoon destination.

Disney World brings to mind the fantasy of the Magic Kingdom and images of Mickey Mouse, Tinkerbell, and a fairy-tale castle. But the Magic Kingdom is just one part of Disney's world. You can also take in the glamour of movie making, visit a world's fair, and travel to 10 foreign countries. You'll find plush hotels, efficiency apartments, and a shopping village. You can enjoy swimming, boating, snorkeling, tennis, championship golf courses, and lakeside white-sand beaches. And you can fill up on fast food, relax in full-service eateries, or enjoy international dining.

Beyond Disney World, Orlando itself offers some high-powered attractions, including Sea World's marine mammals, Universal Studios Florida, family-style nightlife, unique art treasures,

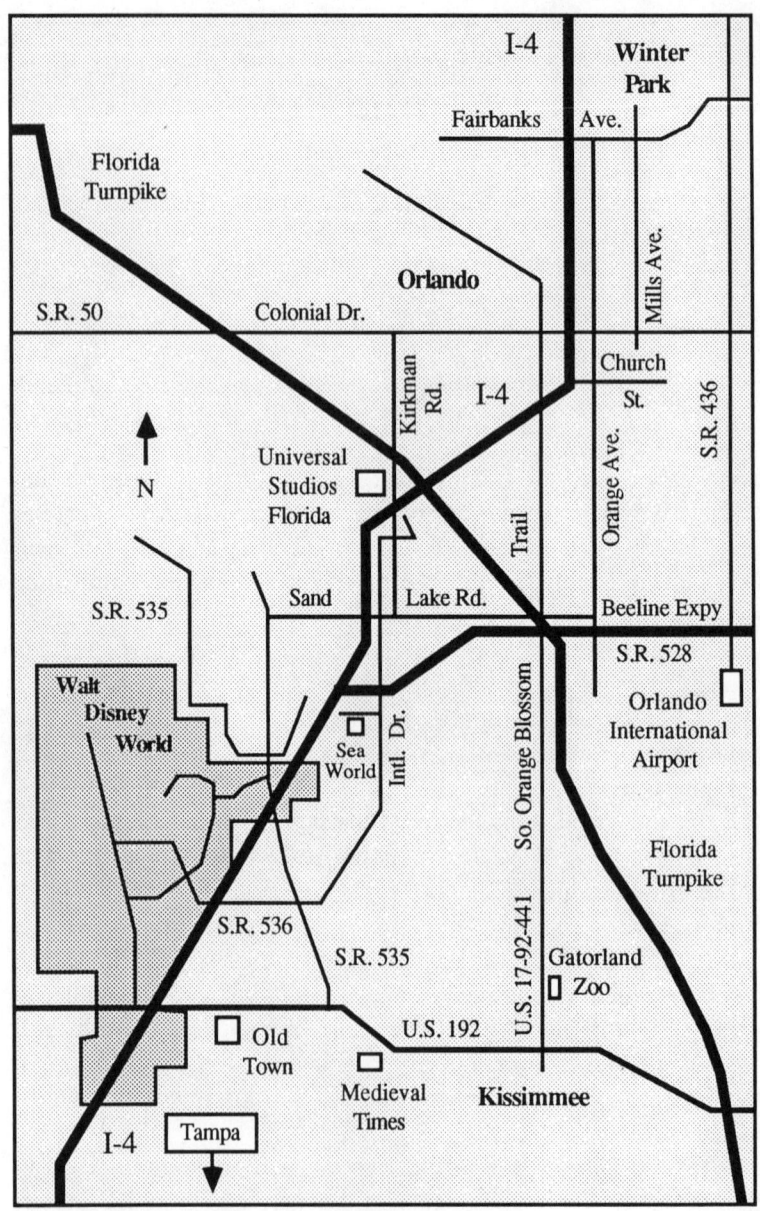

Orlando and Disney World

and even a bit of history. Orlando's shopping is varied and plentiful, ranging from boutiques to factory outlets, from festival marketplaces to themed malls. And the area provides a range of accommodations to fit practically any budget or taste.

Background

Walt Disney World, which occupies 43 square miles southwest of Orlando, opened in 1971. The main focus of early Disney World was the Magic Kingdom, a theme park with rides and attractions divided into six "lands" — Main Street, U.S.A.; Adventureland; Frontierland; Liberty Square; Fantasyland; and Tomorrowland. Early Disney World also featured Discovery Island (a zoological park), River Country (a water park), and a shopping village. And Disney offered its own accommodations in upscale hotels, furnished villas, and a campground.

In 1982 Disney World opened Epcot Center, its first large-scale expansion. Although twice the size of the Magic Kingdom, Epcot contains just two theme areas — Future World and World Showcase. Epcot takes a world's fair approach to its attractions. And since opening, Epcot has steadily added new pavilions to both Future World and the World Showcase.

In recent years Disney World has gone on a building spree. In 1988 Disney opened two new hotels (the Grand Floridian and the Caribbean Beach Resort) and the first new land in the Magic Kingdom (Mickey's Starland). In 1989, three large-scale attractions came on line with the opening of the Disney-MGM Studios (a theme park that includes a working movie-television studio tour), Pleasure Island (a nighttime entertainment complex), and Typhoon Lagoon (Disney calls it the world's largest water park). And 1990 saw the opening of four additional Disney World hotels — the Dolphin, the Swan, the Beach Club, and the Yacht Club.

As Disney World grew, so did Orlando. Competing attractions were drawn to the area, including Universal Studios Florida which opened in 1990. To accommodate the increasing number of visitors, hotel growth mushroomed with lodgings running from small "Mom and Pop" motels to luxury high-rises. A family-style nightlife sprang up offering a variety of unique dinner attractions. And visitors began to notice the native charms of the Orlando area itself. Among them, the world's largest collection of Tiffany stained glass and an inviting downtown that blends modern high-rises with historic buildings from Orlando's past.

Orlando and Disney World continue to grow. New attractions, accommodations, restaurants, and places to shop seem to sprout faster than flowers in a spring garden. And it becomes increasingly difficult to pick and choose and decide what to fit into your schedule. *Orlando and Disney World: A TravelVenture Guide* will help you make those decisions.

How to use this guidebook

When you venture from home to explore the new or to rediscover the old, you need information. *Orlando and Disney World* puts at your fingertips the myriad details that will make your visit run smoothly.

The guide is organized so you can quickly find facts, descriptions of what to expect, and tips from someone who has ventured there before you. Each section of *Orlando and Disney World* opens with a TravelPlanner directory. These directories list attractions by location, type, and time required to see them; shops and malls by location and type; restaurants by location and cuisine; and hotels by location and cost.

The main entry for each attraction, shop, restaurant or hotel begins with the TravelFacts you need — addresses, map references, telephone numbers, hours of operation, prices, how long it will take to see an attraction, what not to miss, restaurant menu summaries, plus other important details. "What to expect" sections then provide background and descriptive information. And to make getting around easy, the guide's 55 simplified maps show the locations of hotels, restaurants, shops, and attractions.

Say, for example, you are staying in the Kissimmee area and

want to take in a nearby attraction. Use the table of contents to locate the "TravelPlanner: attractions" which shows what's available around Kissimmee. Then turning to the pages indicated in the TravelPlanner, you can choose based on each attraction's TravelFacts and "what to expect" section.

If you are interested in a particular subject, perhaps botanical gardens or life in Florida, the TravelPlanner shows which attractions reflect your interests. The TravelPlanners will also help you find accommodations that fit your budget, restaurants that suit your tastes, shops that satisfy your desires, and nightlife that suits your style. Browse through these TravelPlanners and use them to build your itinerary.

Prices and changes

All prices are given in exact dollars and cents and have been verified as close to press time as possible. But prices change. And by the time you read this guide, some prices will undoubtedly be inaccurate. Therefore, treat them only as close approximations. Use them to get a good idea of what your costs will be. But if knowing an exact price is crucial, verify it by calling the telephone number listed in the TravelFacts.

In addition to prices, the other information in this guidebook has also been verified before going to press. But information, too, can change. Use the telephone numbers listed to confirm any information that is important to the success of your visit.

Before you go

Weather

During spring and fall expect warm days — temperatures in the 80s — and cool nights. The weeks just before and just after summer, however, can be hot and humid.

Summer temperatures hover in the low to mid-90s daytime, mid-70s at night. The humidity climbs in early June and doesn't break until well into October. Summer days are also typified by heavy thunder showers in late afternoon and early evening.

TravelVenture tip: For a summer visit bring along a lightweight rain poncho. The late-afternoon showers will greatly thin out crowds at the attractions, but your poncho will let you continue touring.

Winter daytime temperatures generally run in the 70s. Several times each winter, however, you can count on an Arctic air mass to sweep the country and plunge its icy fingers into Florida. These cold snaps can hold the thermometer to a high in the 50s or 60s and push nighttime temperatures below freezing.

What to wear

Dress in Orlando is casual and dictated by the weather. Shorts are acceptable for attraction touring. And during summer shorts are your best bet for beating the heat. You'll be doing plenty of walking, so you'll also need comfortable, broken-in footwear. Evening dress-up normally calls for slacks and shirt or blouse. Unless you're on business, jacket and tie or formal wear for women will rarely be needed.

For a winter trip, you can pack shorts and a bathing suit, but jackets and sweaters are also essential. When a cold spell makes an appearance, you'll need warm clothing.

When to go

Best months for a visit to Orlando and Disney World are early May, late October, November (except Thanksgiving weekend), and the first three weeks of December. The weather should be pleasant and the crowds thinner. Late May, September, early to mid-October, and January run a close second. You'll also find thinner crowds during these months, but late May, September, and early October tend to be hot. In January you run the risk of a cold snap.

Orlando and Disney World have two high seasons. One runs from mid-February through April, the other mid-June through August. During a high-season visit expect large crowds and long lines at attractions. Ultra-high seasons occur during Easter and Christmas. If at all possible, avoid an Easter-week or Christmas-week visit.

Getting there

Airlines: Among the airlines flying into the modern Orlando International Airport are: American, Bahamasair, British Airways, Canadian, Continental, Delta, Eastern, Icelandair, KLM Royal Dutch Airlines, LAV, Mexicana, Midway, Northwest, Pan American, Transbrasil, TWA, United, and USAir.

In the airport's main terminal, reached after a short tram ride from the gates, you'll find an information kiosk, as well as kiosks providing travel agency services, Disney World information, and Sea World information. The terminal also houses a bank, restaurants, car rental counters, and shops — including a bookstore and camera store.

The airport lies southeast of Orlando. Disney World and the main lodging and attractions areas are southwest of Orlando. Airport ground transportation, located just outside the baggage claim area, includes metered taxis and multi-passenger vans. Fares are posted on the outside walls near each exit door. To reach the attractions areas in a cab will cost anywhere from $20 to $34, depending on your destination. Fares to Disney World are at the high end of the range. Vans provide frequent shuttle service at fares ranging from $10 to $18 adults, $6 to $10 for children.

Amtrak: The *Silver Meteor* and *Silver Star* both make daily runs along the East Coast between New York and Orlando. Amtrak trains from Boston, Montreal, and Chicago connect with the *Silver Meteor* and the *Silver Star* at New York, Philadelphia, and Washington. Amtrak's *Auto Train* runs between Lorton, Virginia, near Washington, D.C., and Sanford, Florida, north of Orlando. The *Auto Train* lets you take your car on board with you.

If you will be lodging in downtown Orlando or the International Drive area, ride the train to the Amtrak station in Orlando. But use the Amtrak station in Kissimmee if you will be staying at Disney World, Lake Buena Vista, or in the Kissimmee-U.S. 192 area. The Kissimmee station will put you closer to these destinations. For details on rail service to Orlando-Kissimmee, call Amtrak toll-free at 800-872-7245.

Bus: Greyhound-Trailways bus line serves the Orlando area. As with the Amtrak stations, use the Orlando bus station for downtown Orlando and International Drive-area destinations. For Disney World, Lake Buena Vista, or Kissimmee-U.S. 192 destinations, ride the bus to Kissimmee.

Car: Travelers on the interstate system will head down the Florida peninsula on either I-75 or I-95. On I-95, pick up I-4 west at Daytona. Interstate 4 slices through Orlando and will take you to the main lodging and attractions areas southwest of the city.

To reach Orlando and Disney World from I-75, exit the interstate at the Florida Turnpike, a toll road. Turnpike exit 259 connects with I-4 just south of Orlando. When leaving the turnpike, take I-4 west to reach the lodging and attractions areas. Interstate 4 east leads to downtown Orlando.

TravelVenture tip: Disney maintains an information center alongside I-75 in Ocala, Florida, about 70 miles north of Orlando. You can buy Disney World tickets and passports, make Disney hotel reservations, or get additional information about Disney World.

Car rental: If your travel venture will be confined to lodging at Disney World and visiting only Disney attractions, you can easily get along without a car. Disney provides a fine transportation system that uses buses, boats, trams, and a monorail train to reach all corners of Disney World.

To get the most out of your visit to the world beyond Disney, however, you'll want a car. Competition between Orlando car rental firms is keen, and you can count on getting better rates than in most other areas of the country. Be aware, though, that advertised car rental rates are not likely to resemble your bottom-line cost. This situation is not unique to Orlando, but is typical of the car rental industry nationwide. When shopping for a car rental, determine and compare any additional costs. These could include: a mileage fee, a Collision Damage Waiver charge, a fueling-service charge, or a drop-off charge if you don't return the car to the same location from which you rented it.

Put some of these firms on your shopping list — all have counters on the ground floor of Orlando International Airport.

- Avis: 800-331-1212, (407) 851-7600.
- Budget: 800-527-0700, (407) 850-6700.
- Dollar: 800-421-6868, (407) 851-3232.
- Hertz: 800-654-3131, (407) 859-8400.
- National: 800-227-7368, (407) 855-4170.
- Superior: 800-237-8106, (407) 857-2023.

You can also check a few of these companies, which are located near the airport. They'll pick you up and bring you to their offices. If you don't already have a reservation, or to notify them of your arrival, you'll find direct telephone lines to these firms on consoles at the airport's ground-floor exits.

- American International: 800-527-0202, (407) 851-6910.
- Payless: 800-729-5377, (407) 825-4400.
- Thrifty: 800-367-2277, (407) 380-1002.
- Value: 800-327-2501, (407) 851-4790.

Additional information

As you travel around Orlando's tourist areas you'll spot numerous signs declaring the availability of tourist information. Many of these information centers, even though labeled "official," are operated by business establishments and time share sales organizations. You'll find the most reliable information, however, in the following tourist bureau information centers:

• Kissimmee-St. Cloud Convention and Visitors Bureau, 5260 W. Bronson Hwy. (U.S. 192), Kissimmee 34746, telephone (407) 396-2040. Hours: 8:30 A.M. to 10 P.M. Located at the Fort Liberty attraction (free access).

• Kissimmee-St. Cloud Convention and Visitors Bureau, 1925 E. Bronson Hwy. (U.S. 192), Kissimmee 34744, telephone (407) 847-5000. Hours: 8 A.M. to 6 P.M. Located east of Kissimmee.

• Orlando/Orange County Convention & Visitors Bureau, 8445 International Dr., Orlando 32819, telephone (407) 363-5871. Hours: 8 A.M. to 8 P.M. Located in the Mercado shopping center.

To request information before your arrival, you can write or telephone:

• Kissimmee-St. Cloud Convention and Visitors Bureau, P.O. Box 422007, Kissimmee, FL 34742-2007. (Telephone 800-327-9159, in Florida 800-432-9199.)

- Orlando/Orange County Convention & Visitors Bureau, 7208 Sand Lake Rd., Suite 300, Orlando, FL 32819. (Telephone 407-363-5800.)

- Walt Disney World Co., P.O. Box 10,040, Lake Buena Vista, FL 32830-0040. (Telephone 407-824-4321.)

TravelPlanner: attractions

Attractions by location

Disney World
Discovery Island 21
Disney Learning Adventures 22
Disney-MGM Studios Theme Park 23
Epcot Center 49
Magic Kingdom 81
River Country 104
Typhoon Lagoon 118
Wonders of Walt Disney World 130

International Drive area
Elvis Presley Museums 47
Mystery Fun House 98
Sea World 107
Universal Studios Florida 120
Wet 'n Wild 128

Kissimmee area
Elvis Presley Museums 47
Flying Tigers Warbird Air Museum 73
Gatorland Zoo 75
Kissimmee Livestock Market 77
Medieval Life 97

The Potter Train Museum 103
Tupperware International Headquarters 117
Water Mania 127
Xanadu 131

Orlando central

Leu Gardens and Leu House Museum 78
Orange County Historical Museum 99
Orlando Museum of Art 101
Orlando Science Center 102

Orlando downtown

Downtown Orlando Walking Tour 38

Winter Park

Albin Polasek Galleries 17
Charles Hosmer Morse Museum of American Art 18
Cornell Fine Arts Center 20
Scenic Boat Tour 105
The Sinkhole 114

Attractions by type and interest

Amusement and theme attractions

Disney-MGM Studios Theme Park 23
Epcot Center 49
Magic Kingdom 81
Medieval Life 97
Mystery Fun House 98
Sea World 107
Universal Studios Florida 120

Animals/Birds/Reptiles

Discovery Island 21
Gatorland Zoo 75

Kissimmee Livestock Market 77
Medieval Life 97
Sea World 107
Wonders of Walt Disney World 130

Architecture

Disney Learning Adventures 22
Disney-MGM Studios Theme Park 23
Downtown Orlando Walking Tour 38
Epcot Center (World Showcase) 49
Leu Gardens and Leu House Museum 78
Medieval Life 97
Wonders of Walt Disney World 130
Xanadu 131

Art galleries

Albin Polasek Galleries 17
Charles Hosmer Morse Museum of American Art 18
Cornell Fine Arts Center 20
Disney Learning Adventures 22
Epcot Center (World Showcase) 49
Orlando Museum of Art 101

Botanical gardens

Discovery Island 21
Disney Learning Adventures 22
Leu Gardens and Leu House Museum 78
Wonders of Walt Disney World 130

Florida life

Downtown Orlando Walking Tour 38
Gatorland Zoo 75
Kissimmee Livestock Market 77
Leu Gardens and Leu House Museum 78
Orange County Historical Museum 99
Scenic Boat Tour 105
The Sinkhole 114
Wonders of Walt Disney World 130

Museums

Disney Learning Adventures 22
Elvis Presley Museums 47
Epcot Center (World Showcase) 49
Flying Tigers Warbird Air Museum 73
Leu Gardens and Leu House Museum 78
Orange County Historical Museum 99
Orlando Science Center 102
The Potter Train Museum 103
Tupperware International Headquarters 117

Water parks

River Country 104
Typhoon Lagoon 118
Water Mania 127
Wet 'n Wild 128

Attractions by time to see

2 Days

Epcot Center 49
Magic Kingdom 81

1 Day

Universal Studios Florida 120

8 Hours

Disney-MGM Studios Theme Park 23
Sea World 107

7 Hours

Wonders of Walt Disney World 130

4 Hours

Disney Learning Adventures 22

River Country 104
Typhoon Lagoon 118
Water Mania 127
Wet 'n Wild 128

3 Hours

Leu Gardens and Leu House Museum 78
Orlando Science Center 102

2 Hours

Albin Polasek Galleries 17
Charles Hosmer Morse Museum of American Art 18
Cornell Fine Arts Center 20
Discovery Island 21
Downtown Orlando Waking Tour 38
Gatorland Zoo 75
Medieval Life 97
Orlando Museum of Art 101

1 Hour or less

Elvis Presley Museums 47
Flying Tigers Warbird Air Museum 73
Kissimmee Livestock Market 77
Mystery Fun House 98
Orange County Historical Museum 99
The Potter Train Museum 103
Scenic Boat Tour 105
The Sinkhole 114
Tupperware International Headquarters 117
Xanadu 131

Attractions

Albin Polasek Galleries

TravelFacts

Location: 633 Osceola Ave., Winter Park 32789.
Map: Page 20.
Telephone: (407) 647-6294.
Hours: 10 A.M. to noon and 1 P.M. to 4 P.M. Wednesday through Saturday, 2 P.M. to 4 P.M. Sunday. Closed Monday and Tuesday and from July 1 to October 1.
Time to see: 1 to 2 hours.
Price: Free.

What to expect: an interesting collection of sculptures and paintings. The works of Albin Polasek are not spotlighted in a white-walled exhibition hall. Rather, they're on display in and around Polasek's lakeside Mediterranean-style home.

Entering the grounds, Polasek's work greets you even before you get to the galleries. A 15-foot statue of a man rises from a block of stone encasing his lower legs. He holds a mallet in his fist, his muscular arm upraised, ready to again chisel away at the stone block. The sculpture is titled *Man Carving his Own Destiny*.

Polasek was born in Czechoslovakia in 1879 and immigrated to the United States when he was 22. Already an accomplished sculptor, he earned his living during his first years in the United States by carving religious figures for altars. Polasek later headed the Department of Sculpture at the Chicago Art Institute, and it was in Chicago that he created much of his work.

By the time he retired in 1950, Polasek sculptures were on display around the country in gardens, cemeteries, and buildings — including St. Cecelia Cathedral in Omaha, Nebraska. Polasek moved to Winter Park and brought many of his sculptures and paintings with him. Although retired, he continued to work at a studio in his home until his death in 1965 at age 86.

When you visit the home, you'll be greeted at the door by a guide who takes you on a tour of Polasek's studio, two galleries, and a chapel. The guide is an enthusiastic expert on Polasek and his works. The galleries are small, and you can't walk completely around the statues. So she turns some of the smaller works for you. She points out composition details. She shows where to touch the figures to get a feel for the artistry that went into their making.

One work on display is a Nativity scene with more than two-dozen 8-inch wooden figures that Polasek carved when he was 13. He painted the figures with pigments he ground himself.

In addition to Polasek's work, the galleries and studio contain art works from the sculptor's private collection. This small collection itself would make the Polasek Galleries worth visiting — a couple of paintings by Rubens, a 16th-century icon, 400- and 500-year-old Flemish, French, and Chinese tapestries, European furniture, and a small Tiffany window.

After the tour you can view more Polasek sculptures as you wander through the home's three-acre shaded garden on the shore of Lake Osceola.

Charles Hosmer Morse Museum of American Art

TravelFacts

| *Location:* 133 E. Welbourne Ave., Winter Park 32789, one block east of

Park Avenue.
Map: Page 20.
Telephone: (407) 644-3686.
Hours: 9:30 A.M. to 4 P.M. Tuesday through Saturday, 1 P.M. to 4 P.M. Sunday. Closed Monday and holidays.
Time to see: 1 to 1.5 hours.
Price: $2.50 adults, $1 students and children.
• A small souvenir shop sits off the main gallery.
• A tour guide is available for groups of 12 or more.

What to expect: the world's finest collection of art nouveau works by Louis Comfort Tiffany. Treasure is usually associated with pirates and shipwrecks. But there's treasure right in the heart of the landlocked Orlando suburb of Winter Park — the treasures created by Tiffany.

Although most renowned for his stained glass windows and lamp shades, Tiffany also turned out blown glass vases, pottery, paintings, and even furniture from his home and studio on Long Island, New York.

Tiffany, who died in 1933, made most of his work with the intention to sell it to others. But the Morse collection contains the bulk of the work Tiffany made for himself, including furniture for his Long Island home.

But why is such a treasure in Winter Park, Florida, and not New York's Metropolitan Museum of Art or Washington's Smithsonian Institution? When fire destroyed Tiffany's estate in 1957, Hugh McKean, a Winter Park art collector and former Tiffany student, traveled to Long Island with his wife, Jeannette, to salvage what they could from the rubble. And salvage they did. Today, the results of their efforts have turned into a major portion of the museum's collection of some 4,000 pieces.

However, just a few hundred pieces can be exhibited at any one time, since the Morse Museum is housed in only a modest, 9,000-square-foot building. The museum also exhibits the works of other art nouveau artists and has an important collection of American art pottery.

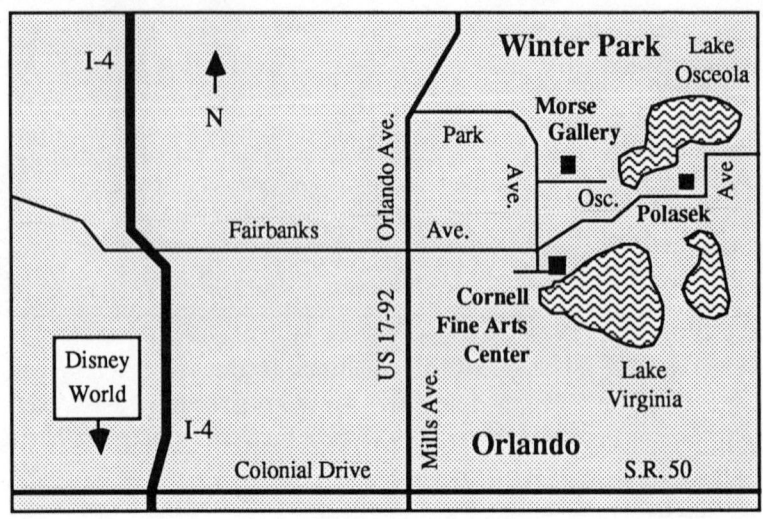

Polasek, Morse, and Cornell Galleries

Cornell Fine Arts Center

TravelFacts

Location: Rollins College Campus, Winter Park 32789.
Map: Page 20.
Telephone: (407) 646-2526.
Hours: 10 A.M. to 5 P.M. Tuesday through Friday, 1 P.M. to 5 P.M. Saturday and Sunday. Closed Monday.
Time to see: 1 to 1.5 hours.
Price: Free.

What to expect: a small but high-quality art museum. The neat, Mediterranean-style building on the campus of Rollins College contains three galleries. These offer both visiting shows and changing exhibits from the museum's permanent collection of 19-century American and European paintings.

Discovery Island

TravelFacts

> *Location:* Walt Disney World, P.O. Box 10,000, Lake Buena Vista 32830-1000, in Bay Lake behind the Contemporary Resort. Catch a boat to the island at the Magic Kingdom boat dock, the Contemporary Resort, the Grand Floridian Beach Resort, the Polynesian Village Resort, or the Fort Wilderness Marina.
> *Map:* Page 23.
> *Telephone:* (407) 824-3911.
> *Hours:* 10 A.M. to 7 P.M. during summer, 10 A.M. to 5:30 P.M. the rest of the year. Call to confirm hours.
> *Time to see:* 2 hours.
> *Price:* $7.95 adults, $4.24 ages 3 to 9.
> • A snack bar and rest rooms are available on the island.

What to expect: an 11.5 acre island containing 100 species of tropical birds and 250 species of exotic plants that create a lush tropical landscape, complete with waterfall. Disney has also populated the island with alligators, monkeys, deer, and giant Galapagos tortoises. In addition to being a certified zoological park, Discovery Island serves, too, as a sanctuary for disabled animals and endangered species.

Shaded pathways wind around and over the island to take you past rope, log, and wire mesh cages and through one of the world's largest walk-through aviaries. But not all the birds are caged. Many are free to roam about — guinea fowl, peacocks, ducks, swans, pink flamingos, pelicans.

Discovery Island's birds are native to lands around the world. Red-billed currasows once called the upper Amazon basin home. Hornbills from Southeast Asia hop along branches in their aviaries. Macaws and scarlet ibis have been transplanted from Central and South America. There are parrots from New Guinea, kookaburras from Australia, cranes from Africa, and Southern bald eagles from the United States, to name just a few.

You can only reach Discovery Island by boat. The boats, except those departing from Fort Wilderness, cut across the

Seven Seas Lagoon before navigating a narrow water bridge that spans an automobile road. The boats then glide beneath monorail tracks and sail past the Contemporary hotel to cruise into Bay Lake.

Disney Learning Adventures

TravelFacts

Location: Epcot Center, Walt Disney World, P.O. Box 10,040, Lake Buena Vista 32830-0040.
Map: Page 23.
Telephone: (407) 345-5860.
Hours: 8:30 A.M. to noon Monday, Tuesday, and Thursday (Gardens of the World). 9 A.M. to 1 P.M. Sunday, Monday, Tuesday, and Friday (Hidden Treasures of World Showcase).
Time to see: 3.5 to 4 hours.
Price: $20 ages 16 and over. Admission price is in addition to the cost of your Disney World ticket or passport.
- Disney Learning Adventures are held only for adults 16 and over. For children's seminars (ages 10 to 15) see "Wonders of Walt Disney World."

Reservations: Required. Call (407) 345-5860.

What to expect: walking tours that take you to parts of Epcot Center you could not reach on your own. Two learning adventures are offered. You can get an insider's view of the "Gardens of the World" or seek out the "Hidden Treasures of World Showcase."

If you find yourself marveling at Disney's gardens and landscaping, take the Gardens of the World tour. You'll learn the secrets of how the Disney horticulturalists work this particular bit of magic. The Hidden Treasures of World Showcase tour gives you a better understanding of the art, architecture, and culture of the World Showcase countries. You also get some surprising behind-the-scenes looks at several pavilions.

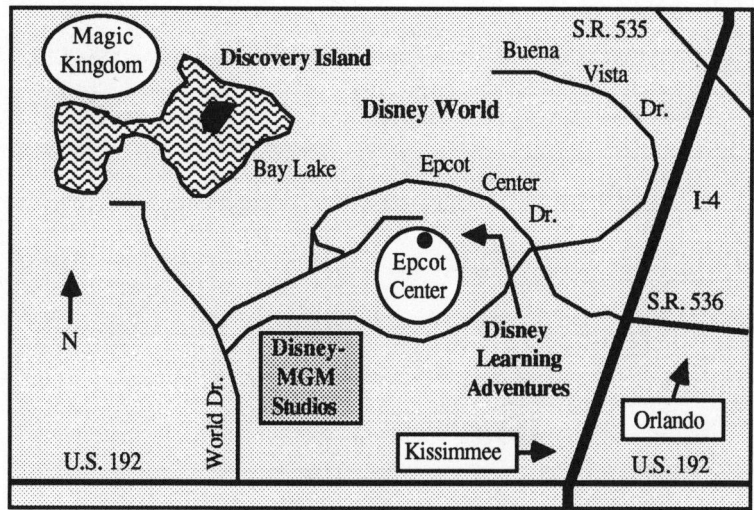

Discovery Island, Learning Adventures, Disney-MGM Studios

TravelVenture tip: If you have a special interest in either of these subjects, consider putting that tour on your must-see list.

Disney-MGM Studios Theme Park

TravelFacts

Location: Walt Disney World, P.O. Box 10,040, Lake Buena Vista 32830-0040.
Maps: Pages 23 and 27.
Telephone: (407) 824-4321.
Hours: Opens 8 A.M. high season, 9 a.m. off season. Closing varies between 7 P.M. and midnight depending on the season. Call for exact time. The Disney-MGM Studios Theme Park's closing time usually differs from that of Epcot Center and the Magic Kingdom.
Time to see: 8 hours.
Price: One Park/One-Day ticket, $32.86 adults, $26.50 children 3

through 9. Ages 2 and under free. 4-Day All Three Parks Passport, $110.24 adults, $87.98 children. 5-Day Plus Super Pass, $143.10 adults, $114.48 children. Admission price gives unlimited access to all rides, attractions, and shows.

One-Park/One-Day tickets are good for entrance to only one park for just one day, either the Disney-MGM Studios Theme Park, Epcot Center, or the Magic Kingdom. Multi-day passports are valid for unlimited admission to the Disney-MGM Studios Theme Park, Epcot Center, and the Magic Kingdom as well as unlimited use of the Disney World transportation system. Multi-day passports carry no expiration date and do not have to be used on consecutive days. The 5-Day Plus Super Pass also includes, after your first use of the pass, unlimited admission for the next seven days to Typhoon Lagoon, River Country, Discovery Island, and Pleasure Island.

Parking: $4 per car parking fee. A tram shuttles between the parking lot and the Disney-MGM Studios Theme Park entrance. Before boarding the tram, be sure to note the number of the row in which you parked.

Credit cards: American Express, Visa, and MasterCard are the only major credit cards accepted at Disney World.

How to see: Monday, Tuesday, and Wednesday are Disney World's busiest days. Sunday, Thursday, and Friday typically have lower attendance. Saturday falls in between. Busiest time of day: 11 A.M. to 5 P.M. The entertainment held throughout the day can add much to your Disney-MGM Studios Theme Park visit. Shows and appearances at the park feature the Muppets, the Teenage Mutant Ninja Turtles, Dick Tracy, and a famous motion picture or television personality who serves as star of the day. Keep track of the day's shows and events by picking up an entertainment schedule at the Crossroads of the World tower just inside the park.

The Disney-MGM Studios Theme Park offers fewer attractions than Epcot Center and the Magic Kingdom. The length of your visit to these attractions, however, is generally longer — two hours for the Backstage Studio Tour for example. Because it has fewer attractions, long lines build quickly. To avoid much time spent standing in line, you *must* arrive early. Plan to be at the entrance gate when the park opens. Upon entering, stop at the Crossroads of the World to pick up your entertainment schedule. Then head straight down Hollywood Boulevard toward the Chinese Theater. As you enter the large, circular Hollywood Plaza in front of the theater, you'll see on your right the park's top restaurant, The Hollywood Brown Derby. If you plan to eat there, walk over and make your reservation. Continue on to the Chinese Theater where you'll board The Great

Movie Ride. Exiting the theater after this 20-minute ride, bear to your left, heading for the Backstage Studio Tour. At this time of day the line, if any, will be short. When you leave the two-hour tour you will have seen two of the park's top attractions, both of which draw lengthy lines. You can spend the rest of the day visiting the remaining attractions, including the outstanding Indiana Jones Epic Stunt Spectacular. This show is held in a 2,000-seat theater at set times throughout the day. Because the theater is so large, there's no need to get in line until about 20 minutes before show time.

During peak seasons, Disney World fills with peak crowds but is open well into the evening. Consider taking a break during the afternoon hours, the most-crowded time of day. Return to your hotel, relax, perhaps enjoy the pool. In the evening, you can return to the theme park refreshed, ready for several hours of less-crowded visiting. This is especially effective during the summer when you'll swap touring during the hottest part of the day for the cooler evening hours.

TravelVenture tip: On both the Backstage Studio Tour and the Animation Tour you will be seeing actual working studios. Most of the work, however, goes on Monday through Friday. On weekends you will see very little activity. Therefore, if possible, schedule your visit to the Disney-MGM Studios Theme Park for a weekday, and take the Backstage Studio Tour and the Animation Tour during normal working hours.

TravelVenture tip: Some attractions include a theater show. Keep in mind that Disney theaters have no bad seats, all offer a good view. But if you would like to sit in the center of a theater rather than toward the side, don't be among the first in. The staff in each theater has everyone move all the way across the rows to fill each and every seat, starting from the far end of the row. Hang back until you're about in the middle of the waiting crowd. When you enter the theater select a row that is already about half full.

Don't miss: The Backstage Studio Tour, the Great Movie Ride, and the Indiana Jones Epic Stunt Spectacular.

Reservations: Mandatory at The Hollywood Brown Derby restaurant and the 50's Prime Time Cafe. After arrival at the park, drop by either restaurant to select your seating time. The park's other eateries are first come first served.

- If you leave the Disney-MGM Studios Theme Park but plan to return that same day or to visit Epcot Center or the Magic Kingdom, be sure to get your hand stamped at the exit.

- Strollers and wheelchairs are available for rent at Oscar's Super Service on your right as you go through the main gate.
- Devices to assist sight- or hearing-impaired visitors are available at the Guest Services Building adjacent to the main gate.
- Coin-operated lockers are located at Oscar's Super Service on your right as you go through the main gate.
- An automated teller machine is located outside the park to the right of the main gate.
- Pets may be boarded at the theme park's kennel (additional charge).
- A baby center equipped to help you care for your infant is located at the Guest Services Building adjacent to the main gate.
- The Darkroom camera center located on Hollywood Boulevard will loan you a camera. You buy the film. You must, however, leave a refundable deposit, using cash or credit card. (You get your credit card slip back when you return the camera.) You can also rent 35mm and video cameras.

TravelVenture tip: You can check at the "Studio Production" information kiosk on opportunities to be part of a studio audience. This kiosk also has information on what is currently in production as well as shooting schedules. The Studio Production kiosk is located adjacent to the main gate. After going through the gate, make a 90-degree right turn and walk straight ahead.

What to expect: a theme park that includes a tour of Disney's movie and television production facilities. At 135 acres the Disney-MGM Studios Theme Park is about half the size of Epcot Center but 35 acres larger than the Magic Kingdom. The studios theme park, though, feels smaller than the Magic Kingdom since about half the park is devoted to production facilities, including soundstages and a backlot.

TravelVenture tip: Both Disney-MGM Studios Theme Park and Universal Studios Florida promote the glamour of movie making. In actuality, however, film and TV production is limited. Consider them both to be primarily theme parks rather than thriving film studios.

Upon entering the Disney-MGM Studios Theme Park you stand at the foot of the **Crossroads of the World,** a 44-foot tower

ATTRACTIONS   27

Main Gate

Crossroads ◯ of the World

Indiana Jones
Epic Stunt
Spectacular

Theater
of the
Stars

Echo Lake

Star Tours

Animation
Tour

Superstar
Television

Monster
Sound
Show

Hollywood
Plaza

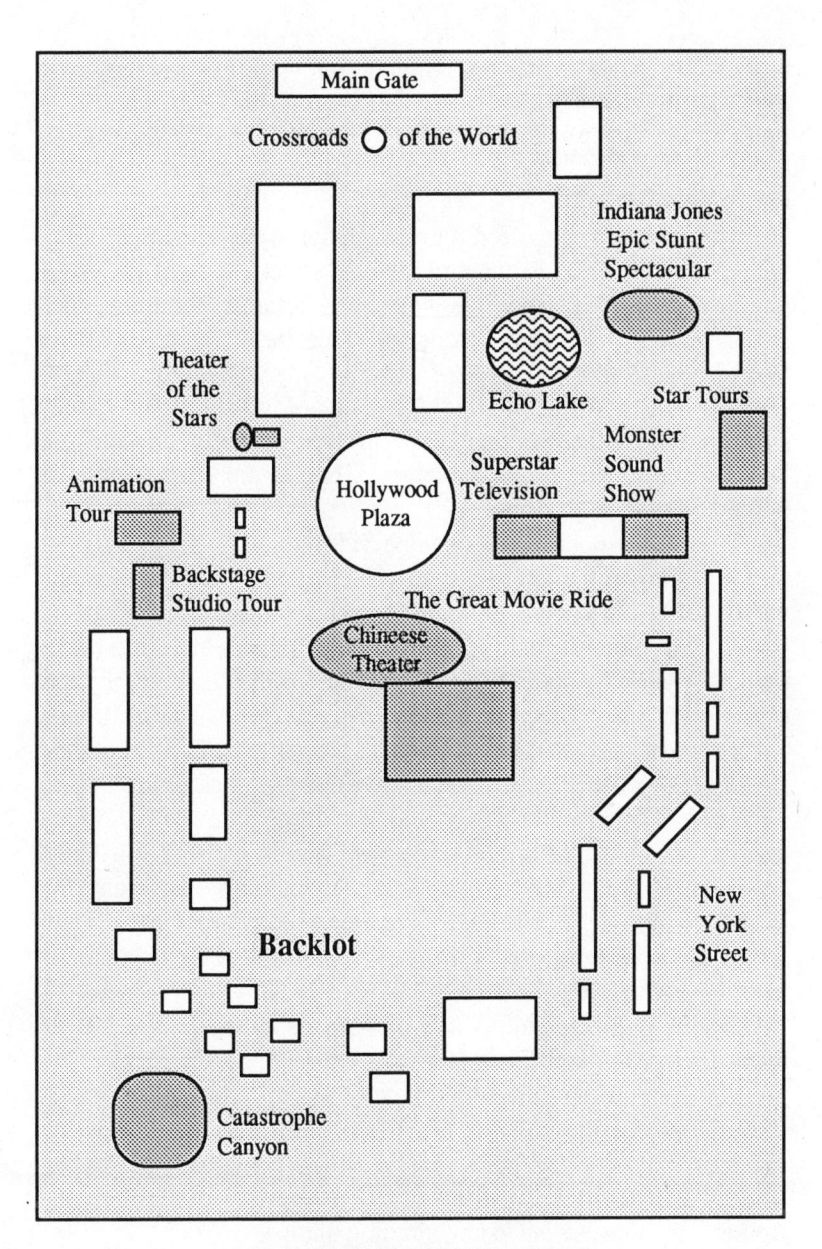

Backstage
Studio Tour

The Great Movie Ride

Chineese
Theater

New
York
Street

Backlot

Catastrophe
Canyon

Disney-MGM Studios Theme Park

crowned by Mickey Mouse standing atop a revolving globe. The tower rises at the head of Hollywood Boulevard, the theme park's main street, and recreates a Hollywood landmark. (The original tower, however, stands — without Mickey — on Sunset Boulevard.)

The art deco and streamline moderne style buildings lining Disney's Hollywood Boulevard give the street a look of the original during the 1930s and '40s. One small building, though, stands out in contrast. To your left as you face the Crossroads of the World, you'll spot the 1920s-style Los Angeles wooden bungalow that houses **Sid Cahuenga's One-of-a-Kind** shop. The Disney story goes that the wooden shop survives because Sid held out and refused to sell to the developers buying up land to fill the boulevard with high rises.

The Hollywood-knowledgeable Sid frequently sits in a rocker on his front porch and chats with visitors. Inside, the shop sells a variety of Hollywood memorabilia such as posters, autographed books and pictures, and personal objects and clothing either owned or worn by stars. While the inventory may change, Sid has offered for sale: Liberace's table napkins ($30 each), Brenda Vacaro's shawl ($95), Cher's belt ($300), Linda Darnell's shoe trees ($500 — that's for a set of two), a pin once belonging to Katherine Hepburn ($1,400), and a complete set of 12 lobby cards (8" x 10" color prints) of James Dean in scenes from *Rebel Without A Cause* ($6,500 — includes matting and framing). While buyers of the pricey curios will probably be serious collectors with fat wallets, you'll want to be sure to browse the shop's intriguing inventory.

On the opposite side of the Crossroads of the World sits an increasingly rare sight in America — an automobile service station, this one going under the name of Oscar's Super Service. A shiny 1947 maroon buick is often parked at the pumps. Another vintage vehicle, a checker cab, sits on the boulevard in front of Mickey's of Hollywood. Mickey's, like most of the Hollywood Boulevard shops, sells Disney clothing and souvenirs.

Across the street from the cab, notice The Darkroom camera store. A portion of one wall resembles a giant box camera. This type of architecture, known as California crazy, was a fad during the 1930s. The theme park sports two more examples of this craze. Halfway down the boulevard Vine Street runs off to the left toward Echo Lake. At the lake you can see a cement dinosaur housing an ice cream parlor (Dinosaur Gertie's Ice Cream of Extinction). On the opposite side of the small lake Min and Bill's Dockside Diner serves fast food from a small tramp steamer permanently anchored to the shore.

Back on Hollywood Boulevard, at the Vine Street intersection, you'll find your opportunity to take a screen test — but only your family and friends will judge the results. **Calling Dick Tracy** lets visitors act in a skit based on the film as a video camera records the performance. You can watch the playback and then, if you like, buy the tape. Even if you don't want to go before the camera, check out the operation. It's fun to watch.

As you stroll along Hollywood Boulevard, you not only mingle with other visitors, you'll probably run into some Hollywood characters — perhaps a gossip columnist, a cab driver, a cop walking his beat, even autograph hounds. Who knows, you may even be mistaken for a star.

Notice the traffic lights. They sit on posts which stand on corners. The red and green lights are backed up with stop and go flags. And when the lights and flags change, a bell rings.

At the foot of Disney's Hollywood Boulevard stands the wide, circular Hollywood Plaza. Immediately on your right you'll see the **Theater of the Stars,** an open-air amphitheater that resembles the Hollywood Bowl. In addition to a variety show held here several times each day, a daily **Star Conversation** is conducted with a film or television personality. (Consult your show schedule for times.)

TravelVenture tip: Call 407-824-4321 to ask which stars are scheduled for the Star Today program while you are visiting Disney World. Then plan your visit to the studios theme park on a day when the star you would prefer to see will be there.

Next door to the Theater of the Stars you'll find Disney's recreation of The Brown Derby, a famed Hollywood restaurant.

You can also spot in the plaza another Hollywood landmark — a full-scale reproduction of the pagoda-roofed **Chinese Theater**. Sid Grauman, a Hollywood showman, built the original — then known as Grauman's Chinese Theater — on Hollywood Boulevard in 1928. It was Grauman who came up with the idea of immortalizing stars in the theater's forecourt by casting their hand- and footprints in cement. The courtyard of Disney's Chinese Theater also boasts cement handprints of stars — Dick Van Dyke, Lauren Bacall, Carol Burnett, John Ritter, Kermit the Frog, Loni Anderson, Audrey Hepburn, Tony Randall, Lucie Arnaz, and Donald Duck among others. Rather than housing a theater, though, Disney's Chinese Theater is home to one of the park's main attractions — The Great Movie Ride.

Exiting the plaza through the massive, towering gate adorned with Mickey Mouse will take you to the studio tours and production facilities. Leaving the plaza on the opposite side will lead you to the theme park area.

The park's tours, rides, and attractions are listed here alphabetically.

Animation Tour (Disney-MGM Studios Animation Tour)

This 30-minute tour takes you into the studio's animation facilities to view artists at work on the other side of soundproof windows. While in a lobby waiting to start the tour, you can take a look at original "cels" (drawings which have been photocopied from paper to clear plastic and then painted). These cels were used in producing some of Disney's animated features. Be sure not to miss the lobby's display case filled with Oscars won by Disney cartoons.

The tour starts in a theater that introduces you to the animation process via a short film starring Walter Conkrite and Robin Williams. The two then continue to guide you, via overhead video monitors, as you watch animators at work and explore the steps in creating a cartoon. And as you would expect, Williams keeps you chuckling and laughing all the way.

The tour ends in a second theater which shows a composite of highlights from classic Disney animated films.

TravelVenture Tip: Since the Animation Tour and the Backstage Studio Tour cover actual, working production facilities, you will see more activity if you schedule your visit to the Disney-MGM Studios Theme Park for a weekday, taking the tours during normal working hours. Try to avoid a Saturday, Sunday, or holiday visit.

TravelVenture Tip: Don't be reluctant to start the two-hour Backstage Studio Tour around meal time. About thirty minutes into the tour you'll be able to grab a bite to eat at the Studio Catering Co. which offers sandwiches and snacks.

Backstage Studio Tour

This tour offers a behind-the-scenes look at movie making from pre-production through production and onto post-production. Plan on about two hours for the tour which consists of two parts: first a tram tour lasting about a half hour and then a guided walking tour of just over an hour. In between, you can take a break and on your own wander backlot streets or grab a light bite to eat.

Should you have to wait in line before starting the tour, easily visible overhead video monitors keep you entertained by running interviews with filmmakers and performers. They won't shorten the time you may have to stand in line, but they will make it quicker mentally.

The tour begins with a tram ride alongside pre-production workshops. You get a through-the-window look at carpenters building sets for sound stages and tailors working on costumes. Disney's large costuming department lets producers order custom designs or catalog shop an inventory of some two million pieces. On display are original costumes, including Michael Jackson's Captain EO spacesuit, a Mary Poppins dress worn by Julie Andrews, and Warren Beatty's big yellow Dick Tracy overcoat.

You also get a look at the 130-foot-high "Earffel Tower" — Disney's landmark for the studios theme park. This simulated watertower is topped with a 28-foot-wide Mouseketeer cap (that's a hat size of 342 3/8, by the way).

The tram moves on to **Residential Street,** a small suburb lined with backlot houses. Herbie the Love Bug is parked in the driveway of one. And another may look familiar as the outside of "The Golden Girls" house. Producers use the relatively inexpensive backlot buildings, which are actually just exterior shells, to film outdoor scenes. Backlot shooting not only saves the expense of going on location, it also gives the producer more control over the setting and the action.

The highlight of the tram tour, **Catastrophe Canyon,** shows just how well filmmakers can fine tune their control over a wild action scene — even with you in it. The aptly named canyon, whose red sandstone walls rise 50 feet, lets you experience three disasters: earthquake, fire, and flood. This is live action. As an earthquake hits the canyon, rocking and swaying the tram, you feel a blast of heat when an oil rig and a tractor trailer burst into flames. And if you're sitting on the left side of the tram, you'll also feel the spray whipped up by the rush of churning, cascading water flooding into the canyon. After the action dies down, the tram pulls alongside the back of the canyon to give a glimpse at how the effects are created.

After Catastrophe Canyon, it's back to the backlot to tour the city streets of a set called, collectively, **New York Street.** As your guide points out the different types of buildings and their uses the Empire State and the Chrysler buildings loom in the background.

The tram drops you off at **Backstage Plaza.** Here you can take a break before continuing with the guided walking tour. Backstage Plaza contains The Loony Bin (a large gift and souvenir shop with an entertaining collection of hands-on sound effects), Toon Park and the Studio Catering Co. eatery. The small Toon Park actually is a park complete with green grass and wooden benches. It also has wooden cut outs of Roger Rabbit and friends with whom you can pose for snapshots.

Backstage Plaza is adjacent to New York Street, and you can

now explore this backlot set at your leisure. If you want to leave the tour, you can return to the theme park via an exit located between Toon Park and New York Street's 8th Avenue.

TravelVenture tip: If you enjoyed Catastrophe Canyon so much that you'd like to experience it again, you can leave the tour at this exit to retake the 30-minute tram portion of the tour. You can then either complete the tour or again leave at the exit. You would, however, want to do this only if you had arrived at the studios theme park early so that the line for the Backstage Studio Tour had not yet built. An alternative method to again see Catastrophe Canyon would be to take the tour's tram ride after 5 P.M. when any line for the tour should be greatly diminished.

The walking portion of the tour covers aspects of film making that take place, for the most part, indoors. The tour demonstrates how special effects are created, takes you through sound stages — some of which may have filming in progress — and gives you a look at how a movie is put together and the finishing touches added. To start the tour, leave the backstage plaza by following the pink, oversized rabbit tracks.

First stop is the **Water Effects Tank.** Entering the show area, you join a group which is assigned a guide who accompanies the group during the tour. The Water Effects Tank offers live demonstrations of how filmmakers use special effects to film ocean battles and storms at sea. To see just how realistic those effects are, you watch video playbacks of the action on overhead monitors. Disney makes good use of overhead video monitors throughout the walking tour. These monitors allow you to see the end result of the film-making techniques demonstrated or explained on the tour.

The **Special Effects Workshop and Shooting Stage** uses a couple of kids from the tour to show how studio shots using a blue-screen background can later be edited to include any desired background.

The tour now moves through the studio's three **Soundstages** where interior scenes are shot. Sound stages are large barn-like structures built with soundproof walls and ceiling. They are actually just a shell with no permanent interior features. But when filming starts, they come to life. Scenery sets are built or moved into the sound stage to be lit by powerful lights hanging from the ceiling. Dolly-supported cameras stand in front of the set. And the sound stage fills with a multitude of actors, actresses, stage hands, camera operators, lighting technicians, and assorted assistants.

What you'll see on the three sound stages depends on what work, if any, is currently in production. The third sound stage does have a long-term tenant with the set for the Disney Channel's "The Mickey Mouse Club." Because you are in an adjacent corridor behind soundproof glass, any shooting going on will continue uninterrupted. And because the corridor is located close to ceiling level, you'll get an excellent view of the action.

The tour uses an entertaining, action-packed short film, *The Lottery* starring Bette Midler, to show how a movie is shot — on the backlot, in a soundstage, using stunt doubles, and with special effects. *The Lottery* was shot both on the backlot's New York Street and in a soundstage at the studio. The studio sets have been left intact. And as you stand among them, overhead video monitors reveal the tricks used in making the film.

The studio's **Post Production Editing and Audio** facilities have the job of bringing everything together. Here technicians add visual and sound effects, and film editors take as many as 100 hours of film and boil it down to a two-hour movie. The unlikely team of Mel Gibson and Pee Wee Herman humorously show how audio technicians work their art to add spice to a film.

The tour ends in **The Walt Disney Theater** where you see previews of newly released Disney films.

The Great Movie Ride

To get to The Great Movie Ride, you make your way through the lobby of the Chinese Theater, walking alongside display cases containing the piano on which Sam played it again in *Casablanca,* Judy Garland's ruby slippers from *The Wizard of Oz,* and costumes from *Alien*. You then wind your way through a theater showing the previews used to promote some of yesterday's renowned films.

At the ride itself, multi-passenger vehicles take you on a 20-minute tour of 11 recreated sound stages. The stages use both live actors and more than a 100 audio-animatronic (robotic) performers to bring to life some of Hollywood's famed film scenes, from musicals to mayhem. You ride by a rain-sodden Gene Kelly clinging to a lamp post and chortling *Singing in the Rain*. Then it's onto Julie Andrews' *Mary Poppins* clinging to her umbrella over the rooftops of London. You also encounter, among others, James Cagney in *Public Enemy,* Sigourney Weaver in *Alien,* and Harrison Ford's Indiana Jones recovering the ark from its sepulcher. The audio-animatronic cast moves, talks, and sings to bring the sets to life. But the action really picks up when an unsavory live character decides to use your ride vehicle to make a getaway.

Things have calmed down again by the time you ride by Bogart's Rick and Bergman's Ilsa playing their farewell scene in *Casablanca*. Standing near the Lockheed Electra 12A waiting to fly Ilsa away, the two say their good-byes as one of the plane's twin engines revs to life. Most movies, though, have a happy ending, and so does your tour of the sets — Dorothy and the gang on the Yellow Brick Road to Oz. The ride itself ends with a short look at film clips of Hollywood stars.

Indiana Jones Epic Stunt Spectacular

This 35-minute exciting, hair-raising, and explosive show is the best at Disney World. The Indiana Jones Epic Stunt Spectacular, held in a 2,000-seat theater, is staged at set times throughout the day. (Consult your show schedule which you picked up at the Crossroads of the World.) The performance consists of a live show in which stunt men and women recreate scenes from *Raiders of the Lost Ark*. These skilled and daring performers carry out stunts involving chases, falls, fights, and explosions.

If you would like to take part in the show, you can volunteer to join the cast as an extra. Before each show the assistant director scouts out 10 volunteers who can fit certain requirements — a Clint Eastwood double ("Okay, you're dirty and hairy."), a courageous type ("You'll do. It takes courage to wear a shirt like that."), an Indiana Jones stand in ("He's more like Pee Wee Herman, but that's okay.") even a Marilyn Monroe look alike.

The show jumps immediately into action as Indiana Jones free falls into a Mayan temple, navigates a field of punji sticks that shoot from the ground at the weight of his steps, and flees a massive rolling boulder. The director then yells, "cut," revealing the show's story line of a film crew shooting the stunt action. And the stage hands wheel the first of the show's three massive sets off to the side.

The scene now shifts to a square in Cairo. And the action picks up again with fights, ladder and rooftop chases, three-story falls, and a truck explosion — while the truck is moving. A fiery finale takes place on the third set as Indiana Jones and a German soldier tangle unnervingly close to an airplane's whirling propeller blades, burning fuel oil, and exploding fuel-storage tanks. As you leave the theater, you'll probably agree that the *Spectacular* in the show's title tends toward understatement.

The Monster Sound Show

Four volunteer guests try their hand at being sound-effects technicians in this 15-minute show. The audience in the 272-seat theater and the four novice technicians watch a short film whose sound effects include thunder, rain, creaking doors, falling chandeliers, foot steps, and door knocks. The film is then rerun, but this time the four audio artists create the effects, trying to sync their efforts to the film's action. The film, with its newly added sound track, is then played back to the audience, generally with quite humorous results.

Leaving the theater, you enter a room containing the **Sound Works.** Here you can try your own hand at creating sound effects. You can also visit **Soundations,** a small booth where you don a set of headphones to listen to seemingly three-dimensional sounds.

Muppet Theater

Scheduled for a 1991 opening, this theater features a three-dimensional Muppet movie.

Star Tours

You enter Star Tours through a recreated Ewok Village. (Remember the Ewoks from the *Star Wars* films?) The village is made up of redwoods, sequoias, and pines which support the treetop homes of the Ewoks. Making your way through a spaceport you spot R2-D2 and C-3PO before boarding a "StarSpeeder" (actually a 40-seat flight simulator theater). After blast off your flight-simulating StarSpeeder banks, turns, and dives in synch to *Star Wars* film footage that takes you on a 4.5-minute journey to the Moon of Endor.

En route, as you watch the action through the cockpit's wide window, your eventful flight plows through an asteroid-like field of frozen ice fragments, combats a massive Imperial Star Destroyer, and battles the Empire's Death Star battle station.

Superstar Television

As its name indicates, this 30-minute show emphasizes television rather than the movies. And it offers you a chance to grab one of some 30 starring roles in TV programs that range from classics to today's hits.

The volunteer stars perform on a set appropriate to their show while the audience seated in the 1,000-seat theater watches. As the TV cameras record the volunteers going through their lines, the live shots are simultaneously integrated into videos of the original programs and projected to the audience on eight overhead screens. Among the roles, budding stars can trade quips with Johnny Carson, act in "General Hospital," play Ethel alongside Lucy on an "I Love Lucy" episode, ride with the boys on "Bonanza," join the castaways on "Gilligan's Island," and swap pies in the face with The Three Stooges.

Downtown Orlando Walking Tour

TravelFacts

> *Location:* The area adjacent to Orange Avenue between Church and Washington Streets.
> *Map:* Page 41.
> *Time to see:* About 1.5 hours, not including time spent in shops.
> *Price:* Free, a self-guided walking tour.
> *Parking:* Municipal parking garages are located on Pine Street (south side, between Orange Avenue and the railroad tracks) and Central Boulevard (north side, between Orange Avenue and the railroad tracks). See map on page 41.

What to expect: an interesting blend of the new and the not-too-distant past. Modern, smart-looking high-rises are taking over downtown Orlando's skyline. But the city has also held onto many of the buildings that have flavored its short history. And recent restorations and renovations of these historic buildings, coupled with a street and sidewalk beautification program, have turned downtown Orlando into an attraction in its own right.

Background

As cities go, Orlando is still young. The first settlers did not arrive until the 1840s. And it was the 1870s before some real growth started when a thriving business district took root along Pine Street. But tragedy stuck in 1884 when fire wiped out many of Pine Street's wooden structures. During the rebuilding, Orlando prohibited wooden buildings on Pine Street, and the new buildings — mostly one- and two-story structures — were built of metal, stone, or brick. Today, downtown Orlando's earliest buildings date from the reconstruction following the 1884 fire.

The downtown skyline began to change around 1910 as three-, four-, and five-story buildings sprang up. Between 1914 and 1925 the shape of downtown itself started changing as the business district shifted from Pine Street to Orange Avenue.

Orlando's buildings were then being built in what was known as the commercial style of architecture, a style popularized in Chicago. During the late 1920s, however, the Mediterranean style captured Orlando with its red-tile roofs and heavy Spanish flavor. The style became so popular that many owners threw a coat of stucco over their existing buildings to give them the Mediterranean look.

This was not to be the last time Orlando covered up original building exteriors to keep pace with the latest trend in architecture. Throughout the '30s and '40s the streamline-shape of art deco swept Orlando. And again some owners gave their buildings a face lift, this time applying a marble veneer to the exterior.

During the '60s and much of the '70s, downtown Orlando followed the pattern of many American cities — as the suburbs grew, downtown withered. The '80s, however, brought a renaissance as businesses began to move back into downtown. In the process, a few historic buildings were lost — leveled to make room for high-rise office towers. But many were spared and renovated. Today, these buildings help preserve the memory of Orlando's past.

Walking Tour

You'll start and finish your tour at downtown's Church Street Station. Starting here is symbolic. Church Street Station gets much of the credit for pumping life back into downtown Orlando. In the early '70s, Bob Snow, creator of Church Street Station, made a daring move. He bought a couple of abandoned, rundown buildings on declining Church Street. Snow renovated his purchases and turned them into **Church Street Station**, the home of **Rosie O'Grady's Good Time Emporium** — a name that sums up the flavor of the attraction. (See the Nightlife section for more information on Church Street Station.) Snow's success in turning derelict buildings into one of Orlando's more popular attractions also helped spark interest in preserving and restoring the city's historic buildings.

Step inside the complex to see what a magnificent restoration job Snow has done. There's no daytime admission charge. On the north side of Church Street, in addition to Rosie O'Grady's, you'll find cathedral-like **Apple Annie's Courtyard** with its dramatic wooden ceiling vaults. Apple Annie's will lead you to the **Church Street Station Exchange,** which opened in 1988. But hold off on the Exchange for now; you're walking tour will wind up there. Instead, bear to the right, towards a disco called **Phineas Phogg's Balloon Works.** Notice the red brick exterior wall, a reminder that these are Snow's once-derelict buildings. After browsing, walk back outside.

You'll often find a 1931 American La France fire engine parked in the street. Notice the street's paving bricks. At one time the city had poured asphalt over them to modernize Church Street. The asphalt, however, has now been stripped away to reveal the original bricks.

Snow's entertainment complex proved to be a success, and it has now grown to occupy buildings on both sides of Church Street. On the street's south side, across from Rosie's, Church Street Station built and opened the **Cheyenne Saloon & Opera House** in 1982. The Nashville Network often videotapes top-name country and western entertainers performing at the Cheyenne. Be sure to step inside and explore. The Cheyenne Saloon's oak interior, 50,000-piece stained glass window, antiques, and western memorabilia must be seen.

From the Cheyenne Saloon, walk east, toward the railroad tracks. Adjacent to the Cheyenne, the **Bumby Arcade** houses a French bakery, eateries, a gift shop, and **The Orchid Garden** ballroom which is filled with ornate wrought iron work. Just before the railroad tracks stands the **Bumby Hardware Building**, dating

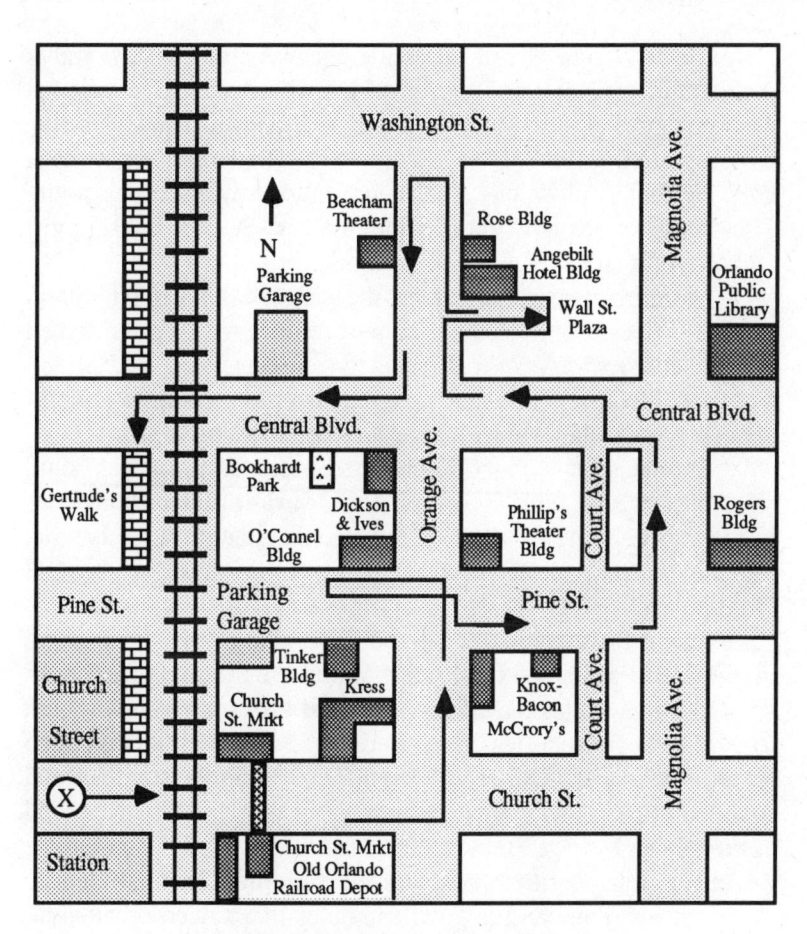

Downtown Orlando Walking Tour

from 1884. For most of its life the building contained one of the largest hardware stores in Central Florida. It now houses Church Street Station's **Buffalo Trading Company**. Inside you'll find a variety of Western goods and paraphernalia.

Continue east and cross the tracks. Amtrak's *Silver Meteor* and *Silver Star* ride these rails four times a day. The turreted **Old**

Orlando Railroad Depot on your right was built in 1889 and is included in the National Register of Historic Places. The terminal was designed by a Russian architect, and it shows in the building's onion dome. The station served rail travelers in days gone by, but Amtrak has located its station several miles south. The old depot has now joined Church Street Station, housing gift and souvenir shops plus an ice cream parlor.

The railroad cars parked on the siding hold Church Street Station offices. Some of these cars were once used on the famed *Orange Blossom Special* that ran between New York and Miami from 1920 to 1953. The steam engine also has a claim to fame. It appeared in a John Wayne movie — *The Wings of Eagles*.

Continue east along Church Street, remaining on the south side. The recently built **Church Street Market** bridges both sides of the street and holds some 40 shops and restaurants. Notice that the the market's architect picked up on the style of the Old Orlando Railroad Depot.

Beyond the market, look to the north side of the street where you'll see a string of red-brick buildings built in 1911. At 15 Church Street stands the art deco **Kress Building**, which was built in 1936 as a five and ten store. During the '30s and '40s art deco architecture, with its streamlined look of smooth surfaces and rounded corners, was popular throughout the United States, and especially in Florida. Between the second and third floors, notice the concrete banner that preserves the building's original identity and purpose. You can see good examples of art deco ornamentation above the second and fourth floor windows and along the roof line. The Kress Building is L shaped, so you'll get another view of it on Orange Avenue.

Next door to the Kress Building, at the corner of Orange Avenue, stands the **First National Bank Building**. Built in 1929, it reflects Egyptian revival architecture. Egyptian revival architects used designs and styles similar to those found on the buildings and landmarks of ancient Egypt. The building now houses a branch of a local community college.

Cross Orange Avenue. Then turn left and cross Church Street. You're now walking north on the east side of Orange

Avenue. Across the street you still have a fine view of the First National Bank Building and the L-shaped Kress Building. The wide, bricked sidewalks with trees at the curb are the result of a downtown beautification program.

The second building beyond Kress was built in 1909. Its owner wanted a safe and sturdy structure, so he built the ground-floor walls 17 inches thick and had fireproof windows installed. These features, though, skyrocketed the building's cost to $5,000.

When you reach the corner, you're at Pine Street, Orlando's original downtown thoroughfare. The **Metcalf Building**, across Orange Avenue on the southwest corner, is one of Orlando's earliest high rises. This 10-story structure was built in 1924 for the Orlando Bank & Trust Co. Although the building survives, the bank didn't survive the depression of the '30s. The Metcalf Building was renovated in 1985. Its lower two floors, below the eight floors of brick, are an example of classical revival architecture, which uses features found in ancient Greek and Roman buildings.

On the northwest corner of Pine and Orange stands one of Orlando's oldest buildings. Built in 1886, two years after the Pine Street fire, the **O'Connell Building** is a lost treasure. You can't see the original exterior. It has been altered and completely covered over, hiding its history under a nondescript facade. The wall on its Pine Street side, however, is brightened by a mural depicting scenes from Pine Street's history.

Cross Pine Street. Then turn left to cross Orange Avenue, walking towards the O'Connell Building. Continue heading west on Pine Street until you are abreast of numbers 16-18 on the opposite side of the street — the **Tinker Building.** Green, blue, and gold tiles spell out *Tinker* across the top of the two-story building. Built in 1925 by Joe Tinker, the building was rescued in 1980 from beneath an aluminium-siding exterior and accurately restored to its original appearance. Today, this box-shaped building is one of Orlando's best examples of the commercial style of architecture so popular in Florida during the 1920s. The Tinker Building has also been added to the National Register of Historic Landmarks.

If you know baseball history, the name Joe Tinker may ring familiar. Tinker was a major league ball player. He achieved fame in the early 1900s as a member of the Chicago Cubs crack double play combination: Tinker to Evers to Chance. Tinker, who had invested his baseball earnings in the land boom sweeping Florida during the 1920s, moved his real estate office into the new building.

Retrace your steps back to the corner of Pine Street and Orange Avenue. On the southeast corner is the streamlined, art deco **McCrory's Building.** McCrory's opened a department store on this corner in 1906. The building you're looking at now, though, was put up in 1942, at the height of art deco popularity. But it no longer houses a McCrory's.

The renovated **Phillip's Theater Building** occupies the northeast corner. The "Dr. Phillip's Theater," built in 1916, was Orlando's first movie house. But the theater, which also staged live shows, went bust four years later and was turned into a store.

Cross Orange Avenue and again cross Pine Street, walking toward McCrory's. Immediately turn left so you are walking east along Pine Street. You're now in the heart of the old Pine Street business district. These buildings are among Orlando's oldest, dating from after the 1884 Pine Street fire. This is a pleasant walk along a wide, tree-lined sidewalk paved with six-sided bricks. Notice, also, that the street itself is paved with red bricks.

The building at number 27, on the opposite side of the street, dates from 1884, the year of the fire. Next door, number 29 was built in 1887. And at number 33, the renovated **Ellis Building** dates from 1885.

On your side of the street you are probably now in front of 32-36 Pine St., the **Knox-Bacon Building.** It, too, was put up in 1884, following the fire. In 1900, the Knox-Bacon Building housed Orlando's first library.

Next door, at 38 Pine St., the narrow, Mediterranean-style **Orange County Building and Loan Association Building** was constructed in 1925.

Cross Court Avenue. On the southeast corner, number 50, stands the renovated **Landmark Bank Building,** which was built in 1923. A massive, walk-in Diebold vault installed in 1925 still remains. You can see the vault from the window in the front door.

Continue east on Pine Street. The three buildings on the north side of the street, numbers 55, 63, and 69, were all built in 1884 and were among the first to be constructed after the fire. The builders of the **Robinson Building** at number 63 kept the fire in mind — the building is reputed to be fire proof.

If you feel like it, at Magnolia Avenue you can take a break. On the corner stands the Cafe Victor, which serves breakfast and lunch Monday through Saturday and has sidewalk tables.

Turn left at Magnolia to cross Pine Street. On the northeast corner of Pine and Magnolia, you'll see the unique, two-story **Rogers Building**. Built in 1887 by an Englishman, Gordon Rogers, the building had a wood frame and stucco exterior, despite the prohibition on wood. Later, the stucco was replaced with pressed tin panels brought over from England. Most of the tin panels still make up the exterior, although a few have been replaced with wood panels.

When first built, the Rogers Building served as a gathering spot for members of a small colony of English immigrants who had settled in the area. It was then known as, appropriately enough, the English Club. The Rogers Building was placed on the National Register of Historic Places in 1983.

Continue north on Magnolia. On the opposite side of the street notice the four boxy, commercial-style buildings.

At Central Boulevard, you can see the **Orlando Public Library** on the northeast corner. Turn left onto Central. The **Orange County Court House Annex** stands across the street.

Walk one short block west on Central to Court Avenue. Turn right to cross Central Boulevard. Then turn left, continuing west on Central past the roaring '20s-flavored mural titled *Elks Club Saturday Night*.

Now you're again approaching Orange Avenue. The five-story building across the street, at the southeast corner of Central and Orange, was built in 1914. With its sidewalk overhang the building has a distinctive look about it. Can you guess what it was built to be? You're right if you thought a department store.

Turn right onto Orange Avenue. Four stores up, on your right, is **Wall Street Plaza**, a small, landscaped pedestrian plaza with a small fountain. Leave the plaza the way you entered, turning right on Orange Avenue. Across the street you can see the old **Beacham Theater**. The building started life in 1921 as a vaudeville theater where acts such as the Ziegfeld Follies played. In recent years it has undergone a variety of transformations — from music hall to laser show to dinner theater — trying to find a niche that would let it thrive in nighttime downtown Orlando.

Continue north to the corner, Washington Street. Turn left to cross Orange Avenue. Again turn left so you're heading south, back down Orange Avenue.

At number 49, on the opposite side of the street, stands the two-story **Rose Building**. Built in 1924 by Walter Rose, a local real estate developer, the Rose Building has fallen victim to architectural fads. Its box shape gives it a commercial-style look. The ground floor exterior, however, has been covered over with a modern veneer of black and green marble. The upper story, though, separated from the lower by a red, Spanish-tile overhang, retains a pink-stucco Mediterranean flavor.

Next door rises the 11-story **Angebilt Hotel Building**. This commercial-style structure, which was modeled after New York's Pennsylvania Hotel (now the Penta), was built in 1923 to house Orlando's finest luxury hotel. It boasted a roof-top garden and a tenth-floor restaurant where folks could dine overlooking downtown Orlando. Unfortunately, the hotel's owners went bankrupt within three months. The Angebilt has recently been renovated and turned into office space. If you're feeling weary, you can rest and take in the Angebilt from any of the sidewalk benches along your side of the street.

Continue walking south on Orange Avenue. At Central Boulevard, notice the renovated six-story building across the street, on the southwest corner. Built in 1920 as a department store, the **Dickson & Ives Building** sports the features of classical architecture and now serves as an office building.

Turn right and walk west on Central. Across the street stands the four-story **Empire Hotel Building,** built in 1913. Today it houses stores and offices. **Bookhardt Park** sits next to the Empire. This small, building-sized park is named for Assistant Fire Chief Calvin Bookhardt. The fire chief died in 1972 fighting the fire that destroyed the building which stood on the park site.

Continue west on Central until just past the railroad tracks. Turn left and cross Central, walking toward the narrow, brick-paved walkway — **Gertrude's Walk.** This pedestrian walk is named for the sister of the man who was Orlando's mayor in 1881. Originally, though, it was not Gertrude's Walk but Gertrude Street. And at 100-feet wide, the widest street in Orlando. But when the railroad came to town, they laid the tracks right down the middle of Gertrude's street. Orlando's once-widest thoroughfare was reduced to a narrow back alley. In 1980, the alley was turned into a pedestrian mall and renamed Gertrude's Walk. On your right, colorful murals decorate one wall of a two-story building.

Continue south along Gertrude's Walk, and cross Pine Street. You're now back at Church Street Station, looking at the latest addition to the complex — **Church Street Station Exchange.** The Exchange is a three-story festival marketplace housing some sixty shops, boutiques, and restaurants. (See the Shopping section for more information.) You can enter the Exchange or continue along Gertrude's walk to Church Street, where you started your tour.

Elvis Presley Museums

TravelFacts

Location: 7200 International Dr., Orlando 32819 and 5770 W. Bronson Hwy. (U.S. 192), Kissimmee 34746. The Orlando museum is on the second floor of Dowdy Plaza which occupies the southeast corner of Carrier and International Drives. The Kissimmee museum is located in the Old Town shopping complex.
Maps: Page 48.

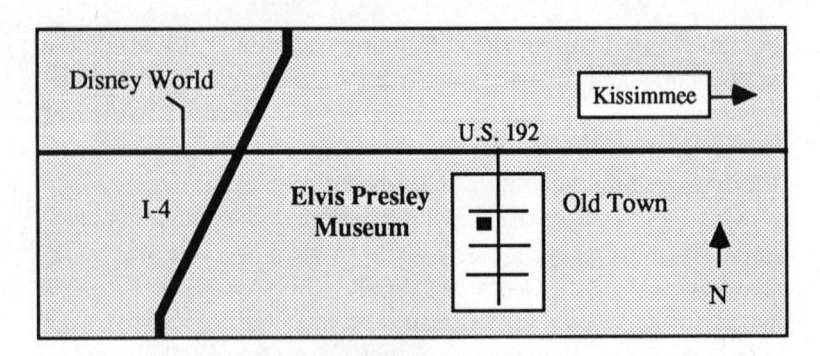

Elvis Presley Museum — Kissimmee

Telephone: (407) 345-9427 (Orlando), (407) 396-8594 (Kissimmee).
Hours: Orlando - 9 A.M. to 10 P.M., Kissimmee 10 A.M. to 11 P.M., daily except Christmas.
Time to see: 30 to 45 minutes.
Price: $4 adults, $3 ages 7 to 12, under 7 free.
• A gift shop offers Elvis T-shirts, photographs, records, and souvenirs.

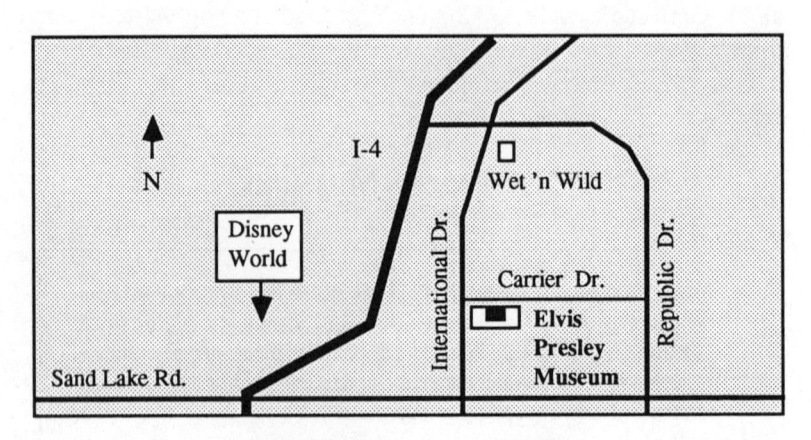

Elvis Presley Museum — Orlando

What to expect: a red-carpeted showroom, Elvis memorabilia, and piped-in Elvis songs. You don't have to be an avid Elvis fan to visit one of the museums. Anyone who has enjoyed his music will find the exhibits of interest.

The museums contain memorabilia ranging from jeweled rings to vehicles. You'll also see furniture, clothes, pistols, paintings, and photos. Some photographs are professional, others snapshots. The most poignant are those showing Elvis as a husband and a father.

Epcot Center

TravelFacts

Location: Walt Disney World, P.O. Box 10,040, Lake Buena Vista 32830-0040.
Maps: Pages 50 and 55.
Telephone: (407) 824-4321.
Hours: Opens 9 A.M. Closing varies between 8 P.M. and 11 P.M. depending on the season. Call for exact time. Epcot's closing time usually differs from that of the Magic Kingdom and the Disney-MGM Studios Theme Park.
Time to see: 2 days.
Price: One Park/One-Day ticket, $32.86 adults, $26.50 children 3 through 9. Ages 2 and under free. 4-Day All Three Parks Passport, $110.24 adults, $87.98 children. 5-Day Plus Super Pass, $143.10 adults, $114.48 children. Admission price gives unlimited access to all rides, attractions, and shows.
One-Park/One-Day tickets are good for entrance to only one park for just one day, either the Disney-MGM Studios Theme Park, Epcot Center, or the Magic Kingdom. Multi-day passports are valid for unlimited admission to the Disney-MGM Studios Theme Park, Epcot Center, and the Magic Kingdom as well as unlimited use of the Disney World transportation system. Multi-day passports carry no expiration date and do not have to be used on consecutive days. The 5-Day Plus Super Pass also includes, after your first use of the pass, unlimited admission for the next seven days to Typhoon Lagoon, River Country, Discovery Island, and Pleasure Island.
Parking: $4 per car parking fee. A tram shuttles between the large park-

ing lot and the Epcot entrance. Before boarding the tram, be sure to note the parking area name and row number where you parked.

Credit cards: American Express, Visa, and MasterCard are the only major credit cards accepted at Disney World.

How to see: Monday, Tuesday, and Wednesday are Disney's busiest days. Sunday, Thursday, and Friday typically have lower attendance. Saturday falls in between. Busiest time of day: 11 A.M. to 5 P.M. The entertainment held throughout the day can add much to your Epcot visit. Keep track of the day's shows, parades, and performances by picking up an entertainment schedule at the Earth Station behind Spaceship Earth.

To cut down on time spent standing in line, be there when the gates open, usually between 8:30 A.M. and 9 A.M. This will give you time to stop at the Earth Station to make any restaurant reservations (see "Reservations" below) and to pick up your entertainment schedule before the attractions open at 9 A.M. Most people line up at Spaceship Earth, the first attraction you come to, and then work their way into the park. For now, skip Spaceship Earth and the CommuniCore. Head deeper into the park to explore The Living Seas, The Land, and Journey into Imagination. Then head for World Showcase. Late

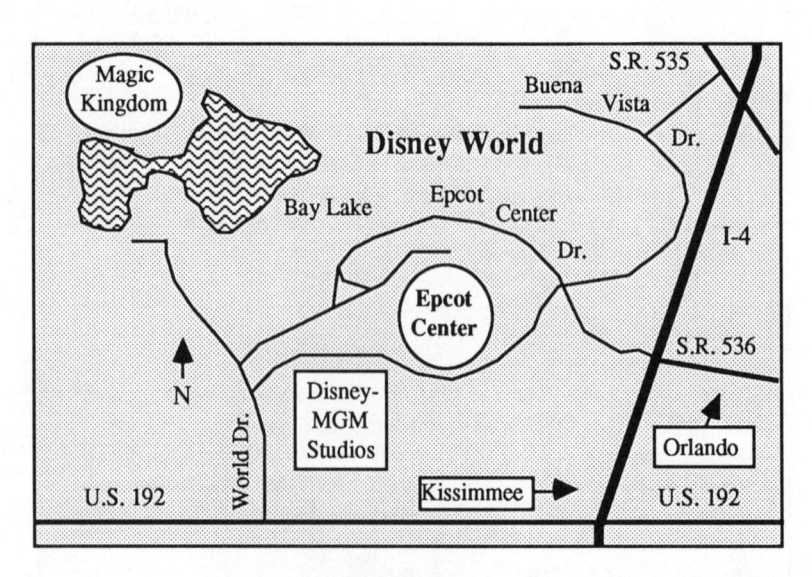

Epcot Center

afternoon or early evening return to Future World to take in the attractions you have not yet seen.

During peak seasons, Disney World fills with peak crowds but is open well into the evening. Consider taking a break during the afternoon hours, the most-crowded time of day. Return to your hotel, relax, perhaps enjoy the pool. In the evening, you can return to Epcot refreshed, ready for several hours of less-crowded visiting. This is especially effective during the summer when you'll swap touring during the hottest part of the day for the cooler evening hours.

TravelVenture tip: Put on your most comfortable walking shoes for Epcot Center — it's twice the size of the Magic Kingdom.

TravelVenture tip: Some attractions include a theater show. Keep in mind that Disney theaters have no bad seats, all offer a good view. But if you'd like to sit in the center of a theater rather than toward the side, don't be among the first in. The staff in each theater has everyone move all the way across the rows to fill each and every seat, starting from the far end of the row. Hang back until you're about in the middle of the waiting crowd. When you enter the theater select a row that is already about half full.

Don't miss: Spaceship Earth, Universe of Energy, The Living Seas' aquarium, Captain Eo (a 3-D film in Journey into Imagination), Mexico's pavilion including its "River of Time" boat ride, Norway's "Maelstrom" boat ride, China's Circle-Vision 360 film and museum exhibit, the Moroccan pavilion, The American Adventure, a performance of either the Renaissance players (United Kingdom pavilion) or Il Teatro di Bologna (Italian pavilion), eating in a World Showcase restaurant.

Reservations: Mandatory at most World Showcase restaurants, but not fast food eateries. (See the Dining section for restaurant information.) If you want to eat in one of these restaurants, be at Epcot when the gates open. Go immediately to the Earth Station. Here you can make reservations for lunch or dinner. You can also make lunch reservations in person at the restaurant. These restaurants are popular, and during high seasons reservations go especially fast at the more popular French, Italian, and Japanese restaurants. Reservations must be made in person on the day you wish to dine. No telephone reservations accepted. An exception to that rule: guests staying at a Disney hotel may make day-before advance reservations at their hotel.

- If you leave Epcot but plan to return that same day or to visit the Magic Kingdom or the Disney-MGM Studios Theme Park, be sure to get

your hand stamped at the exit.
- Strollers and wheelchairs are available for rent on your left as you go through the main gate and at the International Gateway entrance adjacent to the French pavilion.
- Devices to assist sight- or hearing-impaired visitors are available at the Earth Station.
- Coin-operated lockers are located to the right (as you enter Epcot) of Spaceship Earth and at the International Gateway entrance adjacent to the French pavilion.
- A bank is located just outside and to the left (facing Epcot) of the main gate. Hours: 9 A.M. to 4 P.M. daily.
- Pets may be boarded at Epcot's kennel, $4 per day.
- A baby center equipped to help you care for your infant is located near the Odyssey Restaurant between Future World and World Showcase.
- Package pick-up service is available for shoppers. Make your purchases and pick them up at the Entrance Plaza when you leave Epcot.
- The Camera Center by Spaceship Earth will loan you a camera. You buy the film. You must, however, leave a refundable deposit, using cash or credit card. (You get your credit card slip back when you return the camera.) You can also rent 35mm and video cameras.

What to expect: a world's fair focusing on man and the planet we live on. Epcot had long been a dream of Walt Disney's. He pictured a utopian community where people would actually live and work, a sort of Experimental Prototype Community of Tomorrow — EPCOT. When Walt Disney died in 1966, though, Epcot was still just an idea. But that idea continued to germinate within the Disney organization. As it began to take definite shape, however, the idea ran into the practicalities of people calling an experimental community home. So Disney imagineers modified the original idea. They replaced human beings with more than 700 audio-animatronic — robotic — manikins and shaped Epcot as an international showplace of human achievement and future ideas — the Epcot Center that opened at Disney World on October 1, 1982.

Epcot, whose initial costs were almost $1 billion — which makes it one of the largest private construction projects ever undertaken in the United States — is a 260-acre permanent world's fair wrapped around a 40-acre man-made lagoon. Epcot is split into two areas: Future World and World Showcase.

Future World merges history, entertainment, and technology to give a glimpse of the future. It takes a look at the themes of communications, energy, life and health, hi-tech, transportation, imagination, agriculture, and the world's oceans. Future World, in spite of its name, gives you a generous dose of history, but it uses advanced and emerging technology to do so. Solar cells that convert sunlight directly into electricity help power one ride. Another ride shows experimental farming methods that may find use in the future. And the lifelike moving and talking audio-animatronic figures are a visible symbol of the advanced computer technology that drives the whole park.

World Showcase, on the other hand, takes a look at life as it is lived in ten foreign countries — Mexico, Norway, China, Germany, Italy, Japan, Morocco, France, the United Kingdom, and Canada. The country pavilions are a blend of distinctive landmarks and architectural features intended to give you an impression of each country. The Eiffel Tower, a 15th-century Chinese temple, a Mayan pyramid, Venetian gondolas, and a British pub are just a few of the recreations. Shops are filled with the crafts and products of these countries. Many of the employees are natives. And fine-dining restaurants offer you an actual taste of the country.

TravelVenture tip: On-the-spot information about Epcot Center is literally at your fingertips. Spread around Epcot are four World Key Information Service centers.which have a total of 29 computer consoles. You don't have to be a computer expert to operate them. Follow the computer's instructions, and touch the appropriate spot on the monitor screen to direct the computer to retrieve the information you need. If you dislike working a computer, you can call up on the screen an actual person who will answer your questions. World Key Information Service consoles are located in the Earth Station, on the causeway connecting Future World to World Showcase, at World Showcase Plaza, and in front of the German Pavilion. If you don't want to fool with a computer at all, the hosts and hostesses at the Guest Relations booths in Earth Station will also answer your questions.

Future World

Spaceship Earth

Approaching Epcot you'll spot the park's hallmark and one of its must-see attractions — Spaceship Earth. This 180-foot silver sphere looks like a giant golf ball sitting on a tee. Its skin is made up of 954 triangular aluminium panels. Inside, you'll find a continuous chain of "time machine" vehicles. These ride cars take you on a 15-minute journey along a quarter-mile track.

You'll be surprised at just how much Disney imagineers have packed into Spaceship Earth. When you climb aboard, your ride car moves upward into a black void and back in time to the dawn of man. You then begin to journey forward in time. Along the way, audio-animatronic figures demonstrate how communications have progressed through the ages. These advances range from stone-age cave paintings, to Renaissance art, to books, television, and the communications of space station astronauts working beneath a star-filled sky — the top of the sphere.

TravelVenture tip: As your ride car moves past the glowing embers of a fallen Rome, it's not your imagination bringing the stench of smoldering timbers to your nostrils. It's a "smelitzer," a Disney effect that shoots an appropriate aromatic whiff in your direction.

CommuniCore

At the CommuniCore it's please touch and hands on. Two semicircular buildings — CommuniCore East and CommuniCore West — wrap around a fountained plaza. Inside the buildings you'll find a computer playground. You can operate various computers and play video games with an educational twist. In one game you protect your microchip not from space invaders but

ATTRACTIONS 55

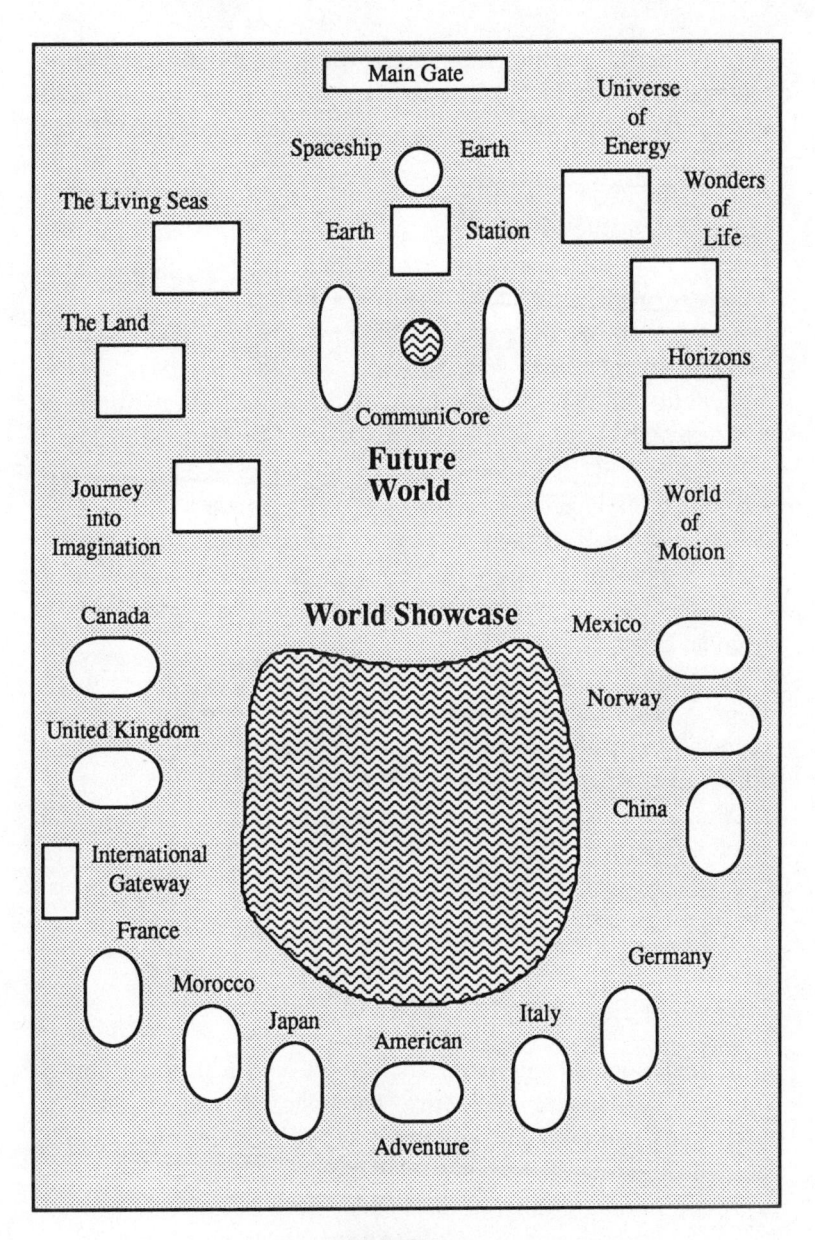

**Epcot Center
Future World and World Showcase**

from its mortal enemies: dust, hair, water, and static electricity. Another computer lets you design your own roller coaster. The computer then visually puts you into the front seat and takes you for a ride.

CommuniCore East offers hands-on energy exhibits and a 20-minute show, **Backstage Magic.** This show gives a short history of computers, offers a well-done, simplified explanation of how computers work, and then gives you a look at Epcot Computer Central. You'll see the computers that run Epcot and serve as the brains for its more than 700 audio-animatronic characters .

Feel like nobody ever listens to your opinion? Then drop in at the **Electronic Forum** in the Future Choice Theater and take part in the Epcot poll. In response to the poll's questions, pressing one of five buttons located on your seat's left arm rest allows you to anonymously express your opinion on current events and contemporary issues. A computer tallies audience answers and gives instant feedback, so you can see how you compare with the rest of the audience.

While at the forum, catch up on what's happening in the outside world. Television monitors display news and information programs from around the world, pulled in by the two satellite dish antennas located just outside CommuniCore East.

Should a particular theme catch your imagination during your Epcot wanderings, visit **Epcot Outreach** in CommuniCore West. Here you can get a computer printout listing additional information sources on your subject.

Universe of Energy

A futuristic-looking building, taller at one end than the other, is home to the Universe of Energy. Thousands of four-inch-square mirror tiles make up the building's facade. On its roof, 80,000 photovotaic solar cells convert Florida sunshine directly into electricity to help power the attraction. These solar cells generate enough energy to meet the needs of 15 single-family homes.

Inside the 30-minute attraction, three theaters feature slide and film shows that give new meaning to the word audiovisual. But the highlight comes in the second theater where the seats split into six separate sections and turn into traveling cars holding almost 100 people each. Guided by an eight-of-an-inch-thick wire imbedded in the floor, and powered with the aid of those rooftop solar cells, the traveling seats transport you to the next theater.

Along the way you take a time journey to look at the earth as it appeared when fossil fuels began to form. Amidst crashes of thunder, flashes of lightning, and the bellows of prehistoric creatures, you encounter grass-chewing brontosauruses, winged reptiles, three-foot-long centipedes, and a tyrannosaur locked in combat with a stegosaur. Bubbling pools hiss steam into the air to herald an erupting volcano. Fingers of glowing molten lava ooze from its cone. Its acrid fumes drift over you — and you know you've been zapped again by the smelitzer.

Wonders of Life

A double-helix tower — resembling the DNA structure of a human cell — rises at the entrance to Wonders of Life. Inside the gold-domed pavilion, you can step into one of four 40-seat theaters to experience **Body Wars.** The theaters are mounted on hydraulic lifts, similar to a pilot's flight simulator. As the lifts rock, roll, and jerk the theater in synch to a five-minute film, you'll take a roller coaster-like ride through the human body. Although the ride takes you on a simulated trip inside a splinter-pierced finger and on through the body's heart, lungs, and brain, the ride emphasizes entertainment rather than education.

TravelVenture tip: Body Wars is actually quite a rough thrill ride. If you don't enjoy thrill rides or are easily prone to motion sickness, you may want to pass it up.

Another theater takes you inside the body less vigorously. The light-hearted **Cranium Command** uses animation, film, and an audio-animatronic figure to take you inside the head of a 12-year-old boy.

The pavilion also houses a collection of hands-on educational exhibits and three health-themed theaters. The **Anacomical Players** theater uses live characters to get its point across while the **Goofy About Health** theater depends on animation. A third theater features a 14-minute film, *The Making of Me*. The film stars Martin Short and shows the development of a fetus as well as an actual birth.

The health theme also carries over into the pavilion's eatery, Pure and Simple, which serves health food.

Horizons

This pavilion shows how Disney imagineers view life in the 21st century — in a city, a desert, outer space, and undersea. To view these future horizons, you climb aboard one of 174 continuous-chain vehicles. The ride's initial mundane effects give way to projections on a 60-foot screen that make you feel as if spinning, flying, and hurtling through space. As you pass a desert landscape turned into a blossoming orange grove, you'll pick up the scent of smelitzer-generated orange blossoms. Returning from the future, you computer-select your environment — air, land, or sea — by touching one of three small screens that light up inside your ride car.

World of Motion

The disc-shaped building alongside Horizons contains the World of Motion. Ride cars take you on a narrated journey among 18 dioramas filled with 139 audio-animatronic figures. What you get is a 14-minute, lighthearted look at the evolution of transportation. Among the scenes: a family of cave dwellers blowing on their swollen red feet (If you've spent much time walking around Epcot, you'll immediately identify with this family.) and Leonardo Da Vinci fiddling with a pair of homemade stick wings while a frowning, foot-tapping Mona Lisa waits alongside her unfinished portrait. After the ride you can look at exhibits and short films on transportation.

Journey into Imagination

The building crowned by the glass pyramids houses Journey into Imagination. Two audio-animatronic characters, Dreamfinder and Figment, guide you on the ride that gives the attraction its name. The Journey into Imagination ride takes you on a 14-minute journey that gives a fanciful look at how imagination works.

On the building's second floor you'll find the entertaining **Image Works.** The works offers various hands-on and electronic exhibits, including a set up that lets you paint by electronics.

The top attraction at Journey into Imagination, and among the best at Epcot, is the **Magic Eye Theater** and its 17-minute, 3-D film, *Captain Eo.* This *Star Wars*-like musical adventure features more than 3-D — it also combines laser lights and projection devices to help pull you into the action. Disney called in some high-powered talent to make the film: George Lucas of *Star Wars* fame is the producer, Francis Ford Coppola *(The Godfather, Apocalypse Now)* the director, and Michael Jackson the star.

Be sure not to miss the fountains outside Journey into Imagination. These imaginative fountains shoot sausage-shaped globs of water from fountain to fountain to land on sponge-like pads. Water globs also shoot over the heads of unsuspecting passersby.

TravelVenture tip: To see *Captain Eo,* you can bypass any Journey into Imagination line that extends outdoors. Keep to the left of the line and enter the building through the three sets of double doors to the right of the fountains.

The Land

At The Land pavilion, whose six-acre building would cover the Magic Kingdom's Tomorrowland, the emphasis is on the fruits of the earth. The main attraction, **Listen to the Land,** is a 12-minute boat ride through a rain forest, past a desert landscape, and alongside a prairie ravaged by locusts and fire. As the boat continues its voyage, it sails through an experimental greenhouse for a look at some of tomorrow's farming techniques. The crops here will crush the ego of most home gardeners — 50-pound squashes and cucumber plants that grow a foot a day.

TravelVenture tip: If these plants intrigue you, sign-up for a guided, behind-the-scenes walking tour of the greenhouse. Make your reservation early in the day at the **Harvest Tour** booth, located on the opposite side of the pavilion from the boat ride. Look for it in an alcove between the Farmer's Market and the Kitchen Kabaret.

The Land also has two theater shows. **Kitchen Kabaret** features audio-animatronic foodstuffs dancing and singing to the tune of proper nutrition. The **Harvest Theater** runs a 20-minute film titled *Symbiosis* which shows man's impact on the environment.

TravelVenture tip: The Harvest Theater has three entrances, two of which you reach by navigating crowded stairways. Here's how to avoid the crowded stairs. When in the lobby waiting to enter the theater, position yourself so that out of the three sets of double doors you'll enter through the set on the right. When the doors open, you'll step into a hallway, and immediately on your right will be another set of doors. Use this set to enter the theater.

Be sure to take time to enjoy the two mosaic murals at the entrance to The Land pavilion. They took three months to create and cover 3,000 square feet with 150,000 individually cut and shaped tiles. The tiles come in 131 colors and are made from marble, granite, slate, smalto, Venetian glass, 14-karat gold, mirror, ceramic, and pebbles.

The Living Seas

At the pavilion's entrance sits a pile of wave-worn boulders. With a loud, deep clap, unseen waves pound the rocks and white spray spews from water-carved tunnels. Inside, the emphasis shifts from the shore and surf to the ocean's depths. You'll move first through a collection of undersea exploration devices — early submarines and deep-sea diving equipment. After viewing an excellent seven-minute film on the sea, you'll ride a trembling "hydrolater" (a Disney underwater elevator) to the floor level of Disney's sea. This 28-foot-deep sea, contained by clear acrylic panels, is made up of 5.7 million gallons of salt water. And it's home to some 200 species of marine life, including sharks, barracudas, rays, dolphins, sea turtles, eels, grouper, snapper, angel fish, and other tropical marine animals found in a Caribbean coral reef. A sea cab ride takes you through a clear underwater tunnel for a close-up look at this marine life. The three-minute ride ends at Sea Base Alpha. Here, observation decks on two levels let you check out life in this coral reef at a more leisurely pace.

Sea Base Alpha is designed to give the feeling of being in an underwater research station. You can talk with marine scientists and see diving demonstrations. You'll also find myriad educational exhibits, including a model that shows how waves form and tanks of zooplankton and phytoplankton, the basic ingredients required for life to exist undersea.

World Showcase

Jules Verne sent Phileas Fogg around the world in 80 days, Disney will send you around the world in about 8 hours. World Showcase offers a slice of life from ten foreign countries: Mexico, Norway, China, Germany, Italy, Japan, Morocco, France, the United Kingdom, and Canada. You'll also find a bit of America.

World Showcase gives you a taste of world travel without the worry of shots, visas, or airline tickets. All you need is a day and your Disney World passport. The country pavilions line World Showcase Promenade, a mile-long roadway that rings the World Showcase Lagoon. Double-decker buses make frequent circle trips around the roadway, while boats similar to those that ply the canals of Amsterdam crisscross the lagoon.

Mexico

Moving clockwise around the lagoon, you'll travel first to Mexico, whose attractions are housed in a recreated five-tiered Mayan pyramid. Similar pyramids dot the Mexican and Central American countryside. Some experts speculate that Mexico still has thousands of pyramids yet to be discovered. These pyramids were built as religious temples by Indian cultures such as the Toltecs, the Aztecs, and the Mayans — whose civilization mysteriously collapsed some 500 years before Columbus came to America.

Just inside the entrance to Mexico's pyramid is an exhibition hall displaying exhibits of Mexican artworks. Deeper inside the pyramid you'll find the Plaza de los Amigos. Regardless of the time of day, the plaza sits under a darkened evening sky. Peddler stands fill the plaza, and shops line one side. Their wares include pottery, clothing, metal and copper crafts, straw items, and leather goods.

At the end of the plaza flows a river. A pyramid rises from the far bank. You can board a boat in one corner of the plaza for an eight-minute sail past this pyramid, alongside a glowing volcano, and down **The River of Time.** The voyage shows you the country's many faces — ancient Mexico, rural Mexico, vacation Mexico, and Mexico City.

Back in the plaza, candle-lit tables on the patio of the San Angel Inn Restaurante overlook the River of Time, the pyramid, and the volcano. The San Angel is patterned after its namesake in Mexico City. The original is an exclusive and popular restaurant located in an 18th-century hacienda that was once a stagecoach stop.

The rhythms of mariachi and marimba bands add to the Mexican atmosphere, both in the plaza and outdoors in the pavilion. Check your show schedule.

Norway

Your around-the-world journey now takes you to Europe and the northernmost Scandinavian country — Norway. A long, narrow land next door to Sweden, Norway's fjord-laced coastline extends for thousands of miles. And the sea plays a prominent part in Norwegian life.

Norwegians are the descendants of ancient seafaring Vikings. And many Viking skills still find use today, including wood working, shipbuilding, and fishing. A modern sea-borne activity is also significant — extracting oil from beneath the wild waters of the North Sea.

At the entrance to the Norwegian pavilion stands a replica of a wooden church. As the Viking age drew to a close and Viking kings adopted Christianity, churches were built throughout Scandinavia. However, this distinctive type of wooden building, called a stave church, is found only in Norway. Only a handful of these churches still survive today. Epcot's stave church is patterned after one of these survivors, the Gol church built around 1250. The Norwegians dismantled the original Gol church and moved it to the Oslo suburb of Bygdoy. Here they reassembled it at the Norwegian Folk Museum, an open-air collection of ancient buildings gathered from throughout Norway. Inside the Epcot stave church you can view an exhibit of Viking artifacts.

On the opposite side of the pavilion, across the cobblestone plaza from the stave church, looms a replica of Akershus Castle. The original in Norway stands on a rocky hillside jutting into Oslo harbor. It was first built around 1300 and rebuilt in the 17th century. The Epcot castle stretches the length of the pavilion and houses the Restaurant Akershus. The restaurant offers an authentic Norwegian buffet at both lunch and dinner.

Also inside the castle is the **Maelstrom,** a short but exciting boat ride. After boarding a dragon-prowed Viking craft, you enter a tunnel to sail back in time. Your boat takes you past a 10th-century Viking village and through a forest inhabited by trolls. Should you incur the wrath of a particular three-headed troll, his spell will send your boat backwards on a rough journey over white-water rapids, past polar bears, and alongside fjords. With luck, just as the boat's stern approaches the top of a waterfall, it will shake the spell and reverse direction — only to plunge into the wind-whipped spray of the North Sea. After rounding an offshore oil rig, you reach safe harbor in a typical Norwegian coastal town of today. A theater in the town shows a five-minute film on Norwegian life and culture.

Upon leaving the theater, you can stroll through the pavilion's shops. These stores are housed in wood buildings typical of those found in Bergen, Alesund, Oslo, and the farm country around Setesdal. Their wares include Norwegian merchandise such as troll dolls, wooden toys, games, wood carvings, pewter tableware and candle holders, glassware, jewelry, blankets, and clothing.

As you leave the pavilion, be sure to walk over to the World Showcase Lagoon. Here *The Norseman* lies at anchor. Made from spruce planking on spruce and fir ribs, the 49-foot vessel is an historically accurate replica of a 10th-century Viking craft. *The Norseman* was built in Afjord, a small Norwegian town, as a gift from the people of Norway to the people of the United States.

China

To reach the People's Republic of China from Norway requires a trek across the European-Asian landmass. At Epcot it's just a short stroll. Enter the pavilion through one of three portals in the delicately sculptured and brightly painted Gate of the Golden Sun, which is styled after the gate to Beijing's summer palace. Once through the gate you'll see gardens and reflecting ponds similar to those found in the Chinese city of Suzhou. The Chinese design their gardens and ponds to symbolize the order and discipline of nature.

A three-tiered, round red building with blue shingle roofing dominates the pavilion. The building is a half-size replica of Beijing's Hall of Prayer for Good Harvest. The actual hall in China was built in 1420 and is just one of several temples built in Beijing's Tian Tan Park between 1406 and 1420. Collectively, the buildings are known as the Temple of Heaven.

At the doorway a Chinese man or woman will greet you. As you step inside, immediately notice the intricate carvings and colors on the walls and ceiling. Farther inside, a Circle-Vision

360 film, *Wonders of China,* takes you to the Beijing Opera, along the Yangtze River, through bustling Shanghai, among the surreal mountain peaks of Guilin, up to the 12,000-foot altitudes of Lhasa, Tibet, and along the 2,500-year-old Great Wall. The film, which took seven months to make, reveals China's vastness through scenes as diverse as a camel caravan crossing the Gobi desert and man-made ice sculptures in a frozen landscape.

Exiting the theater, you'll enter the *Xing fu Jie* — the Street of Good Fortune. A row of red-painted buildings line one side of the street. The buildings actually house a single large store whose merchandise includes furniture, jade, jewelry, silk paintings, and clothing.

Be sure not to miss the *Liu Yin Ge* — **House of the Whispering Willows.** It's easily overlooked, sitting between the Street of Good Fortune and the Hall of Prayer for Good Harvest. The house is actually a museum exhibiting Chinese art treasures, many of which have never before been shown outside China.

Germany

From China, Epcot leaps back to Europe. Bavarian-style buildings with gables and towers circle round a cobblestone *platz* or plaza. From a fountain in the center, a column rises to support a statue of St. George slaying the dragon. At the back of the pavilion rises a medieval castle whose design is a combination of features from two German castles — the Eltz on the Mosel River and the Stahleck on the Rhine River. The castle houses Germany's Biergarten restaurant.

Shops in the pavilion offer such German products as Hummel and porcelain figurines, cookies, candy, and toys. There's also a wine cellar plus an art and book store whose exterior derives from the 16th-century Kaufhaus or merchants hall in the town of Freiburg.

Italy

Next door to Germany's pavilion you'll find another European country — Italy. The flavor of Venice predominates the pavilion. Venetian-style bridges overlook gondolas tied to candy-striped poles rising from the lagoon. As you enter the *piazza* — the plaza — a replica of the Doge's Palace in Venice sits on your left. The Epcot version, like the original which sits in St. Mark's Square, is a three-story building of Gothic arches and "marble" facades (actually fiberglass). Its top story displays three shades of pink tiles.

Doge is the name for Venice's ruling official, and since the 9th century the palace has been the residence of the doges. The palace as it looks today, however, dates from the 14th century when it was rebuilt after fire destroyed the previous building.

Alongside the Doge's Palace rises another St. Mark's Square landmark — the Campanille. Epcot's 105-foot red-brick bell tower is modeled after Venice's 324-foot structure which was built in 1902. Actually, though, a bell tower has been on that site in Venice since the 10th century.

While Venetian landmarks predominate, you can also see influences from other Italian cities. The stairway and portico adjoining the Doge's Palace are typical of those in Verona. The Neptune fountain duplicates an original in Florence which was crafted by Bernini, the famed 17th-century Italian sculptor. The garden wall enclosing the piazza resembles walls in Rome and Florence. And the highlight of the pavilion, L'Originale Alfredo di Roma Ristorante (Alfredo's), is also reminiscent of Florentine architecture. Alfredo is the man who gave the world fettucine Alfredo. Of course, the dish is among the restaurant's specialties.

Don't miss the entertainment in the Italian pavilion. An all-seriousness-aside troupe of players from **Il Teatro di Bologna** (rough translation: The Baloney Theater) perform outdoors in the center of the piazza. Dressed in Italian peasant costumes, the players put on skits with the aid of performers selected from the audience.

TravelVenture tip: If you'd rather spectate than participate, hang around the back of the gathered throng.

The shops in the Italian pavilion offer Murano glass, alabaster figurines, pottery, jewelry, and leather goods.

The American Adventure

After Italy you take a break from your foreign travels and jump back to America and The American Adventure. Located halfway around the lagoon, directly opposite Spaceship Earth, The American Adventure is housed in an early-American, red-brick building. Like other World Showcase pavilions, The American Adventure is a composite. The pavilion has just one building, done in just one architectural style — Georgian, which was developed during the reign of Great Britain's King George III. But the building blends Georgian features from such buildings as Philadelphia's Independence Hall, the Old State House in Boston, and Thomas Jefferson's home at Monticello, Virginia.

Inside, in a thousand-seat theater, audio-animatronic figures of Ben Franklin and Mark Twain host a show that uses film clips and 35 audio-animatronic characters to take a look at America. The show moves from the landing of the pilgrims at Cape Cod to the landing of the astronauts on the moon. The American Adventure also boasts a Disney first — a walking audio-animatronic figure (Ben Franklin).

Alongside the lagoon you'll find the **America Gardens Theater,** an outdoor theater that uses the World Showcase Lagoon and Spaceship Earth as a backdrop. Varied entertainers perform here daily. A small billboard at the theater lists performance times. You can also check your show schedule.

Japan

From America it's back overseas, this time to Japan. A red torii gate, similar to one that stands in Hiroshima Bay, rises from the waters of the lagoon. Typically, the Japanese build torii gates at approaches to Shinto shrines.

As you enter the pavilion, a five-tiered pagoda stands on your left. The Epcot structure was inspired by the pagoda built in the 7th-century Horyu-ji Buddhist monastery at Nara. The structures in Japan's Horyu-ji monastery are the world's oldest surviving wooden buildings.

To your right sits a long, massive two-story structure built to resemble elaborate aristocratic houses called *shindens*. This type of building developed in Kyoto, Japan, during the 9th century. Typically, as at Epcot, the shinden is a lakeside building. The ground floor of the shinden is given over to the Mitsukoshi Department Store, one of Japan's leading retailers. Merchandise includes toys, Japanese dolls, books, jewelry, china, prints, and kimonos. The Mitsukoshi Restaurant and the Matsu No Ma Lounge occupy the second floor. Patrons in the lounge get a superb view of the lagoon, Future World, and the other World Showcase pavilions.

On the opposite side of the plaza you can walk through a small, pleasant garden to a thatch-roofed, fast food restaurant called the Yakitori House. The building duplicates a teahouse at the 17th-century Katsura Imperial Villa in Kyoto. Notice the simplicity of the building's architecture, which reflects the spirt of the tea ceremony. Some of the wood in the Yakitori House even retains its bark.

In the background, towering over the whole scene, stands a moated feudal castle. Two massive wooden doors fill its entrance. Just inside, two statues of Japanese warriors on horseback keep vigil. As you can see from looking around the pavilion, wood is the favored Japanese building material. Japan's only large stone buildings were its 16th- and 17th-century castles, like this one at Epcot. The Epcot structure is patterned after the Himeji Castle built in the late 16th century. Don't overlook the collection of Japanese art works at the **Bijutsu-kan Gallery** inside the pavilion's castle.

Morocco

Your Epcot journey now takes you to the northwest corner of Africa and the Kingdom of Morocco. Both the Atlantic Ocean and the Mediterranean Sea wash the sands of Morocco's beaches. And although Morocco's eastern and southern frontiers are landlocked, there's also sand there — the sands of the Sahara Desert.

If Morocco brings to mind the exotic and the romantic, it's only natural. The country is home to Casablanca, Tangier, and Marrakech, three cities whose very names are synonymous with mystery, intrigue, and adventure.

At first glance the Moroccan pavilion appears quite small. Red sandstone-like walls, similar to those surrounding parts of Marrakech, enclose a small courtyard. A fountain decorated with small blue and white tiles occupies the center. Buildings flank the courtyard on two sides. One houses the **Gallery of Arts and History,** an exhibit of Moroccan cultural artifacts. The other, the Moroccan National Tourist Office.

The tall, square tower rising from the corner is a replica of the minaret at Marrakech's 12th-century Koutoubia Mosque. Minarets are a feature of mosques throughout the world. Five times a day, a *muezzin* climbs to the minaret's top to call the faithful to prayer.

A two-story wall closes off the back of the courtyard. The wall, however, is pierced by three horseshoe-arch gateways. The wall and its gateways recreate the *Bab Boujoulaoud,* a gate built in 786 at the Moroccan imperial city of Fez. It's behind Epcot's Bab Boujoulaoud that the heart of the Moroccan pavilion unfolds. Here you'll find the old quarter, or *medina.*

The typical medina contains a labyrinth of narrow, winding streets — some so narrow you can extend both arms and touch the buildings on each side. Morocco and Disney have faithfully recreated the spirit and feeling of a North African medina. As you explore it, you may even feel a momentary uneasiness that you have lost your way.

Once through the Bab Boujoulaoud and into the medina, you can visit the **Fez House** to your left. This traditional Moroccan home is constructed in a style developed in the 14th century. The two-story house is built around a fountained courtyard. Notice the carved wooden arches made from Moroccan red cedar and the handcrafted tile work.

One of the pavilion's most striking features is this abundance of tile work. Forbidden by religion to reproduce images, Moslems developed patterns of intricate geometric designs using tiles, some of which are as small as an inch. To ensure the pavilion's tile work would be authentic, craftsman came over from Morocco, bringing with them some nine tons of tiles which they hand cut and laid. In the process they turned the entire pavilion into a work of art.

Next door to the Fez House is a carpet shop selling handmade Moroccan rugs. At times throughout the day you can watch a Moroccan woman's flashing hands weave a rug on a large wood loom. As you exit the carpet shop, just down the curving street to your left you'll find the Restaurant Marrakech.

The remainder of the pavilion is taken up by the shops of the *souk,* or bazaar. Portions of the souk's walkways are shaded by a roof of bamboo poles as is done in the old quarter of Fez. Skeins of wool yarn dyed blue, purple, green, red, and yellow hang from the poles. Much of the merchandise flows out of the shops to make the walkways even narrower. Among the goods for sale are inlaid-wood jewelry boxes, wood carvings, leather goods, colorful Moroccan clothing, handmade jewelry, brass and copper items, and pottery.

Moroccan musicians and dancers perform frequently throughout the pavilion and in the Restaurant Marrakech. You'll also see Moroccan craftsman at work.

France

From Africa you again travel to Europe, this time to France. As you approach from Morocco, you'll spot the maroon awning that shades the tables of the Au Petit Cafe — a sidewalk cafe where waiters in white shirts, black trousers, and bow ties scurry about balancing large trays on their fingertips. If you approach from the opposite direction, you'll cross a bridge similar to those that cross the Seine River in Paris.

Around the corner from the Au Petit Cafe, European-style buildings border a fountained plaza. You're now in a France intended to resemble the late 19th and early 20th centuries, *La*

Belle Epoque — the beautiful time. It was a time of French impressionist painters like Monet and Renoir. A France of Toulouse-Lautrec, La Moulin Rouge, and the Paris world's fair of 1892 which introduced the Eiffel Tower.

The French pavilion's Eiffel Tower rises 100 feet in the background. It's an accurate, one-tenth replica built according to Gustaf Eiffel's original blueprints. Unlike the original in Paris, however, only the upper stages are visible, and you can't ride an elevator to the top. But you can get a feel for what that ride would be like. *Impressions de France,* a 200 degrees-wide film shown on five screens will take you up the Eiffel Tower so realistically that you may cringe and clutch your armrests. The film also produces an impression of motion as it moves you along on board a boat, in a hot-air balloon, perched on a flower vendor's cart, and clinging to the very front of a railroad locomotive. The London Philharmonic provides the background music for this 18-minute look at the beauty of France.

TravelVenture tip: Unlike most World Showcase films, *Impressions de France* is held in a sit-down theater. Seek it out when you need to relax and be entertained in air-conditioned comfort. If you've been touring most of the day, your feet will think it's almost heaven.

The French atmosphere is further reinforced by the pavilion's entertainers. These can include a white-faced mime performing in the streets and the fountained plaza, a singing organ grinder, and a trio of musicians in berets and black and white striped T-shirts who fill the air with strains of accordion music.

The emphasis in the French pavilion is on food. In addition to the Au Petit Cafe, there's two first-class restaurants — Les Chefs de France and Le Bistro de Paris. Just down the street from the Bistro, the Boulangerie Patisserie serves up such goodies as croissants, brioche, eclairs, and napoleons. You can take your bakery purchases to tables and chairs located in a nearby Epcot version of Les Halles, a former Paris farmers market.

Many of France's shops continue the pavilion's preoccupation with food. Their wares include table cloths, baking pans, copper cooking pans, mustard, cook books, and wine. Other shops offer French perfumes, jewelry, scarves, books, and art prints.

United Kingdom

While you don't cross the English Channel when departing France, you do move on to a land of British accents and Scottish woolens. The United Kingdom pavilion brings a bit of Britain to Epcot through eight different architectural styles. The earliest styles are found at the foot of Tudor Street. As you move down the street, deeper into the pavilion, the buildings reveal British architecture from increasingly later periods. The buildings range from medieval structures — a 15th-century, thatch-roofed, masonry cottage and a timber-and-plaster building whose upper floors protrude increasingly out over the sidewalk — to 19th-century brownstone row houses. At the far end of the pavilion, you'll find a quiet, out-of-the-way corner with a wee bit of London's Hyde Park, complete with bandstand.

TravelVenture tip: This small park is a rare, peaceful, shaded, uncrowded refuge. If you feel the need to get far from the madding crowd, seek it out.

As you browse in the stores, notice that the interior architecture and decor also grows more sophisticated as you move farther down Tudor Street. The wares in these shops include tea, candy, jellies, soap, Royal Doulton figurines and dinnerware, toys, and Scottish woolens.

The hungry and the thirsty can find solace at the Rose and Crown pub. A typical British pub, the Rose and Crown offers more than beer; you can also get a hearty meal. Although British pubs serve their beer warm, the Rose and Crown has made a concession to American tastes and offers cold beer.

If you missed Il Teatro di Bologna in the Italian pavilion, be sure to catch the **Renaissance Street Theater.** These players put on an equally good, British version of the audience-participation skit staged in Italy.

TravelVenture tip: Same tip here as in Italy; if you'd rather spectate than participate, hang around the back of the gathered throng.

Canada

Setting out from the United Kingdom you'll be on the last leg of your journey around Epcot's world. You're destination now is North America and Canada. The Canadian pavilion has a rugged, north-woods look — a rock mountain with cascading waterfall, totem poles, and a log cabin trading post. Inside the trading post, the Northwest Mercantile, the shelves are stocked with lamb-skin rugs, animal pelts, wool sweaters and jackets, leather goods, raccoon hats, moccasins, jewelry, maple syrup, and maple sugar candy.

An impressive replica of a metal-roofed, chateau-style hotel towers over the pavilion. A prominent feature in many Canadian cities, Epcot's building is modeled after Ottawa's Chateau Laurier. The pavilion's replica, however, contains a boutique rather than a hotel. The building's lowest level houses Le Cellier, a cafeteria that features Canadian specialties in a rathskeller-like setting. Across from Le Cellier you'll find Victoria Gardens, which is patterned after the Butchart Gardens in Victoria, British Columbia.

The main attraction at Canada is a nine-screen wraparound movie called *O Canada*. You reach the theater by entering a gold mine tunnel. This 17-minute CircleVision 360 film shows Canada to be a country packed with terrific scenery.

Flying Tigers Warbird Air Museum

TravelFacts

Location: 231 N. Hoagland Blvd. (formerly Airport Road), Kissimmee 34741.
Map: Page 74.

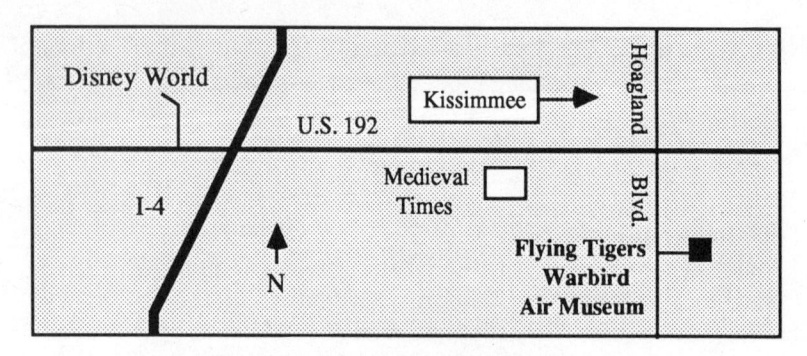

Flying Tigers Warbird Air Museum

Telephone: (407) 933-1942.
Hours: 9 A.M. to 5:30 P.M. Closing may vary, call to confirm.
Time to see: 30 minutes.
Price: $5 adults, $4 ages 11 and under and 60 and over.

What to expect: a look at a vintage aircraft restoration facility and the aircraft housed in its hangar. Tours are assembled in the office of Reilly Aviation. While waiting for your tour to start, you can inspect the museum's small collection of World War II memorabilia. The collection includes a B-25 nose bubble equipped with an anti-aircraft machine gun and bomb site, bandoliers of anti-aircraft ammunition, hats, goggles, a flight jacket, an Army Signal Corps radio transmitter and receiver, C rations, first aid kit, even an unopened green, gold, and red pack of Lucky Strikes. If you flew in World War II, you'll find some memories here.

The museum also houses a collection of original aviation paintings and an exhibit of 450 aircraft models that depict the history of flight.

The 20-minute guided tour takes you into the restoration hangar. On display are anywhere from 12 to 18 restored aircraft as well as several in-progress restorations. The rebuilt aircraft are in excellent shape and flyable condition. What you'll see may vary as restorations are completed and moved out but will probably include P-51 Mustangs, T28 and PT-22 trainers, and cloth-covered bi-planes including a 1940 DeHavilland Tiger Moth.

Gatorland Zoo

TravelFacts

Location: 14501 S. Orange Blossom Trail (U.S. 17-92), Orlando 32821, just north of Kissimmee.
Map: Page 77.
Telephone: (800) 777-9044, (407) 855-5496.
Hours: Opens 8 A.M. Closes between 6 P.M. and 8 P.M. depending on the season.
Time to see: 2 hours.
Price: $7.95 adults, $4.95 ages 3 to 11, under 3 free.
- A Gator Jumparoo show is held periodically throughout the day. Call (800) 777-9044 for recorded information on the show schedule.
- Souvenir shop available. Wares include Gator Chowder and alligator-skin boots, handbags, and attache cases.
- Snack bar available. Fare includes fried alligator meat.

What to expect: snakes, crocodiles, and alligators. The cute and the cuddly take a back seat at this zoo. At the entrance you get right into the alligator theme — you have to walk through a giant replica of open alligator jaws. To reach the real thing, a boardwalk leads out over a pond filled with the reptiles.

But don't build your expectations of alligators too high. They won't be roaring or lumbering about like prehistoric movie monsters. At the zoo they may be sitting on the pond bottom in shallow water, floating along in deeper water, or just sunbathing on one of the two wooden platforms anchored in the pond. You may get the impression that alligators are Florida's foremost sunbathers.

Don't let this turn you away from the Gatorland Zoo, though.

What these creatures lack in activity is made up by their sheer numbers — some 5,000 of them throughout Gatorland. With so many gators around, when you spot out of the corner of your eye one of the life-size replicas, you'll probably jump with a start.

You can get a look at alligators in action by taking in the zoo's **Gator Jumparoo** show. During the 20-minute performance, you'll see alligators leap from the pond to snatch hunks of meat or chicken hanging from a cable stretched 4 feet above the water. A gator trainer fills you in on alligator lore and also entices alligators to jump from the water, jaws open, for a hunk of meat held in his hand. If you want to see still more flashing and snapping jaws, you can buy dead fish at the zoo to feed the gators.

Some of these alligators are movie stars. You saw them near the end of *Indiana Jones and the Temple of Doom*. The film's gators were feasting on the bad guys who fell into the river when the footbridge broke. Actually, the alligators were filmed close up in their Gatorland Zoo pond while they devoured a dummy stuffed with raw meet.

The far side of the pond is lined with open-air cages and pens whose inhabitants include: macaws, monkeys, sheep, raccoons, pygmy goats, a peacock, European spotted deer, ostriches, turtles, a zebra, and a Florida black bear. There's also almost two-dozen cages of snakes — including each type of Florida's poisonous snakes. An open-air snake pit with natural landscaping also holds a generous helping of eastern diamondback rattlesnakes and Florida cottonmouth moccasins.

The pond's far side also has — you guessed it — more alligators. The largest is a 13-foot giant weighing some 1,000 pounds. The smallest will be a pile of scrambling foot-long babies playing a gator version of king of the hill. Gatorland Zoo breads alligators for commercial purposes and also sells them to zoos around the world. The zoo has gained some renown with its successful experiments artificially inseminating alligators.

A swinging wood-plank bridge crosses over alligator breeding ponds to a swamp walk. Here, a 2,000-foot boardwalk curves and winds through a thickly forested, natural cypress swamp. The walk is intended to give you a look at Florida plant life, so Ga-

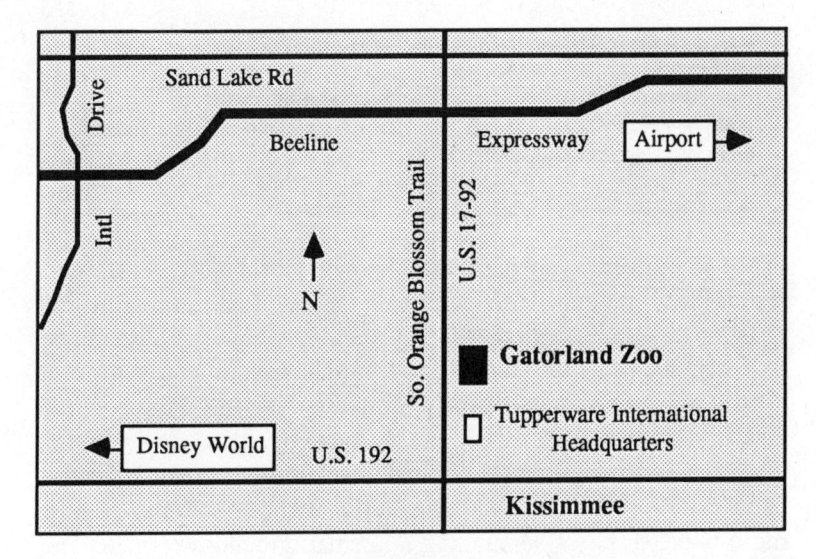

Gatorland Zoo

torland hasn't stocked the swamp with any wildlife. But as for Mother Nature, who knows?

No newcomer to the Florida attractions scene, Gatorland Zoo started out in 1948. Today, it can give you a glimpse of Florida's wilder side.

Kissimmee Livestock Market

TravelFacts

Location: 150 E. Donegan Ave. (P.O. Box 2329), Kissimmee 32742-2329, about one mile east of Orange Blossom Trail (U.S. 17-92).
Map: Page 79.
Telephone: (407) 847-3521.
Hours: Open Wednesdays only starting at 1 P.M. Auctions last for several hours.
Time to see: 30 to 45 minutes.
Price: Free.

- A snack bar serves sandwiches, snacks, and soft drinks.

TravelVenture tip: While the auction lasts until the cattle are sold, you don't have to stay until the end. The atmosphere is informal, and you can enter and leave as you please.

What to expect: a slice of little-known Florida life. Fast food restaurants, motels, and souvenir shops make up one of Kissimmee's faces. Another is cows and cowboys — Kissimmee is the center of cattle ranching in Central Florida. You can get a look at one facet of cattle ranching by dropping in on the Kissimmee Livestock Market for its weekly auction.

The auction building's ground level is given over to cattle pens. To view the auction, you climb a flight of stairs to enter a room with bleachers descending to a small ground-level pen. The first two ringside rows, with the cushioned seats, are reserved for bidders. Most of the men seated ringside wear cowboy hats and clean, pressed jeans. Those in the first row rest their polished boots on the metal railings that rise above the pen. Occasionally, a man leans forward to spit a jet of tobacco juice into the hay strewn about the pen's floor.

A gate in one wall opens and a bull, a calf, or a cow bolts into the pen. After the bidding, a gate in the opposite wall opens and the animal charges out.

TravelVenture tip: For the uninitiated, the rolling sing song of the auctioneer is difficult to decipher. It's almost as difficult to detect the subtle signals from the bidders. If you watch closely, though, you can spot a lifted finger, a slight wave, or an almost-imperceptible nod of a head.

Leu Gardens and Leu House Museum

TravelFacts

Location: 1730 N. Forest Ave., Orlando 32803.

ATTRACTIONS 79

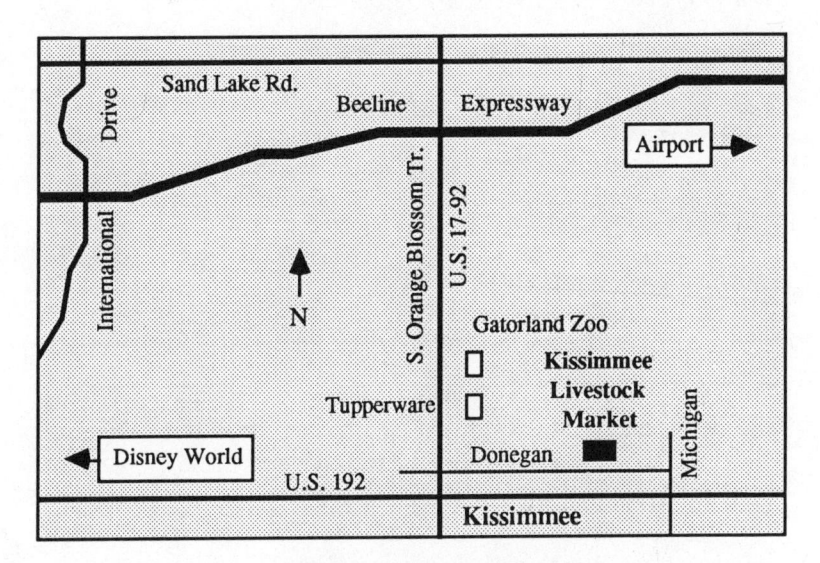

Kissimmee Livestock Market

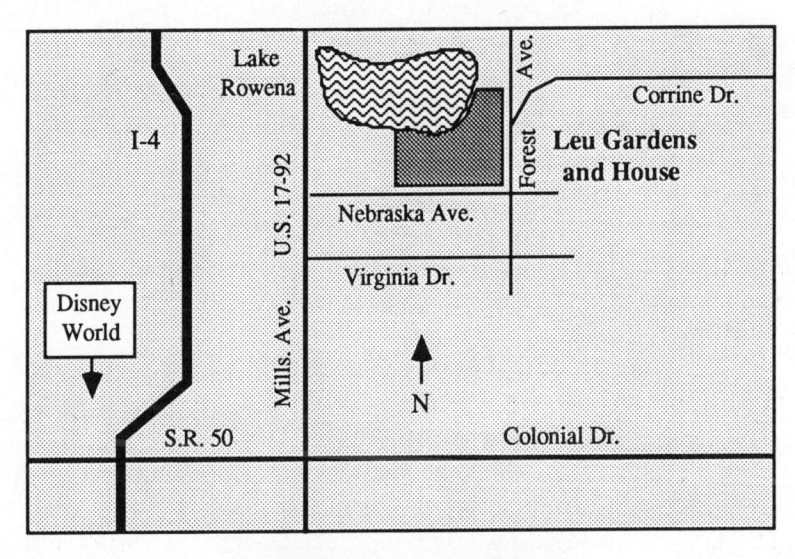

Leu Gardens and Leu House Museum

> *Map:* Page 79.
> *Telephone:* (407) 849-2620.
> *Hours:* Gardens - 9 A.M. to 5 P.M. daily except Christmas. House - 10 A.M. to 3:30 P.M. Tuesday through Saturday, 1 P.M. to 3:30 P.M. Sunday and Monday. House tours generally start every half hour.
> *Time to see:* 2 to 2.5 hours.
> *Price:* $3 adults, $1 ages 6 to 16, under 5 free.
> • A small gift shop contains plants and gardening books.
> • Wheelchair available.

What to expect: a 100-year-old house and 56 acres of trees, shrubbery, and flowers at the south end of Orlando's Lake Rowena. Two-and-a-half miles of walkways shaded by bamboo, magnolia trees, pines, dogwoods, and oaks wind through the gardens like the yellow-brick road to Oz. Thick-stalked split-leaf philodendrons climb tree trunks while ivy ground covers creep through the shade. Special gardens are set aside for camellias, palms, azaleas, lilies, various annuals, and more than an acre of rose bushes. There's even a half-acre desert habitat.

A conservatory stands at one end of the gardens. Inside, the air is heavy with the sweet aroma of purple, white, yellow, and salmon orchids in hanging baskets. Water trickles down small waterfalls and a stream cuts through the conservatory's bromeliads, ferns, dracenas, guava, and rubber plants.

The gardens are named for an Orlando businessman, Harry P. Leu (pronounced "loo"). A botanical buff, Leu purchased the house and the land in 1936 and filled the property with plants from around the world. He donated both the gardens and the house, which also served as his home, to the city of Orlando in 1961.

The property was originally deeded to Angeline and David Mizell in 1862. With the help of family and friends, Angeline built a log cabin on the land. At the time, David was off fighting for the Confederacy. After the war David became sheriff of Orange County. Unfortunately, he was gunned down in 1870 while checking out a cattle rustling complaint. David was buried in a small graveyard that still stands in the gardens.

In 1888, Angeline and her son built a small two-story farmhouse on the property. Subsequent owners added on over the years until the house stood at 10 rooms. Today, the Leu House is one of Orlando's oldest buildings and has been restored, refurbished, and turned into a museum that reflects a Florida home from about 1910 to 1930.

TravelVenture tip: A knowledgeable guide escorts you through the Leu House. In the gardens, though, you're on your own. At the entrance, be sure to pick up a map of the gardens. This will allow you to take a self-guided tour.

Magic Kingdom

TravelFacts

Location: Walt Disney World, P.O. Box 10,040, Lake Buena Vista 32830-0040.
Maps: Pages 82 and 85.
Telephone: (407) 824-4321.
Hours: Gates open at 8:30 A.M., attractions at 9 A.M. Closing varies between 6 P.M. and midnight, depending on the season. Call for the exact time. The Magic Kingdom's closing time usually differs from that of Epcot Center and the Disney-MGM Studios Theme Park.
Time to see: 2 days.
Price: One Park/One-Day ticket, $32.86 adults, $26.50 children 3 through 9. Ages 2 and under free. 4-Day All Three Parks Passport, $110.24 adults, $87.98 children. 5-Day Plus Super Pass, $143.10 adults, $114.48 children. Admission price gives unlimited access to all rides, attractions, and shows.
One-Park/One-Day tickets are good for entrance to only one park for just one day, either the Disney-MGM Studios Theme Park, Epcot Center, or the Magic Kingdom. Multi-day passports are valid for unlimited admission to the Disney-MGM Studios Theme Park, Epcot Center, and the Magic Kingdom as well as unlimited use of the Disney World transportation system. Multi-day passports carry no expiration date and do not have to be used on consecutive days. The 5-Day Plus Super Pass also includes, after your first use of the pass, unlimited admission for the next seven days to Typhoon Lagoon, River Country, Discovery Island, and Pleasure Island.

Parking: $4 per car. A tram shuttles between the large parking lot and the Transportation and Ticket Center. Before boarding the tram, be sure to note the parking area name and row number where you parked

Credit cards: American Express, MasterCard, and Visa are the only major credit cards accepted at Disney World.

How to see: Monday, Tuesday, and Wednesday are Disney's busiest days. Sunday, Thursday, and Friday typically have lower attendance. Saturday falls in between. Busiest time of day: 11 A.M. to 5 P.M.

To cut down on time spent standing in line, get there early. The parking lot and the Transportation and Ticket Center open about 7 A.M. Plan to arrive at the parking lot between 7:30 A.M. and 7:45 A.M. Buy your ticket and take the monorail to the Magic Kingdom's entrance. While official opening time is 9 A.M., the entrance gates and Main Street may open as early as 8 A.M. The rest of the attractions, however, will remain closed until 9 A.M. Use your hour as follows. Stop at the City Hall Information Center to pick up a show schedule. Also, visit the Hospitality House in Town Square to reserve a seat, if desired, for The Diamond Horseshoe Jamboree. Then spend the remaining time exploring Main Street and its shops.

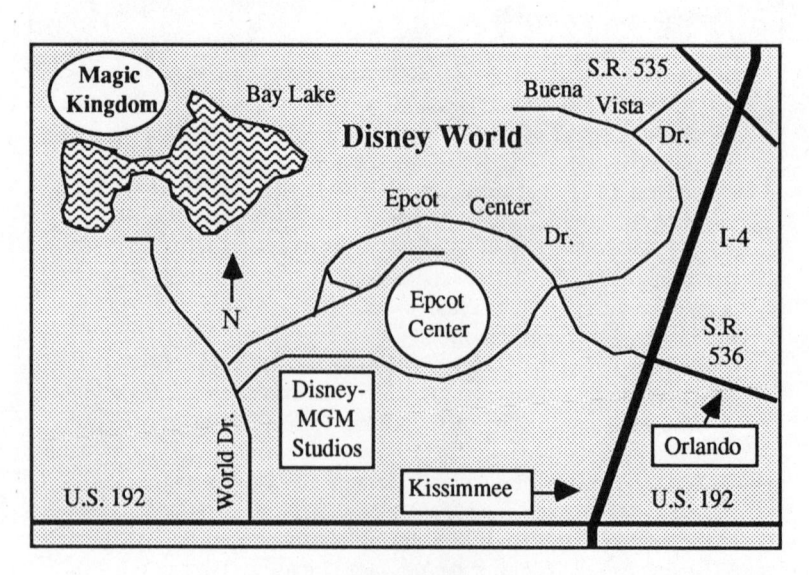

Magic Kingdom

At 9 A.M., be at the foot of Main Street. When the rope barring further entrance into the park is taken down, head for the attractions that have the longest lines: Jungle Cruise, 20,000 Leagues Under the Sea, Big Thunder Mountain, Country Bear Jamboree, the Haunted Mansion, and Space Mountain. The lines at Fantasyland's storybook rides also get quite lengthy. Try to visit these either early in the morning or in the evening.

During peak seasons, Disney World has peak crowds but is open later in the evening. Consider taking a break during the most-crowded afternoon hours. Return to your hotel to relax, perhaps enjoy the pool. In the evening you can return to the Magic Kingdom refreshed for several hours of less-crowded visiting. This is especially effective during the summer when you'll swap touring during the hottest part of the day for the cooler evening hours.

TravelVenture tip: Many attractions have two lines. As a general rule, the line on the left tends to get you to the attraction faster. There is, however, an exception: the right line is shorter at the Grand Prix Raceway ride.

TravelVenture tip: Some attractions include a theater show. Keep in mind that Disney theaters have no bad seats, all offer a good view. But if you'd like to sit in the center of a row rather than toward the side, don't be among the first in. The Disney staff has everyone move all the way across the rows to fill each and every seat starting from the far end of the row. Hang back until you're in the middle of the waiting crowd. When you enter the theater, move into a row that is close to about half full.

TravelVenture tip: Magic Kingdom parades start out in Town Square, head down Main Street, enter Liberty Square, and terminate in Frontierland. Town Square and Main Street draw the most crowds. For less-crowded viewing pick a spot in Liberty Square or Frontierland.

Don't miss: Jungle Cruise, Pirates of the Caribbean, Big Thunder Mountain Railroad, Country Bear Jamboree, The Haunted Mansion, The Hall of Presidents, It's a Small World, Fantasyland Theater's *Magic Journeys* 3-D film, Main Street Electrical Parade (seasonal), Fantasy in the Sky fireworks (seasonal).

- If you leave the Magic Kingdom but plan to return that same day or want to visit Epcot Center or the Disney-MGM Studios Theme Park, be sure to get your hand stamped at the exit.
- A bank is located in Town Square, next to the city hall. Hours: 9 A.M. to 4 P.M. daily.

- Coin-operated lockers are available beneath the Main Street Railroad Station.

  TravelVenture tip: Shops get mobbed near closing time. Shop early and put your purchases in one of these lockers.

- A Baby Center, equipped to help you care for your infant, can be found next to the Crystal Palace Restaurant, just off Main Street.
- Strollers and wheelchairs are available for rent at the Magic Kingdom's entrance.
- Devices to assist sight- or hearing-impaired visitors are available at City Hall Information Center.
- In the Camera Center at the corner of Main Street and the Town Square you can buy film and flashbulbs. If you forgot your camera, they'll lend you one. You buy the film. You must, however, leave a refundable deposit, using cash or credit card. (You get your credit card slip back when you return the camera.) You can also rent 35mm and video cameras.
- Pets can be boarded at the Magic Kingdom's kennel, adjacent to the Transportation and Ticket Center.

What to expect: fun and fantasy in the ultimate theme park. When you enter the Magic Kingdom, it's not required that you deposit your everyday cares and concerns in a repository at the gate — they just have a way of slipping from mind. The Magic Kingdom is made up of shops, eateries, and 40 attractions divided into seven theme areas: Main Street, U.S.A.; Adventureland; Frontierland; Liberty Square; Fantasyland; Mickey's Starland; and Tomorrowland.

From the Magic Kingdom parking lot, Disney trams take you to the Transportation and Ticket Center. To reach the Magic Kingdom, you then take either a ferry or a monorail train. The monorail is normally faster and takes you through the lobby of the Contemporary Resort and past life-size topiary sculptures.

TravelVenture tip: If you leave the Magic Kingdom at closing time, the line for the monorail will be quite long. Take the ferry; it will be quicker. Even if the ferry landing looks packed, head there anyway.

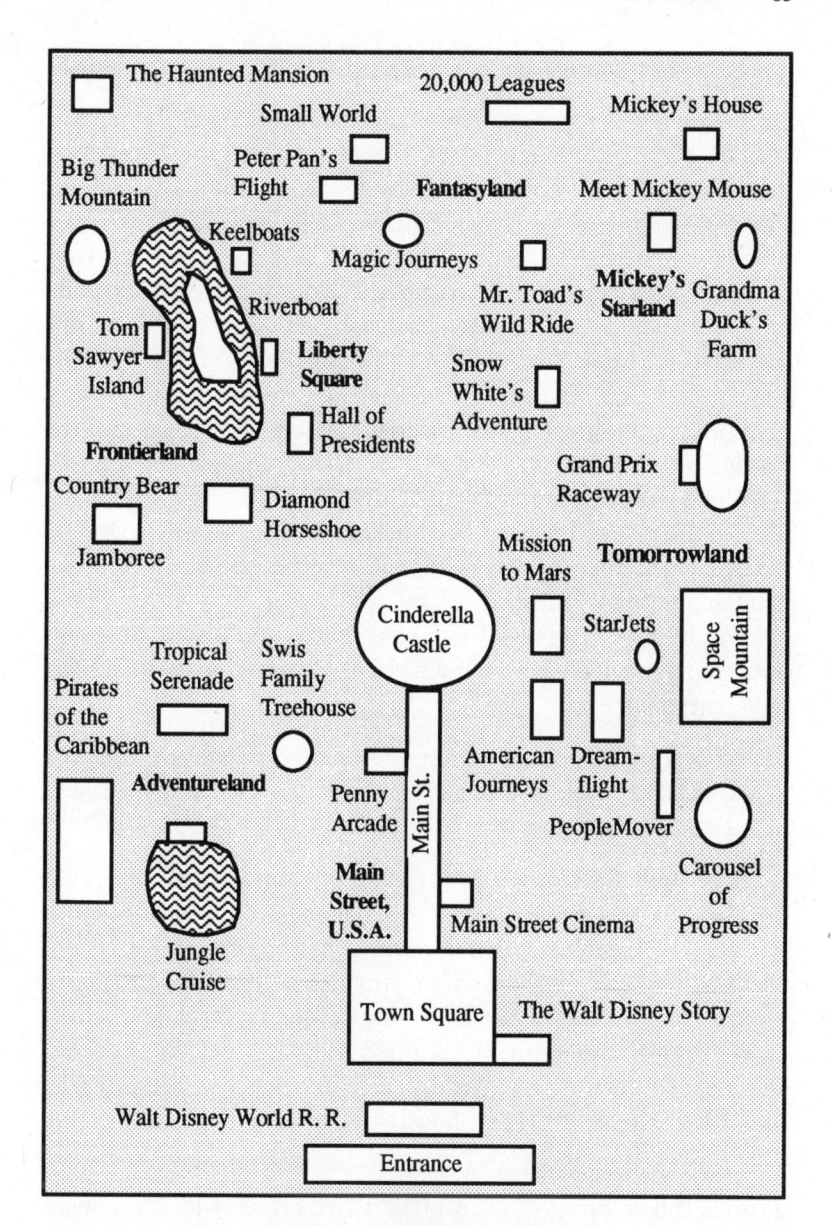

The Magic Kingdom's attractions

Main Street, U.S.A.

Once through the gate to the Magic Kingdom, walk under the railroad overpass to Main Street, U.S.A. — a street that recreates the flavor of turn-of-the-century America. In front of you the street wraps around the Town Square. At its far end Main Street rolls into a circle at the foot of Cinderella Castle.

The Town Square is a busy place. Horse-drawn trolleys, antique automobiles, and double decker buses — all of which run the length of Main Street — pull up to load and off-load passengers. Band concerts take place in the square, parades pass through, and during the Christmas season the Town Square sprouts a giant Christmas tree. City Hall fronts on the square. And, like city halls around the country, it has its share of characters. Disney's characters — Mickey Mouse, Goofy, Dopey, Donald Duck, and the others — will also be glad to shake your hand and pose for pictures.

Inside the City Hall Information Center, you'll find a roll-top desk, antique telephones, and a staff of Disney experts to answer your questions.

TravelVenture tip: Be sure to ask for a copy of the show schedule, which lists times and locations of the day's entertainment and parades.

Fire Engine Company Number 71 sits in one corner of Town Square. The red-brick fire house is home to a small, red fire engine — when it's not out hauling passengers up and down Main Street. The fire house also provides a good introduction to typical Disney detail. Wooden chairs surround a black pot-bellied stove. On the floor sits a bucket filled with large chunks of coal; a small shovel rests on top. Nearby, a crank telephone hangs on the wall. At the rear of the fire house a floor-to-ceiling brass sliding pole gleams from one corner.

TravelVenture tip: As you explore Disney World look for these details. They're everywhere, and their subtle impact adds greatly to the atmosphere.

In the corner of Town Square opposite the fire station you can learn about the man responsible for Disney World. **The Walt Disney Story,** a 30-minute film much of which is narrated by Walt himself, traces his life and work. While waiting in a lobby for the film to start, you can view an interesting collection of Disney photos, posters, awards, and letters — including letters from Winston Churchill, Harry Truman, Dwight Eisenhower, and Richard Nixon.

Town Square is backed by the **Walt Disney World Railroad** station. The railroad boasts four restored steam locomotives which were originally built between 1916 and 1928. At one time these steam engines hauled freight cars filled with sugar, jute, and hemp through Mexican jungles. Now they pull open-air passenger cars from the Main Street station on a 1.5 mile journey around the edge of the Magic Kingdom. The train stops at Frontierland and Mickey's Starland, but you can remain on board and make a circle trip to get an overview of the park.

Main Street between Town Square and Cinderella Castle is a turn-of-the-century version of a mall. The street is lined with two-story buildings whose ground floors house shops, eateries and a couple of attractions. Among the merchandise offered along Main Street: Disney souvenirs, hats, jewelry, clocks, clothing, candy, and greeting cards. There's also a shop selling Christmas ornaments, year round.

At the **Main Street Cinema** you get more than a double feature. They're offering six continuous and simultaneous showings of early Mickey Mouse cartoons, including *Steamboat Willie,* Mickey's first film. Across the street stands a **Penny Arcade** with old-fashioned hand-crank movies and arcade games from yesterday. A couple of video games have also infiltrated the arcade. You can use a penny here, but most games are hungrier and want nickels, dimes, or quarters.

Adventureland

Getting to Adventureland takes only a short walk over a wooden bridge, but it's a long-distance journey in time and imagination. The sound of jungle drums reverberates through the air. And the architecture of the place runs from early treehouse to contemporary Timbuktu. Adventureland takes you to the fringes of civilization.

In 1805, the story goes, a family from Switzerland named Robinson were the sole survivors of the wreck of the good ship *Swallow*. The Robinsons set about using bamboo and whatever they could salvage from the *Swallow* to turn a massive Banyan tree into a safe refuge. Disney has recreated this refuge in the **Swiss Family Treehouse**.

As you climb a steep stairway up, around, and down the Spanish moss-draped tree, you'll marvel at the ingenuity the Robinsons — and Disney — used to turn this refuge into a home with all the comforts expected of an early 19th-century high rise. It even has running water. A sense of adventure, an urge to get away from it all, and a desire to move right in may grip you as tight as you grip the handrail when you look down and see how high you are.

A narrow river runs by the treehouse. Its banks are jungle-thick with green foliage. Downstream, a bend curves the river out of sight. For a look at what's around that bend you have to book passage on the **Jungle Cruise**. Boats leave from an outpost landing with shipping crates stacked about awaiting transport to such destinations as Lincoln, Nebraska, and Saco, Maine.

On board the *Nile Nellie, Senegal Sal,* or any of the other *African Queen*-looking launches, the captain's pun-filled patter narrates you around herds of elephants and hippos, past head-hunters, and through a cobra-filled Cambodian temple. The grit, daring, and seamanship of these captains courageous are tested daily. They're generally equal to the task, bringing their passengers back safely — but not uneventfully.

At the far end of Adventureland the atmosphere turns Caribbean Spanish. Spanish-style houses line one side of a tranquil plaza. Fountains are scattered about. On occasion a steel band sends calypso and reggae rhythms cascading into the plaza.

But the tranquility is not to last. From a Spanish fort filling one side of the plaza, cannon barrels jut from between battlements. Their bark as they send cannon balls hurtling seaward signals trouble ahead.

When you enter the **Pirates of the Caribbean** the sun may be shining outside, but inside night has fallen. The orange glow of wrought iron lamps lights a walkway that winds through the fort and leads down to a boat landing.

TravelVenture tip: Take your time along this walkway so you won't miss more of that Disney detail. You may hear shouted commands and marching boots as the guard is changed. Or, perhaps, a sentry cry, "Sound the alarm," as he sights a pirate ship on the horizon. Peer through the barred windows. In one, two skeletons seated in a dimly lit dungeon study a chess board. When you reach the darkened boat landing, listen for the seagulls. And notice the lights of the schooner anchored offshore.

At the landing you board a small boat to sail several hundred years back in time. The craft moves into a cave and sails past a sandy beach strewn with skeletons left over from a buried treasure party. After a brief spell of bad weather and rough water, your boat sails right down the middle of an artillery duel between a pirate ship and the fort. The mouths of the pirate cannons flash orange as the captain orders a broadside. The Spanish gunners answer back. And cannonballs fall short of their targets to splash uncomfortably close to your boat.

As the boat glides into town, it's apparent that sentry's cry of alarm came too late — dozens of audio-animatronic pirates have overrun the city. They've taken the townspeople prisoner. Drunken pirates recklessly fire their pistols. The far end of the town is in flames. The scene is so realistic that it takes singing pirates and frequent touches of Disney humor to keep the atmosphere light.

Adventureland also has a tamer side. You can find it by taking in the **Enchanted Tiki Birds** and their Tropical Serenade, a musical fantasy featuring hundreds of audio-animatronic birds and flowers singing in a tropical setting.

Frontierland

Frontierland and its companion theme area, Liberty Square, take you back to the time of wooden sidewalks, frontier forts, and colonial red brick. This is the land of early America and also the land of some of the Magic Kingdom's more popular attractions.

One of the most popular is the **Big Thunder Mountain Railroad** whose red-sandstone hills clutch the fossilized bones of long-gone dinosaurs. Deep within these hills is a gold mine where you can board an ore train. Consisting of a miniature steam engine and a half-dozen open cars, the train takes you on a tour of the mine.

But things go amiss. The train, apparently out of control, hurtles along the tracks racing up and down the sandstone buttes. The ride also takes you through a cave-in amidst huge crashing boulders.

TravelVenture tip: As roller coasters go, the Big Thunder Mountain Railroad is relatively tame. But it's still a roller coaster, and you may want to watch the train go through it's paces before you climb on board. Instead of entering the ride, move around the mountain to your right. Here, at the ride's exit, you can get a good look at the train in action.

The **Country Bear Jamboree** is another Disney don't miss. This show can be summed up as cute, cleaver, and comical. An audio-animatronic menagerie puts on an entertaining, 15-minute country music show. Even rock 'n' rollers will like this one.

Here's an attraction for the kids: a trip to **Tom Sawyer Island.** It actually is an island, and to get there you have to board a raft — how else would you expect to get to Tom Sawyer Island? Once there, the kids can explore Injun Joe's cave, cross a wobbly barrel bridge, or run up to Fort Sam Clemens to fire air muskets that send volleys of sound crashing down on imaginary invaders. While the kids are knocking themselves out, you can relax on Aunt Polly's back porch, grab a beverage and a snack, and look out across the Rivers of America.

TravelVenture tip: Keep in mind that Tom Sawyer Island closes at dusk, even when the Magic Kingdom remains open later into the evening.

The Diamond Horseshoe Jamboree takes you into an old-West saloon, complete with brass-railed bar, for some dance hall entertainment. This 40-minute show offers singing, dancing, comedy, and audience participation. The only way you're going to see the jamboree, though, is to have reservations. To make yours, stop early in the morning at the Town Square's Hospitality House on your way into the Magic Kingdom. Once inside the Diamond Horseshoe, while waiting for the show to start, you can order hot dogs, sandwiches, and snacks.

TravelVenture tip: Consider scheduling your visit to The Diamond Horseshoe Jamboree during the hour you'd like to eat lunch.

TravelVenture tip: If Frontierland is the last stop on your day's visit to the Magic Kingdom, board the Walt Disney World Railroad for a ride back to Main Street's Town Square and the park's exit. After a day of walking around the Magic Kingdom, to sit down, rest your feet, and ride to the exit is sheer delight.

Liberty Square

Liberty Square gives you a chance to take to the water. You can board a stern-wheel riverboat at the **Liberty Square Riverboat** landing and cruise down the Rivers of America and around Tom Sawyer Island. For something more offbeat, try a keelboat. Remember these from Disney's Davy Crockett films? You can board the small, double-decked boats at the **Mike Fink Keelboats** landing.

The Hall of Presidents is the Magic Kingdom's audio-animatronic showcase. After a wide-screen film that looks at the political history of the United States, the screen slides away to reveal a stage filled with life-size audio-animatronic figures, each portraying one of the country's presidents. A few are seated, but most stand. And all wear the clothing of their time. As a spotlight picks them out of the crowd, each president is introduced. Abraham Lincoln then stands and delivers a speech.

TravelVenture tip: During Lincoln's speech, watch the other presidents for the subtle movements that help create this attraction's life-like quality — an arm lowered, a head turning to whisper a word, or a shifting of weight from one leg to the other.

Directly across from the entrance to The Hall of Presidents stands a replica of the original Liberty Bell which hangs in Philadelphia. The Liberty Square bell was cast from the same mold as the original.

TravelVenture tip: Liberty Square possesses the best-kept secret in the Magic Kingdom — a shaded, secluded, and tranquil rest area. Right next to a small stand selling soft drinks and snacks — the Fife and Drum snack bar (open seasonally) — are a half-dozen wrought iron tables and chairs that sit in the shade of sycamore and pine trees. Its off-the-beaten-track location keeps the area hidden from most Disney visitors, and the place is seldom crowded. To reach this secluded nook, turn left just as you step off the foot bridge that leads to Liberty Square from the circle in front of Cinderella Castle. From Liberty Square itself, take the walkway that runs alongside the Silversmith shop.

Tucked away in a remote corner of Liberty Square is an old mansion. As you approach, the house looks deserted, only a dog howls from somewhere nearby. The Disney people, however, claim not only that the building isn't deserted, but that it's packed with 999 ghosts, ghouls, and goblins. They call it **The Haunted Mansion.**

At the door you'll be greeted by a stern-faced butler or maid who escorts you through a room with cobwebbed chandeliers. It looks as if they brought the interior decorator over from Transylvania. You're lead into a second room where candle-holding gargoyles jut from the walls beneath a series of portrait paintings. They cut corners to build this room. After you and the other visitors are packed inside, you'll discover the room has no door. And if you think that's strange, wait until the ceiling starts to rise...or is the floor descending?

When you get out of that room, you'll head for the ride cars that take you on a tour through the mansion. Your car will take you past an invisible piano player — invisible except for his shadow on the floor — beneath dusty chandeliers, alongside a ghostly banquet, and into a spook-filled cemetery. The whole ride is so thick with haunting characters you'll think Disney's count of 999 to be on the conservative side. It's surprising one doesn't hop right into your ride car.

The audio-animatronic figures get most of the glory at Disney World, but at The Haunted Mansion the outstanding special effects steal the show. The attraction, however, is not really scary; touches of humor keep it light and amusing.

Fantasyland

This is the land of fairy tales, story books, and Cinderella Castle. Banners, flags, and pastel-colored awnings give one section of Fantasyland the appearance of a medieval country fair. A jousting knight would not be out of place. Another section, though, has an Alpine look, and still another, English Tudor.

At first glance Fantasyland may appear to be strictly for kids. Actually, it's for kids of all ages. To get into a Fantasyland mood, make your first stop **It's a Small World.** Here you'll take a boat ride along a winding canal on a musical journey around the world. As you float by brightly-painted landscapes, two-foot-high dolls in native costumes dance and sing to the tune "It's a Small World." Musical accompaniment ranges from Swiss bells to the beat of jungle drums to the whine of a Hawaiian steel guitar.

For a bit more adventure in a water journey, head for **20,000 Leagues Under the Sea.** Boarding Captain Nemo's *Nautilus,* to take a seat before your own private porthole. You know the submarine doesn't actually dive under water, but as the diving Klaxon squeals and those bubbles rush up past your window on the sea, the effects can be convincing. During the voyage, you'll spot on the wet side of your porthole: mermaids, seahorses, and even the lost continent of Atlantis.

Fantasyland could not be Fantasyland without fairy-tale attractions. **Peter Pan's Flight** flies you over London, as the city's lights twinkle below, and then through a capsule version of the tale. Other storybook rides will take you among the witches, skeletons, and vultures lurking about in **Snow White's Adventures** and will carry you wildly through London town in **Mr. Toad's Wild Ride.** Here you end up driving bumpily down a railroad track — as a train speeds towards you.

Don't miss the **Fantasyland Theater** and its film *Magic Journeys.* You take these journeys via a 15-minute 3-D movie whose effects are so good that it turns into an audience-participation film. You and the other viewers will find yourselves flinching, ducking, reaching out to touch, oohing, aahing, and bursting into applause.

Fantasyland also has several typical amusement park rides: the spinning tea cups of the **Mad Tea Party;** an airborne **Dumbo, the Flying Elephant** for the young set; and the 90-horse **Cinderella's Golden Carrousel.**

The attraction that visually dominates not only Fantasyland but the whole of the Magic Kingdom is the almost 300-foot-tall **Cinderella Castle.** The castle is made from rectangular blocks of gray "stone" (fiberglass, actually). Its slim towers are topped by blue-shingled cones. Some of the uppermost towers take on a Gothic look. On the castle's second floor you'll find King Stefan's Banquet Hall, a reservations-required restaurant. (For more information on King Stefan's see the Dining section.) Before you leave the castle area, be sure to see the five floor-to-ceiling mosaic murals covering almost one wall of the walkway that cuts through the castle. The murals use a million squares of colored glass to depict the Cinderella story.

If, after you've done Fantasyland, you want to move on to Tomorrowland, you can take the **Skyway** cable cars and get an aerial view of both lands.

Mickey's Starland

This newest land at the Magic Kingdom opened in 1988.

Mickey's Starland is made up of a miniature town called Duckburg. The buildings, which include **Mickey's House,** are built in a cartoon-like style of architecture. Mickey's House is open to the public. And as you walk through, you can view the living room, kitchen, and a study filled with Mickey's memorabilia. You can also take in a live skit staring Mickey and other Disney characters.

If you want to personally **Meet Mickey Mouse,** step over to Mickey's Hollywood Theater. In front of the theater, immortalized in concrete, are the hand and foot prints of Donald, Pluto, Goofy, Mickey, and Minnie. Inside, you'll be escorted into Mickey's backstage dressing room where he'll greet you and pose for pictures.

Mickey's Starland also boasts a playground, with slides and a hedge maze, and **Grandma Duck's Farm.** This petting zoo has a variety of animals including: goats, ponies, sheep, pigs, rabbits, turkeys, and ducks.

Tomorrowland

The attractions in Tomorrowland will take you around a raceway, around America, and around outer space. To get around outer space, you'll need to be daring enough to hop aboard one of the rocket-type cars in **Space Mountain.** Housed in a UFO-shaped building, Space Mountain gives the feel of a full-fledged roller coaster as it hurls you up, down, and around the black void of outer space.

If you think this trip through space may be too much for you, take a ride on the **WEDway PeopleMover.** The PeopleMover gives you a glimpse of Space Mountain's ride so you can decide for yourself. The PeopleMover is a chain of four-passenger open cars powered by a linear induction motor that has no moving parts. The ride takes you in or alongside most Tomorrowland attractions. The PeopleMover has found use as more than a theme park ride. It was the model for a people mover system installed at the Houston Intercontinental Airport.

TravelVenture tip: The PeopleMover is ideal for the foot weary and the line weary. Its line, if any, is generally short and always fast moving. When you need a sit-down-and-relax ride, seek it out.

The **Mission to Mars** offers a more down-to-earth trip to outer space than does Space Mountain. After a tour of the Mission Control center, staffed by an audio-animatronic crew, you'll board a rocket to take a seat that tilts and vibrates you through a simulated voyage to Mars.

For your trip around the United States, take in the Circle-Vision 360 *American Journeys.* Inside, in a circular stand-up theater, you'll be completely surrounded by nine movie screens. The film, which was made using a ring of nine 35mm movie cameras shooting simultaneously, gives you a look not only at what's in front but what's on either side and in back. The 360-degree screen gives the illusion of putting you right in the middle of the action.

Dreamflight, another ride with a short, fast-moving line, uses dioramas and film to give you a glimpse of air travel — past, present, and future. You ride through a fanciful landscape of early aircraft, through a large clipper aircraft of the 1930s, and through the sky at a simulated speed of some 3,800 miles per hour.

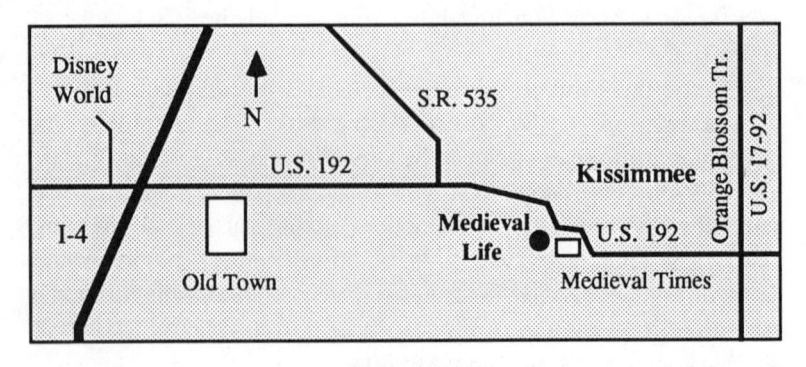

Medieval Life

At the **Carousel of Progress** you'll visit four dioramas populated by an audio-animatronic family. Each diorama portrays how life in the home has evolved over the years thanks to electricity. It takes no effort, however, to view these dioramas. The seated audience revolves carousel-like to the next scene.

A couple of amusement park rides round out Tomorrowland's attractions: the **Grand Prix Raceway,** slow-moving, drive-yourself race cars; and the **StarJets,** a dozen high-flying rockets.

Medieval Life

TravelFacts

Location: 4510 W. Vine Street (U.S. 192), P.O. Box 2385, Kissimmee 34742-2385.
Map: Page 96.
Telephone: (407) 396-1518 (Kissimmee), (407) 239-0214 (Orlando), 800 327-4024, in Florida 800 432-0768.
Hours: 9 A.M. to 9 P.M.
Time to see: 2 hours.
Price: $6 adults, $4 ages 3 to 12.

What to expect: an excellent recreation of a village from 1,000 years ago, complete with crafts people. Set alongside the white stone walls of a medieval castle (home of the nighttime attraction Medieval Times), the village gives you an idea of life in the 11th century.

Your walk through the village starts in the home of the village architect. There a robed, sandal-clad curator tells you a bit about 11th-century people and the life they lived. He also fills you in on the village's background. Then your on your own to wander through the dozen and a half buildings that encircle a cobblestone courtyard.

The stucco buildings have roofs of slate, tile, or wooden

shingles. One even has a roof of live green grass. Room interiors appear authentic, with stuccos walls, wood beam ceilings, wooden windows, and metal-hinged wooden doors. Most of the hand tools and much of the wooden furniture filling the rooms are antiques brought over from Europe. The rooms really come to life, though, with knowledgeable crafts people in period costumes working at and explaining their trades. You'll find carpenters, basket weavers, glass blowers, cloth weavers, potters, candle makers, coppersmiths, and blacksmiths. And in the village square, you can see demonstrations of how birds of prey and hunting dogs were used in the Middle Ages.

The Village also contains a dungeon packed with recreated but authentic-looking medieval torture instruments. Small signs detail how they were employed.

TravelVenture tip: When touring the dungeon, you may want to take only a cursory look at the exhibit. If you pause, read the signs, and dwell on the instruments, you'll find the exhibit horrifying.

Mystery Fun House

TravelFacts

Location: 5767 Major Blvd., Orlando 32819.
Map: Page 99.
Telephone: (407) 351-3355.
Hours: 10 A.M. to 10 P.M. Box office closes at 9 P.M.
Time to see: 1 hour.
Price: $7.95 adults and children, under 4 free.
- The attraction includes a miniature golf course.
- Starbase Omega, a computer-scored laser-tag game, carries a $5.95 additional charge.
- Snack bar, souvenir shop, and large game room available.

TravelVenture tip: If you're in the International Drive area, look for the free trolley that runs to the fun house.

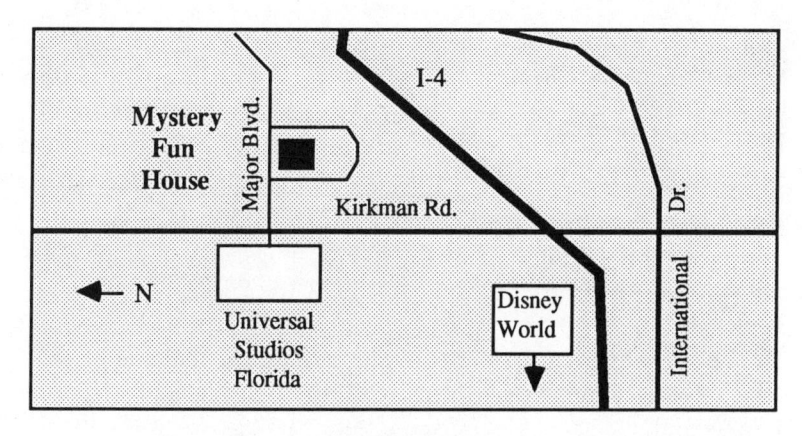

Mystery Fun House

What to expect: mystery, fun, and surprises. The cashier says, "Step into the fireplace and walk through the wall." On the other side of the fireplace, you'll find the first of the fun house surprises — a maze of mirrors. By the time you leave the Mystery Fun House, you'll have bumped your way through that mirror maze, climbed out of a topsy-turvey room whose floor is built at a steep angle, negotiated a giant revolving barrel, and groped about in a couple of lightless rooms.

Orange County Historical Museum

TravelFacts

Location: 812 E. Rollins St., Orlando 32803, in Loch Haven Park.
Map: Page 100.
Telephone: (407) 898-8320.
Hours: 9 A.M. to 5 P.M. Tuesday through Friday, noon to 5 P.M. Saturday and Sunday. Closed Monday.
Time to see: 1 hour.

Price: $2 adults, $1 children.
• Small snack bar available.

What to expect: a look at Orlando's short, hundred-year past. Exhibits include replicas of a general store and a newspaper hot-type composing room, as well as furnishings, clothing, photographs, and other memorabilia from the late 19th and early 20th centuries.

The highlight of the museum sits outside the building at the far end of a small courtyard. Here you'll find the actual two-story brick building that was Orlando's Fire Station No. 3. Built in 1926, the station was active for more than 40 years before being moved to the museum and restored. Inside are photographs, memorabilia, and fire-fighting equipment — an 1885 hose cart

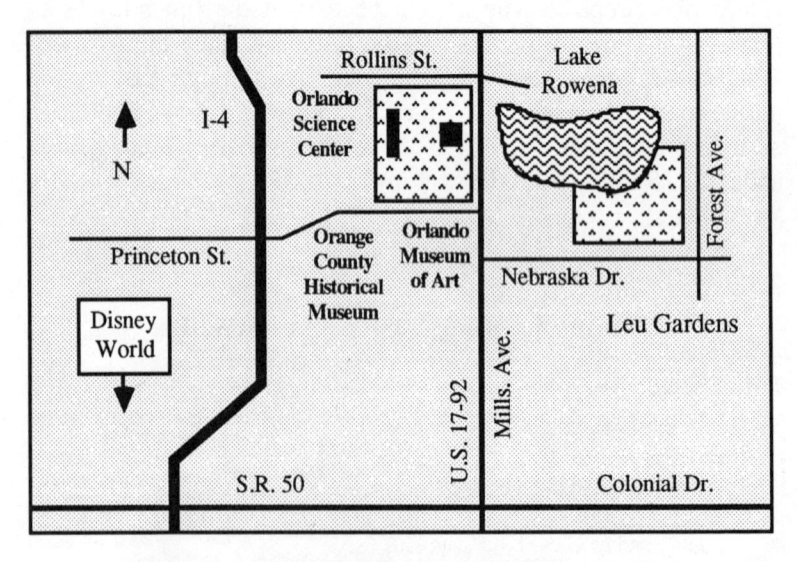

Orange County Historical Museum, Orlando Museum of Art, Orlando Science Center

with five-foot spoked wooden wheels, a 1908 horse-drawn steamer, and a 1915 American La France fire truck.

TravelVenture tip: The museum is located in the same building as the Orlando Science Center and near the Orlando Museum of Art. The trio make a good rainy-day excursion.

Orlando Museum of Art

TravelFacts

Location: 2416 N. Mills Ave., Orlando 32803, in Loch Haven Park.
Map: Page 100.
Telephone: (407) 896-4231.
Hours: 9 A.M. to 5 P.M. Tuesday through Thursday, 9 A.M. to 7:30 P.M. Friday, 10 A.M. to 5 P.M. Saturday, noon to 5 P.M. Sunday. Closed Monday.
Time to see: 1 to 2 hours.
Price: $3 adults, $2 ages 6 to 18, under 6 free.
• Small bookstore-souvenir shop available.

What to expect: a fine art collection housed in a contemporary building at Loch Haven Park. The Orlando Museum of Art boasts a permanent collection that includes African, pre-Columbian, and 20th-century American art. Among the works in the American collection are paintings by Georgia O'Keeffe, Thomas Moran, and Charles Sheeler. The collection also features photographs by Ansel Adams and Yousuf Karsh.

In the Museum's Pre-Columbian Art and Culture Gallery, an eight-minute slide show gives a quick background on pre-Columbian artifacts, history, and development. Exhibits include pottery and stone sculptures.

The art museum's spacious galleries also host changing exhibits.

TravelVenture tip: The Orlando Museum of Art is located near the Orlando Science Center and the Orange County Historical Museum. The trio make a good rainy-day excursion.

Orlando Science Center

TravelFacts

Location: 810 E. Rollins St., Orlando 32803, in Loch Haven Park.
Map: Page 100.
Telephone: (407) 896-7151.
Hours: Museum - 9 A.M. to 5 P.M. Monday through Thursday, 9 A.M. to 9 P.M. Friday, noon to 9 P.M. Saturday, noon to 5 P.M. Sunday. Planetarium shows - 2 P.M. Monday through Friday, 2 P.M. and 4 P.M. Saturday and Sunday. Planetarium Cosmic Concerts - 9 P.M., 10 P.M., and 11 P.M. Friday and 6:30 P.M., 7:30 P.M., 9 P.M., 10 P.M., and 11 P.M. Saturday.
Time to see: 2 to 3 hours.
Price: Science center - $4 adults, $3 ages 4 to 17 and 55 and over, under 3 free. Maximum charge per family $10. Planetarium shows - $1.50. Cosmic Concerts - $4.
• Small snack bar available.

What to expect: The main feature of the Orlando Science Center is not what it has, but what it doesn't have — and that's DO NOT TOUCH signs. Many exhibits are hands-on working displays such as a bicycle-powered electrical generator, a gravity well, and a microscope to examine computer chips. One exhibit lets you sit down at a computer and, by entering answers to questions, determine your susceptibility to heart disease.

You'll also find natural history exhibits, a solar system slide show, and a collection of live Florida snakes, turtles, fish, and frogs.

The science center has a planetarium which is named for Astronaut John Young, commander of the first space shuttle flight and an Orlando native. The John Young Planetarium offers daily star shows and on weekend evenings puts on Cosmic Concerts which feature laser lights and rock music.

TravelVenture tip: Kids find the participatory exhibits especially appealing. The science center is located in the same building as the Orange County Historical Museum and near the Orlando Museum of Art. The trio make a good rainy-day excursion.

The Potter Train Museum

TravelFacts

> *Location:* 5770 W. Bronson Hwy. (U.S. 192), Kissimmee 34741. Located in the Old Town shopping complex, inside The Great Train Store & Exhibit.
> *Map:* Page 104.
> *Telephone:* (407) 396-7120.
> *Hours:* 10 A.M. to 10 P.M. daily.
> *Time to see:* 20-30 minutes.
> *Price:* By donation, $3 adults or $5 per family suggested.

What to expect: an interesting collection of hand-made wooden train models. Not the kind you'd see on a track around a Christmas tree, but well-detailed models about a foot high and up to 12 feet long. The models are patterned after actual trains that rode the rails from the early 1800s to the mid 1900s. Except for a Penn Central streamliner, all engines are steam locomotives.

The collection includes a three-car model of the funeral train that carried Abraham Lincoln's body from Washington, D.C., to Springfield, Illinois; a replica of the first steam engine used in the United States; and a model of the first passenger car built for the Pennsylvania Railroad in 1835. You'll also see several inlaid-wood horse-drawn carriages, and a model of the original Fort Knox.

The trains are the work of Walter T. Potter of Pigeon Forge, Tennessee. Potter, a stone mason, started making the models at age 59 after the death of his wife. He continued with his hobby until he died in 1983. Potter built his models using 17 kinds of wood, including white birch, ebony, mahogany, olive wood, teak,

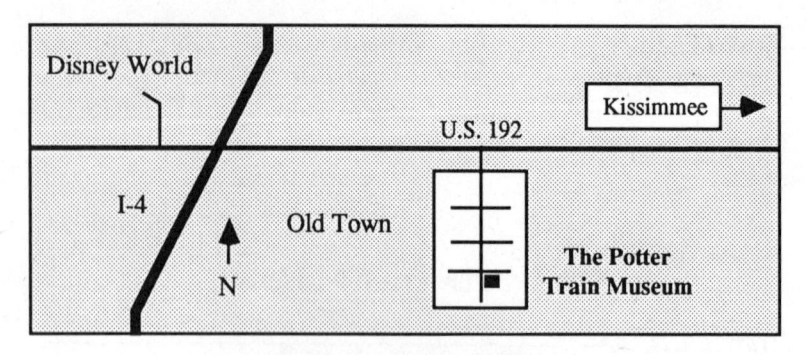

The Potter Train Museum

tulipwood, and walnut. He put only clear varnish on the trains, but used light and dark wood to add color and contrast.

The collection is well documented. Small signs identify each model, giving details on both the model and the actual train it represents. In addition, a taped narration plays continuously to fill you in on the collection's history.

River Country

TravelFacts

Location: On Bay Lake near Fort Wilderness Campground, Walt Disney World.
Map: Page 105.
Telephone: (407) 824-2760.
Hours: Opens, 10 A.M. closes between 5 P.M. and 8 P.M. depending on the season. May close from January to mid-February.
Time to see: From several hours to an entire day.
Price: $12.46 adults, $9.81 ages 3 to 9, under 3 free. Two-day admission $18.82 adults, $14.58 ages 3 to 9. Late-afternoon reduced admission available in summer.
• Fast food and picnic area available.
• Lockers, small towels, dressing rooms, and sundries available.

What to expect: a lakeside water park offering swimming and water slides. Disney bills River Country as an old-fashioned swimming hole. While you can swim in a lake and cut an arc on a tire swing, River Country updates the old swimming hole with water slides, a heated pool, and an inner tube ride down whitewater rapids. River Country also boasts a sand beach and Kiddie Cove, a section with water slides for younger children.

TravelVenture tip: Disney offers a Discovery Island and River Country combination ticket. The ticket costs $15 adults, $11 ages 3 to 9 and saves about 25% over separate admissions to each attraction.

Scenic Boat Tour

TravelFacts

Location: 312 E. Morse Blvd., Winter Park 32879.

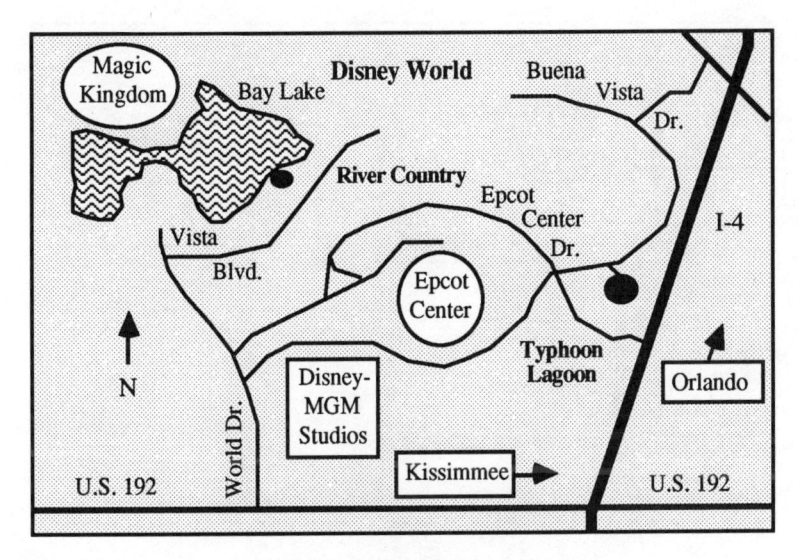

River Country and Typhoon Lagoon

> *Map:* Page 106.
> *Telephone:* (407) 644-4056.
> *Hours:* 10 A.M. to 4 P.M. daily, except Christmas. Boats generally leave the dock on the hour.
> *Time to see:* 1 hour.
> *Price:* $5 adults, $2.50 ages 2 to 11.

What to expect: a pleasant cruise offering a different view of Winter Park, an upscale Orlando suburb. The open boats set out from their dock on Winter Park's Lake Osceola and transit a shaded canal to also explore Lake Virginia. The voyage is narrated. The helmsman-guide identifies the birds and trees and fills you in on the stories behind many of the million-dollar-plus estates that dot the shoreline. On Lake Osceola the boats sail past the home and gardens of the late sculptor Albin Polasek. Some of the artist's work stands on display in the gardens.

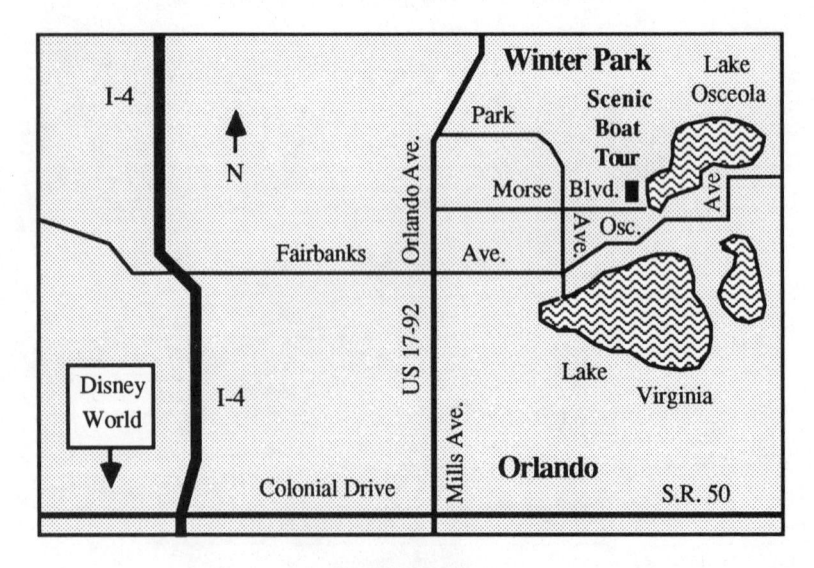

Scenic Boat Tour

Sea World

TravelFacts

Location: 7007 Sea World Dr., Orlando 32821.
Maps: Page 109.
Telephone: (407) 351-3600.
Hours: Opens 9 A.M. and closes between 7 P.M. and midnight, depending on the season. Call for exact closing time.
Time to see: 8 hours.
Price: $27.03 adults, $23 ages 3 to 9. Under 3 free. All shows are included in admission price. A "Sea World Week Long Pass" costs $31.99 adults, $28 ages 3 to 9. The pass is good for unlimited admission during seven consecutive days. If while visiting Sea World you decide the Week Long Pass would be appropriate, the ticket you've already bought will be credited toward your purchase of the pass.

- An Animal Lover's Tour of Sea World is available for an additional $5.75 adults, $4.95 ages 3 to 11. The two-hour tour includes behind-the-scenes visits to Sea World's breeding and research areas.

Don't miss: Whale and Dolphin Stadium show, Shamu Stadium show, Sharks, Atlantis Theater Water Ski show, Seal & Otter Stadium show.

- Fast food eateries and souvenir shops are spread throughout the park.
- A full-service restaurant, Al E. Gator's, is located inside the park. It's lunch and dinner menu includes sandwiches plus beef, chicken, and seafood entrees. The menu also offers an alligator-meat appetizer.
- A Polynesian luau is held each evening. Reservations required. Call (407) 351-3600, or stop at the Information Desk just inside the park's entrance.
- A ride to the top of a "400-Foot Sky Tower" is available at an additional charge.
- Strollers and wheelchairs may be rented at the Information Desk located just inside the main gate.

TravelVenture tip: Sea World offers wheelchair-bound visitors excellent access to most shows. Ramps are plentiful, space is set aside for wheelchairs, and adjacent seating is reserved for those accompanying the wheelchair visitor.

- Free pet kennels available.
- Pay lockers are located near the Information Desk.
- Cameras are loaned free at the Shamu Emporium near the park's en-

trance. You buy the film.and leave a refundable deposit (cash or credit card).

TravelVenture tip: Remember where you park your car. Sea World's parking lot is quite large, and the last thing you'll want at the end of your visit is to wait until everyone else drives off so you can spot your car.

What to expect: fascinating exhibits and shows held at set times throughout the day. But don't think you'll be hanging around bored waiting for shows to start, there's always something going on. And you'll seldom stand in line.

TravelVenture tip: After you pass through the main entrance, stop at the information counter on your left to pick up a copy of the day's show schedule and a map of the park. Walk to one of the nearby benches, and look over both the map and the listing of show times. Whether you're a planner who wants to work out a detailed itinerary or the footloose type who wants to wing it, you'll benefit by time spent browsing the map and schedule.

The order in which you visit Sea World's attractions will depend upon show schedules and which performance you choose. The park's attractions are listed here alphabetically.

Atlantis Theater Water Ski Show

Several times a day, a dozen skillful and accomplished water skiers perform acrobatics, somersaults, mid-air spins, and crossovers while putting on the skit that makes up this show. Some skits have called upon these talented performers to ski backwards, on one ski, and even on no skis at all. A must see.

Cap'n Kids' World

If young kids bursting with energy are wearing you down, take them over to **Cap'n Kids' Fun Ship** and give yourself a rest. Here

ATTRACTIONS 109

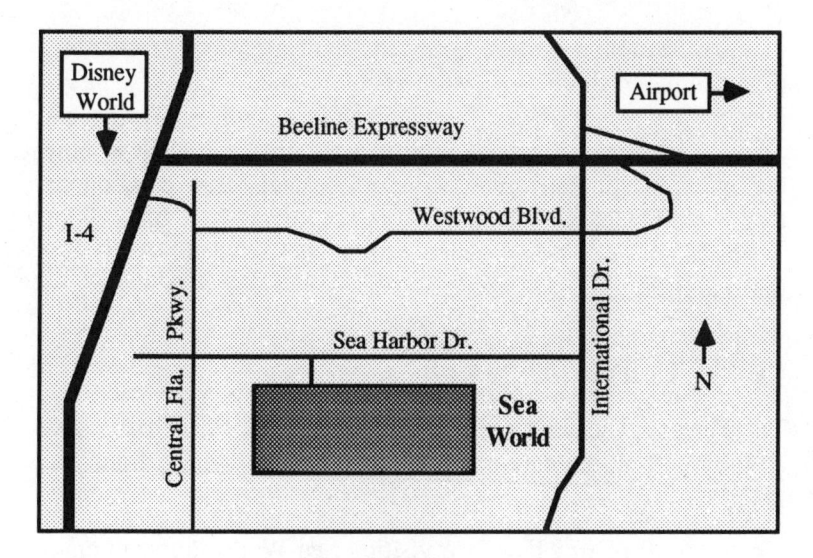

Sea World

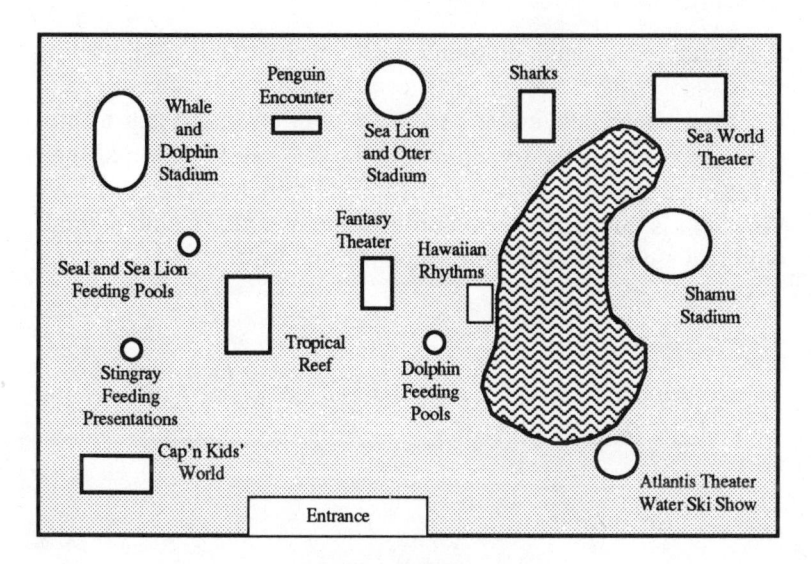

Sea World attractions

they can scramble up a rope net to board a 55-foot replica of a pirate ship. On shore they can monkey around on monkey bars or duel with water muskets. Younger children will enjoy the ball crawl — a large cage whose floor is made up of red, yellow, blue, and green plastic balls piled about a foot deep. They can bounce, flop, roll, or just bury themselves in the hundreds of balls. Foot-weary Moms and Dads can take it all in from shaded bleachers on the sidelines.

Fantasy Theater

The Fantasy Theater stages varied shows that, in the past, have employed film, animation, costumed characters, black light, and people.

TravelVenture tip: If you're visiting Sea World in the summer, save this show for the heat of the afternoon — it's indoors in an air-conditioned theater.

Feeding Pools

Seals, sea lions, and dolphins each inhabit their own feeding pool. Fish vendors are on hand to provide dead fish for the feeding. And attendants are on hand to answer questions and to provide a seemingly endless stream of facts — seals can hold their breath and stay underwater for 20 to 25 minutes; sea lions have vocal cords and bark, seals don't; dolphins are sociable animals who will aid a sick dolphin to keep it from drowning.

Hawaiian Rhythms

Polynesian entertainers perform songs and dances native to Hawaii and to South Pacific islands.

Penguin Encounter

On a hot day, the thought of changing places with these penguins will probably cross your mind. The air temperature in their recreated antarctic environment ranges from 38 to 42 degrees. Even a dip in their 160,000-gallon pool would cool you off to between 50 and 55 degrees. The best you can settle for, though, is the air conditioning that greets you upon entering the encounter.

A 120-foot moving sidewalk takes you alongside the clear panels enclosing several hundred penguins and their saltwater pool. From the sidewalk you get both an underwater and an on-land view of the penguins, which represent six out of the 17 penguin species. To help the penguins feel at home, special lighting simulates sunlight in the Southern Hemisphere's Antarctica, and 6,000 pounds of snow a day are blown over their ice shelf.

Penguin Encounter also includes a Northern Hemisphere exhibit of Arctic sea birds — puffins, auks, and murres.

Sea Lion and Otter Show

At this show a couple of California sea lions, a walrus, and an otter team up with a couple of people to put on a 30-minute skit. This is a "wonder" performance — when you see the antics of these animals you wonder how they get them to do it. Which is harder, to train a walrus or an otter?

TravelVenture tip: Arrive 15 minutes early for this performance so you can watch the pre-show escapades of a white-faced mime.

Sea World Theater

This massive outdoor theater seats 3,100 people and has a stage stretching 100 feet across. On occasion, entertainment is brought into the park especially for the theater. Normally, though, the Sea World Theater presents a show that gives a light-hearted look at some of the ideas behind Sea World's animal-training methods.

Shamu Stadium

The stars here are Shamu, Kandu, and Kandu's offspring — Baby

Shamu. Born in September 1985, Baby Shamu is the first killer whale to be born and raised in captivity. During the show, these graceful giants leap, dance, and splash their way around the stadium's pool.

Sharks

With all the hulabaloo since the *Jaws* movies, you might think people would be tired of sharks by now. Not so. This is a popular attraction.

Upon entering, you step into a theater to sit before a 40-foot-wide screen for a slide show designed to acquaint you with sharks. Forget about the neighbor's slide show of little Johnny's third birthday party. This show uses multiple projectors to give the illusion of swimming, moving sharks. It takes you as close to the world of sharks as it can without you actually going underwater — that comes later.

The slide show goes beyond entertainment and slips in some education. Did you know that sharks inhabited the earth millions of years before man, that sharks are designed for speed and have been clocked at up to 40 miles per hour, and that the nerve endings in a shark's snout can detect the slightest movement of its prey? The narrator also points out that sharks are actually a misunderstood fish only doing what comes naturally — being an efficient eating machine.

After the show you move into a second theater to sit before a band of clear, horizontal panels that let you view a continuous parade of live sharks. To prepare you for your close-up look at these sharks, the attendant points out some of the different species, including man-eaters. Don't be concerned, though, only a relatively few species are known to attack humans. Then the attendant announces, Boris Karlof-like, that the sharks are waiting.

You move down a semi-darkened corridor to turn a corner and stand before a giant, half-million-gallon tank filled with sharks. Stretching along the bottom of the tank is a 124-foot tunnel, made of four-inch-thick, clear acrylic panels. A moving sidewalk slowly takes you through the tunnel.

Although 18 feet underwater with sharks just inches away — the largest is about 14-feet long — your trip through the tunnel is more fascinating than frightening. The sharks appear quite uninterested in the spectators. If they weren't, that tunnel might get you to wondering just who's the spectator and who's the spectatee.

After the tunnel, at the exit, instead of leaving you can turn to the right to enter a viewing room for a longer, more leisurely look at the sharks in the tank. If you've had enough sharks for one day, though, don't feel obligated to join those who go into the viewing room. They probably went to see the *Jaws* movies twice, too.

Sting Ray Feeding Presentations

If you've already seen the Sharks exhibit and enjoyed being just inches away from those denizens, you'll love the pool of sting rays — you can stick your hand in the water and pet them. "They're very gentle creatures," the attendant claims. "They only have a bad reputation."

The attendant is right. These saucer-shaped fish are rather docile. They're just not lovable. If you get your courage up, you can buy a carton of dead fish, hold one on the bottom of the shallow pool, and let a ray glide over and suck the fish from your hand. (Just keep telling yourself they're gentle creatures.)

Tropical Reef

A semi-circular corridor leads you alongside this reef. The corridor's inner wall is made up of a 160,000-gallon, floor-to-ceiling aquarium which contains a coral reef. Some 2,000 fish from 100 species call this reef home. Periodically, a diver wearing a microphone-equipped helmet enters the water to feed the fish and identify some of the species.

Smaller aquariums line the outer wall. They contain even

more exotic varieties — four- and five-inch long seahorses and their snake-like babies, venomous marine animals, a Pacific octopus, moray eels, chambered nautiluses, and brilliant-red and deep-maroon anemones. Some real beauties swim in these tanks, but so do some real beasts.

Across from the Tropical Reef you'll find the **Tide Pool** which contains a smaller reef and some of the brightly colored fish and marine life typically found living in such an environment.

Whale and Dolphin Stadium

Teams of dolphins and whales dance, somersault, twist, and jump their way through this entertaining show. These animals appear to respond so willingly to their trainers that the whole show looks like a piece of cake. Actually it's not. It has taken patient work to build a bond of trust and affection between trainers and animals. At Sea World the old idea of rewarding an animal's behavior with a bite to eat has given way to a new approach which uses variable rewards.

The reward may be a rub on the head, a bit of food, a scratch on the belly. Sometimes there is no reward at all. By varying the reward the trainer increases the animal's motivation and interest — it doesn't know what the trainer will do next. When you see this show, you'll see that this approach works.

The Sinkhole

TravelFacts

> *Location:* Comstock Avenue and Denning Drive, Winter Park.
> *Map:* Page 116.
> *Hours:* During daylight hours.
> *Time to see:* 15 minutes.
> *Price:* Free.

> **TravelVenture tip:** You can get a good look at the sinkhole during daylight from Comstock Avenue (one block north of Fairbanks Avenue) where it stops at the hole's west side. There's plenty of parking space as well as a bulletin board containing color photographs of the sinkhole's early stages.

What to expect: Central Florida's latest lake. On the evening of May 8, 1981, the ground opened up in Winter Park and swallowed a 40-year-old sycamore tree. But that was just an appetizer. Twenty-four hours later the hole had gulped down a house, three Porsche sports cars, half a municipal swimming pool, seven trees, the back walls of a couple of buildings, and large stretches of two streets. The great Winter Park sinkhole was born, and it began to grab headlines and spots on the evening news around the world.

When the sinkhole stopped growing, it was some 375 feet across and 100 feet deep. Over the years, the hole has filled with water. Comstock Avenue still ends abruptly where it fell into the hole. But the sinkhole's east side has been filled in and built up to allow Denning Drive, which also crumbled into the cavity, to be repaved. The swimming pool, its concrete back broken, has been bulldozed into the sinkhole. Behind the buildings that front on Fairbanks Avenue — one of Winter Park's main thoroughfares — concrete rubble has been poured down the steep bank to stabilize it and keep the bank from eroding away.

In late 1987, Winter Park named the sinkhole Lake Rose after Mae Rose Williams, the lady who lost her home when the lake was born. But just over a month later Mother Nature showed she's not yet finished with Lake Rose. One morning, whatever was plugging the hole popped free and about 20 feet of water drained away, taking with it some 25 feet of bank from the Fairbanks Avenue side.

Are sinkholes a rare occurrence? Not particularly. As you travel around Central Florida, notice all those lakes and ponds splashed throughout the area. Many started out as sinkholes.

Limestone caverns riddle the ground beneath Central Florida.

116   ORLANDO AND DISNEY WORLD

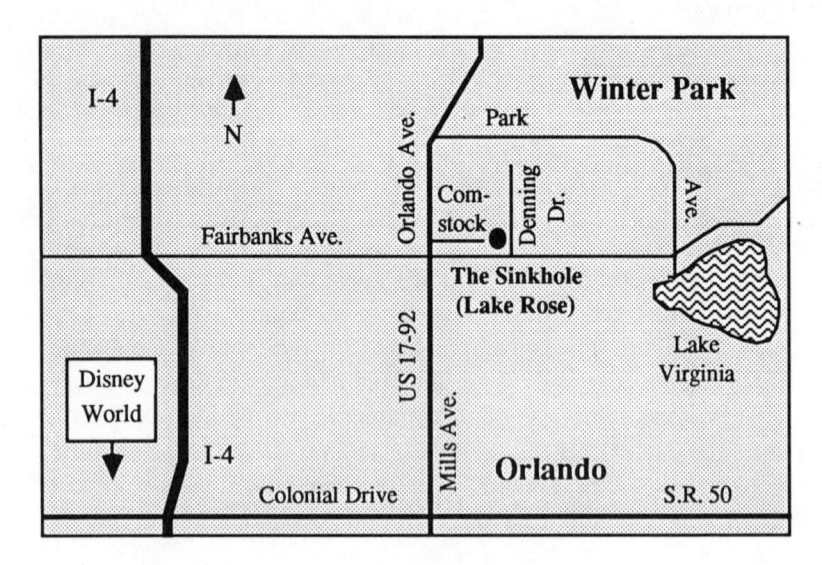

The Sinkhole

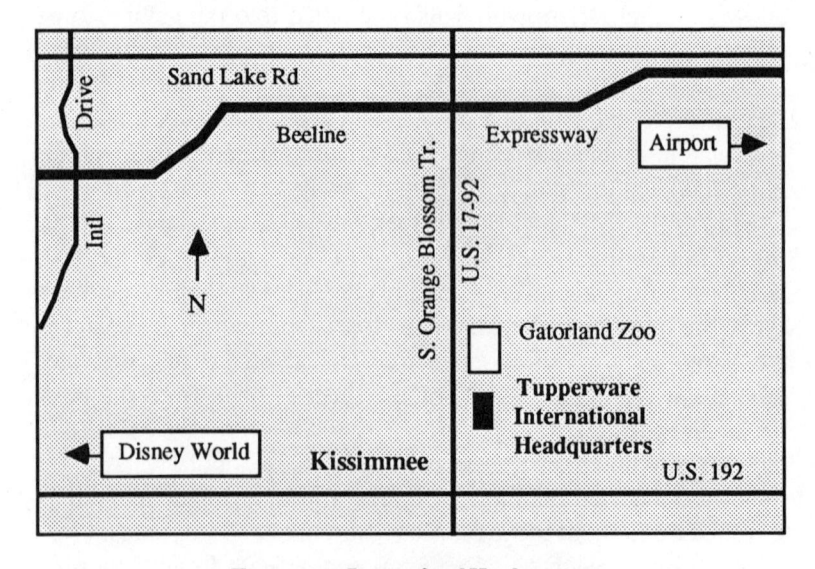

Tupperware International Headquarters

Normally, these caverns are below the water table and are filled with water. During a drought, as occurred in 1980-81, the water table can drop below a cavern. The now dry sand above can trickle through any cracks in the cavern's roof, like sand through an hour glass. Also, when the sand directly above an exposed cavern is no longer bouyed by water, its weight can collapse a weak cavern's roof, allowing sand to pour in. Trickle in or pour in, the sand still gets sucked from the surface. Result: sinkhole. Not all holes, though, are as large as the Winter Park sinkhole. Nor do they have its urban location.

Tupperware International Headquarters

TravelFacts

Location: U.S. Highway 441-17-92, (South Orange Blossom Trail), Kissimmee 34741, located just north of Kissimmee.
Map: Page 116.
Telephone: (407) 847-3111 (Kissimmee), (407) 826-5050 (Orlando).
Hours: 9 A.M. to 4 P.M. Monday through Friday only.
Time to see: 30 minutes.
Price: Free.

What to expect: a short tour which includes a museum of containers. Since this is a convention and office center, Tupperware is not manufactured nor sold here, and on the tour Tupperware is demonstrated but not pushed.

The tour takes place in a contemporary two-story building at the north end of the complex. White swans swim in ponds at the front of the building, and hanging gardens spill from an upper level. At the entrance sits a gift from Australia — a fountain duplicating one in Sydney.

Inside, visitors are assembled into a group. A tour guide escorts the group and explains, with the aid of a series of large color transparencies lining one wall, the Tupperware manufacturing process from design to finished product. The tour then leads into a spacious mock-up of a contemporary home where the guide points out how Tupperware products can be used.

The tour ends in a small museum of containers. Large glass display cases hold a collection of wood, stone, basket, metal, porcelain, and glass containers used through the ages. The earliest is an Egyptian earthen jar from 4,000 B.C. Each tour participant receives a Tupperware sample.

Typhoon Lagoon

TravelFacts

Location: Walt Disney World, P.O. Box 10,040, Lake Buena Vista 32830-0040.
Map: Page 105.
Telephone: (407) 560-4100 or (407) 560-4073.
Hours: 10 A.M. to 7 P.M. summer, 10 A.M. to 5 P.M. rest of the year. May close from January to mid-February. Call (407) 560-4100 for operating hours.
Time to see: From several hours to an entire day.
Price: $19.35 adults, $15.37 ages 3 to 9, under 3 free. A two-day pass sells for $31.80 adults, $25.44 ages 3 to 9.
• Changing areas, lockers, and shower facilities available.
• Fast food available.
• Gift shop offers souvenirs, swimsuits, and sundries.

What to expect: a 56-acre water park boasting a third-of-a-mile-long meandering creek, a 95-foot volcanic mountain, and a lagoon twice the size of a football field.

According to Disney legend, Typhoon Lagoon was born when an earthquake, its resulting tidal wave, and a typhoon converged on what later became Disney World. The extraordinary devastation scooped out a lagoon large enough to hold an ocean liner and left a landscape feature quite unusual in Florida — a mountain, Mount Mayday. And nature has continued its unusual activity. Water gushing down the mountain has carved both roaring flumes and a gentle creek. And to this day some sort of geothermal activity still generates powerful tremors, rocking Mount Mayday and sending waves rolling across Typhoon Lagoon.

Upon entering the water park, you make your way through a ramshackle tropical town. Reminders of the legendary cataclysm are everywhere. Windblown thatch- and tin-roofed wooden buildings stand askew. Trees are bent at awkward angles. Scattered about are cargo and marine wreckage. A car perches on a tree's branches. A surfboard pierces a tree trunk. And a boat sits impaled on the peak of Mount Mayday. That shipwreck is what's left of the shrimp boat *Miss Tilly* which used to sail out of Safen Sound, Florida.

When you take to the water you can choose from a variety of adventures. The lagoon offers body and inflatable-raft surfing on what some claim to be the best surf east of Hawaii. Waves in the lagoon normally run about 2.5 to 3.5 feet. But when the surf's up, they can hit six feet. Mount Mayday lets you choose among the Humunga Kowabunga's two speed slides or the Storm Slides' three curving body slides. You can also shoot the rapids on one of three raft rides, one of which is designed for families to ride together.

For a slower pace, try the 3-foot-deep Castaway Creek which lets you ride an inner tube on a leisurely, one-third mile tour. Skirting the lagoon, the 15-foot-wide creek carries you through a rain forest and into a hidden grotto.

You can also stop in at the Dive Shop, pick up snorkeling gear (no additional charge), and head for Shark Reef. Exploring this salt-water coral reef, which legend says the typhoon blew in from the tropics, you'll encounter a half-sunken tanker and hundreds of Caribbean fish, including snappers, angelfish, groupers, and parrot fish. Yes, Shark Reef does have a couple of sharks swimming about. Lucky for you, though, they're not great whites but small non-aggressive bonnet and nurse sharks. If you'd rather not snorkel, you can climb aboard the bottoms-up tanker and peer at the underwater scene through the ship's portholes.

The park also offers Ketchakiddee Creek — slides and a raft ride for young children — a sand beach, and a picnic area (you can bring a cooler with food but no alcohol or glass containers). If you want to try your hand at a non-water adventure, take the Mount Mayday Scenic Trail. The trail crosses a rope and wood-plank bridge over Castaway Creek and winds its way up the mountain the *Miss Tilly* now calls home.

Universal Studios Florida

TravelFacts

Location: 1000 Universal Studios Plaza, Orlando 32819, off Kirkman Road.
Maps: Pages 122 and 123.
Telephone: (407) 363-8000.
Hours: Opens at 9 A.M. Closing varies between 7 P.M. and 11 P.M., depending on the season. Call for the exact time.
Time to see: 1 to 1.5 days.
Price: One Day Studio Pass, $30.74 adults, $24.38 ages 3 to 11. Under 3 free. Two Day Studio Pass, $51.94 adults, $41.34 ages 3 to 11. Admission price gives unlimited access to all rides, attractions, and shows.
Parking: $3 per car. Be sure to note the row number where you parked.
Credit cards: American Express, MasterCard, Visa, Discovery Card.
How to see: Universal Studios Florida has long, slow-moving lines, even in off season. You encounter your first slow-moving line paying your parking fee at the Parking Toll Plaza, then another getting your parking spot, and another buying your admission ticket. On one not-too-crowded, off-season day, the wait in line to buy a ticket was 40 minutes. Then you get inside the park, where the off-season line for some rides may be in excess of one hour.
To cut down on time spent standing in line, you must get there early. The Parking Toll Plaza and admission ticket booths open at 8:15 A.M. Be there when they open, so you will have parked and purchased your ticket before the main gate opens at 9 A.M. Head immediately for the Kongfrontation ride in the "Production Central" area of the park. Then move on to the adjacent "On Location" area for the Earthquake and Jaws (to open in 1991) rides.
You will now have taken in three of the park's five major attractions.

Spend the rest of your time visiting the other major attractions — the E.T. Adventure and Back to the Future (to open in 1991) — and the lesser attractions.

Several attractions are shows given at set times throughout the day. Consult the "Preview of Today's Rides & Shows" given to you at the entrance to plan fitting these shows into your schedule.

Don't miss: Kongfrontation, Earthquake, Jaws, Back to the Future, and E.T. Adventure.

- If you leave Universal Studios Florida but plan to return that same day, get your hand stamped at the exit.
- Coin-operated lockers are available in "The Front Lot" area, adjacent to the exits.
- Diaper changing facilities are located in restrooms.
- Strollers and wheelchairs may be rented in "The Front Lot" area just inside the main entrance.
- The Lights, Camera, Action photo shop located just inside the main entrance rents video cameras and loans still cameras — you buy the film.
- Pets can be boarded at the Studio Kennel adjacent to the Parking Toll Plaza.

TravelVenture Tip: Before entering the main gate, walk over to Guest Relations located just inside the main entrance to check their chalkboard which lists production activities and shooting schedules. To be part of a television studio audience, ask at the Guest Relations window for tickets. Kids who want to audition for a role in a Nickelodeon television show should check with the Nickelodean sound stage in the "Now Shooting" area of the park for audition availabilities and times.

What to expect: a behind-the-scenes tour with almost double the attractions and shows of the original Universal Studios tour in Los Angeles. The 444-acre Universal Studios Florida is a working studio and backlot — the largest outside of Hollywood — producing both motion pictures and television programming. Universal designed their studio to give you an insider's look at film and television production by allowing you to explore it on foot without interrupting any shooting that may be going on.

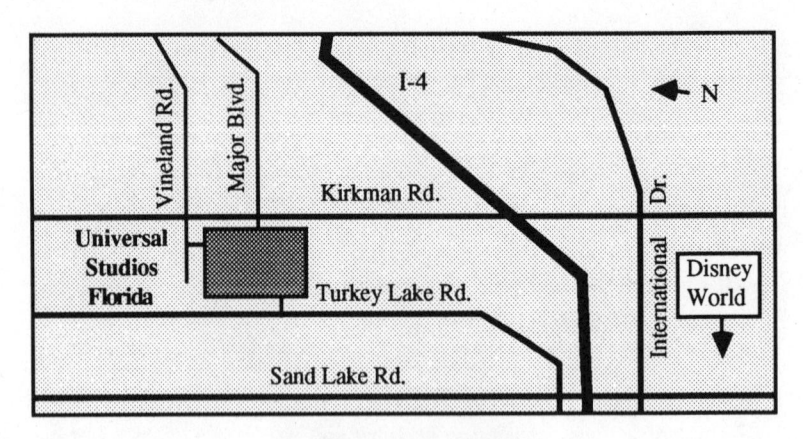

Universal Studios Florida

TravelVenture tip: Both Universal Studios Florida and Disney-MGM Studios Theme Park promote the glamour of movie making. In actuality, however, film and TV production is limited. Consider them both to be primarily theme parks rather than thriving film studios.

Universal Studios Florida appears to be practically one big backlot. Producers use backlot buildings, which are usually only exterior shells, to film outdoor scenes. Backlot shooting not only saves the expense of going on location, it also gives the producer more control over the setting and the action. Universal, however, has also designed as potential shooting locations all its rides, attractions, streets, and restaurants (including Mel's Diner from *American Graffiti,* a recreated Schwab's Pharmacy with its soda fountain where Lana Turner was discovered, and a guitar-shaped Hard Rock Cafe).

The studio's 51 working backlot sets recreate locales from films past and will serve as scenes for future films. Sets include a New England village, New York City's Upper East Side, Central Park, Brooklyn's Coney Island, a world's fair site, San Francisco's Ghirardelli Square and Fisherman's Wharf, Hollywood Boulevard, Beverly Hill's Rodeo Drive, Cambodia's an-

ATTRACTIONS 123

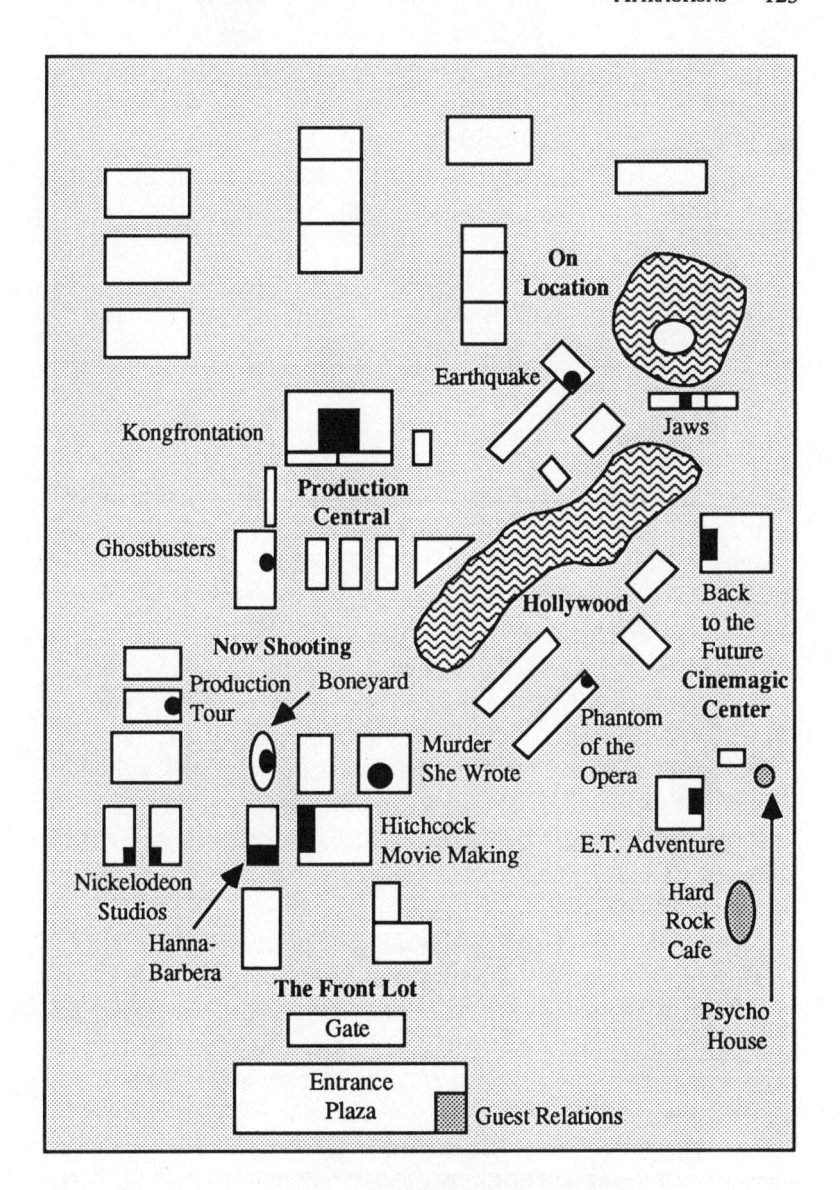

Universal Studios Florida attractions

cient ruins at Angkor Wat, and the infamous *Psycho* house. The house is an exact replica of the one on Universal's California backlot where Alfred Hitchcock shot the original film. The Universal Studios Florida house, which looks down on the Bates Motel from its perch on a 22-foot-high hill, starred in *Psycho IV*.

Universal Studios Florida divides itself into six theme areas. After passing through the first theme, **The Front Lot,** actually the park's entrance plaza, you move into the attractions areas.

Now Shooting

As its name implies, the Now Shooting area gives you a look at film and TV production. **Alfred Hitchcock: The Art of Making Movies** let's you see how the master of suspense made some of his classic thrillers. You'll experience a flight of attack birds reminiscent of Hitchcock's film *The Birds*. You'll also see how Hitchcock shot the *Psycho* shower scene, and you may even get to play a part in such films as *Vertigo* or *Rear Window*.

"Murder She Wrote!" Post Production gives you an idea of how a film comes to life in its post-production phase. A volunteer producer takes on the task of wrapping up an episode of TV's "Murder She Wrote," by editing the takes, arranging the music, and adding the sound effects. The rest of the audience has the pleasure of viewing the finished production.

The Funtastic World of Hanna-Barbera takes you into the world of cartoons with ride cars and 70 mm large-screen animation. You'll encounter such Hanna-Barbera creations as the Jetsons, the Flintstones, and Yogi Bear. After the ride you can see how animated films are made and try your own hand at working on a cartoon.

To get a look at Universal's production facilities, you can take the **Production Studio Tour** or, if you have kids along, the **Nickelodeon Studios Production Tour.** Both will give you a look at working sound stages.

TravelVenture tip: Kids wanting to audition for a role in a Nickelodeon television show should check at the Nickelodean sound stage for audition availabilities and times.

The Now Shooting area also contains **The Boneyard** — an outside storage lot for movie and TV props. You can inspect a variety of actual props, including a *Ben Hur* chariot and the great white shark used in *Jaws*.

Production Central

Production Central is made up entirely of New York City backlot sets. The main attraction here is **Kongfrontation.** You'll meet that famed oversize gorilla King Kong as he's hanging around New York's Queensboro bridge. Don't worry about being able to get a good look at the 30-foot-tall Kong, you'll be seated in an aerial tram that gets so close he could reach out and touch you.

For a look at special effects, Production Central offers the **Ghostbusters** show held at set times — usually every 30 minutes — throughout the day. (Consult your Preview of Today's Rides & Shows.)

On Location

This backlot area includes sets capable of shooting scenes in a Louisiana bayou, San Francisco, and New England. The New England sets include Amity village and harbor. Your remember Amity, don't you?.

You can ride an inflatable pontoon boat on a tour of Amity's harbor. And if you haven't recalled the town by now, you'll readily connect it with **Jaws** as the boat in front of you sinks, and a 24-foot great white makes a move on your pontoons.

TravelVenture tip: The Jaws attraction is scheduled to open during 1991.

On Location's other attraction is also one of the park's major rides — **Earthquake, The Big One.** After a show demonstrating how producers achieve earthquake effects, you board a San Francisco subway car. The Big One then rumbles through San Francisco at 8.3 on the Richter scale just as you're train pulls abreast of a station platform. The train starts rocking — up and down and side to side. The stress proves too much for the station's concrete roof, and a large portion of it collapses with a crash. A propane truck traveling the street above slides into the chasm and catches fire. As you feel the heat from the flames, another disaster arrives. A flood of water rushes down the station's steps with the force of a small tidal wave.

Cinemagic Center

Another two major rides are located here. The **E.T. Adventure** lets you climb on a simulated bicycle — one of nine mounted on each ride vehicle — for a trip to E.T.'s home planet. And when it opens in 1991, Doc Brown's time-traveling car will blast you back to the dinosaur age and then give you a trip **Back to the Future.** On the trip, in an eight-passenger, flight simulator-like car, you'll encounter Leonardo da Vinci in Venice and the Wright brothers at Kitty Hawk among others.

At the **Animal Actors Stage** you can see stars of a different breed. This show introduces you to an acting menagerie that includes dogs, cats, a horse, chimpanzees, and alligators, all of whom sport an impressive list of movie and TV credits.

Among the backlot sets in Cinemagic Center are Doc Brown's Science Center and Norman Bates' motel and nearby home — the Psycho House.

Hollywood

The Hollywood area's backlot sets are capable of supporting films requiring scenes such as Rodeo Drive and Hollywood Boulevard. This backlot also holds **The Phantom of the Opera Horror Make-Up Show.** Here you can see what goes into creating faces such as those of the Phantom, Frankenstein, and London's American werewolf.

Water Mania

TravelFacts

Location: 6073 W. Bronson Hwy. (West U.S. 192), Kissimmee 34741, about 1.5 miles east of Interstate 4.
Map: Price 127.
Telephone: (407) 396-2626.
Hours: Vary with the season. Generally opens at 9 A.M. in summer, 10 A.M. the rest of the year. Closing varies between 5 P.M. and 9 P.M. Call to verify hours. The park usually closes for extended periods during winter.
Time to see: From several hours to an entire day.
Price: $16.95 adults, $14.95 ages 3 to 12, under 3 free. Admission is discounted late in the afternoon. Call 396-2626 to determine starting time for discounted admission.
• Snack bar and picnic area available.
• Rafts, rental lockers, showers, changing facilities, gift shop, and game room available.

What to expect: a water park with speed and toboggan slides, twisting flumes, and a free-fall slide — The Screamer. The 14-foot-wide Anaconda takes four people in a circular raft along a 400-foot slide. Water Mania also offers a heated wave pool and two children's pools with slides. Land activities include volleyball, a miniature golf course, and a 90-foot-square walk-through

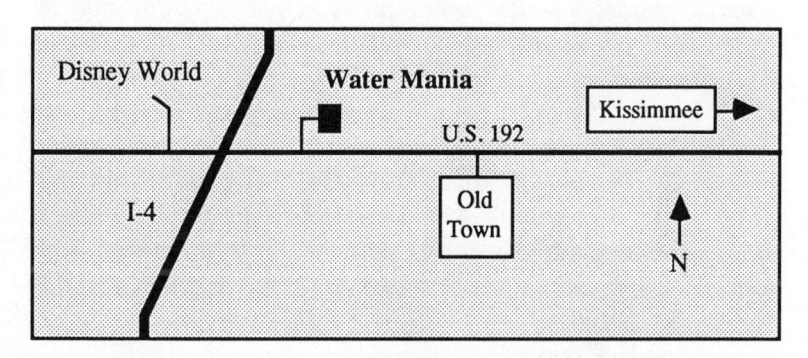

Water Mania

maze. You can also sunbathe on white sand as well as relax and feast in a woodsy, shaded picnic area. Water Mania welcomes coolers, but not alcoholic beverages or glass containers.

Wet 'n Wild

TravelFacts

> *Location:* 6200 International Dr., Orlando 32819.
> *Map:* Page 129.
> *Telephone:* (407) 351-9453 or (407) 351-3200.
> *Hours:* Vary with the season. Generally opens 9 A.M. in summer, 10 A.M. the rest of the year. Closing varies between 5 P.M. and 9 P.M. Call to verify hours. Usually closes from November through mid February. During winter, if daytime temperatures are not expected to reach the mid-60s, the park may not open.
> *Time to see:* 3 to 4 hours minimum, but you can easily spend the day.
> *Price:* $17.95 adults, $15.95 ages 3 to 12, under 3 free. A half-price admission is offered late in the afternoon. Call to determine starting time for discounted admission.
> - Fast food available.
> - Towels, rental lockers, rafts, changing rooms, lifeguards, showers, a gift shop (swimwear, T-shirts, suntan lotion), a game room, and miniature golf course (additional charge) available.

What to expect: a water park with slides ranging from mild to frightening. "Orlando's beach within reach," is Wet 'n Wild's claim to fame. And while it may not give you the tang of salt water, it does offer rolling surf, white sand, and some watery fun.

Wet 'n Wild is a 25-acre water park made up of pools, water slides, and a water playground. Its largest pool, called Surf Lagoon, holds 570,000 gallons of water which are whipped into a four-foot rolling surf. The park also has a smaller, wave-less pool. For the young set, there's a water playground with shallow pools and what could pass as a junior commando obstacle course — a wood-plank bridge, a ropeway, and water cannons.

That's the wet. On the wild side are the attraction's water

slides such as the Mach 5, the Corkscrew, and the Kamikaze among others. The Kamikaze, for example, starts out six stories up and sweeps the fearless along its 300-foot slide to a pool at the bottom. If you pass that test, head for Der Stuka, a high-speed slide 76-feet high that starts out with almost a sheer drop.

The water park's latest slide, the Black Hole, sets out from a flying saucer-shaped structure 55 feet above the ground. Riding in either a one- or two-person inflatable vehicle, you make a 30-second descent through 500 feet of twisting, nearly dark tubes. Fiber-optic lights mark the turns in the tubes while spaceshiplike sounds add realism.

A little less wild are the park's Raging Rapids and Kneeski. You navigate the rapids in an inner tube. The Kneeski uses a cable to tow you around a small lake.

On the tamer side, a white sand beach dotted with palm trees borders the lake. Here you can relax and sun bathe. While fast food is available, you may also want to bring your picnic cooler (but no alcoholic beverages or glass containers). The beach offers shady areas and covered pavilions come equipped with tables and chairs.

TravelVenture tip: Water Mania and Wet 'n Wild are both water

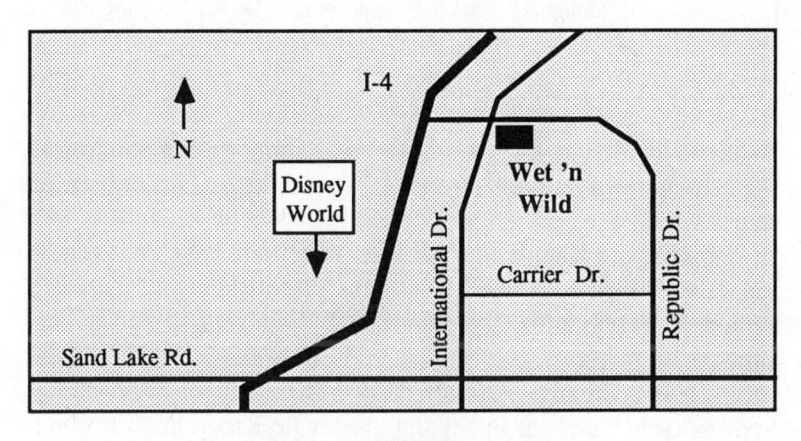

Wet 'n Wild

parks. Wet 'n Wild is the larger, offering more variety in its slides. But Wet 'n Wild also gets extremely crowded during high seasons, and you'll spend much time waiting in line. Water Mania makes an excellent alternative. If you're willing to settle for less variety, you'll gain by spending more time sliding and less time bucking the crowds.

Wonders of Walt Disney World

TravelFacts

Location: Disney World, P.O. Box 10,040, Lake Buena Vista 32830-0040.
Telephone: (407) 345-5860.
Hours: 8:45 A.M. to 3:30 P.M. or 9:30 A.M. to 4 P.M.
Time to see: approximately 6 hours.
Price: $75, includes theme-park admission, books, use of a camera, and lunch.
Reservations: Required, call (407) 345-5860.
- The program offers three seminars: "Exploring Nature: A True-Life Adventure," Tuesday and Thursday. "Art Magic: Bringing Illusions to Life," Monday, Wednesday, and Friday. "Show Business Magic: The World of Entertainment," Monday through Thursday.
- Wonders of Walt Disney World programs are open only to children ages 10 through 15. For adult seminars see "Disney Learning Adventures."

What to expect: small classes, 14 maximum, offering children an educational look at parts of Disney World they could not see on their own.

• Exploring Nature: A True-Life Adventure explores Discovery Island, Disney's wildlife sanctuary, and some of Disney's protected wetlands to take a look at Florida's plant and animal life.

• Disney Creative Arts offers a fine-arts tour of artist studios and backstage areas at Epcot and the Magic Kingdom. The seminar studies Disney techniques in drawing, costuming, and architecture.

• The Walt Disney World of Entertainment features interviews with characters, choreographers, lighting experts, musicians, and performers. The seminar includes performances by a steel-drum band and a barbershop quartet.

TravelVenture tip: These courses have been nationally recognized for their educational value and may qualify for school credit. Check with your child's school back home.

Xanadu — Home of the Future

TravelFacts

> *Location:* 4800 W. Bronson Hwy. (U.S. 192), Kissimmee 34741, near the intersection with S.R. 535.
> *Map:* Page 131.
> *Telephone:* (407) 396-1992.
> *Hours:* 10 A.M. to 10 P.M., daily.
> *Time to see:* 30 minutes.
> *Price:* $5.95 adults, $4.95 ages 3 to 12, under 3 free.

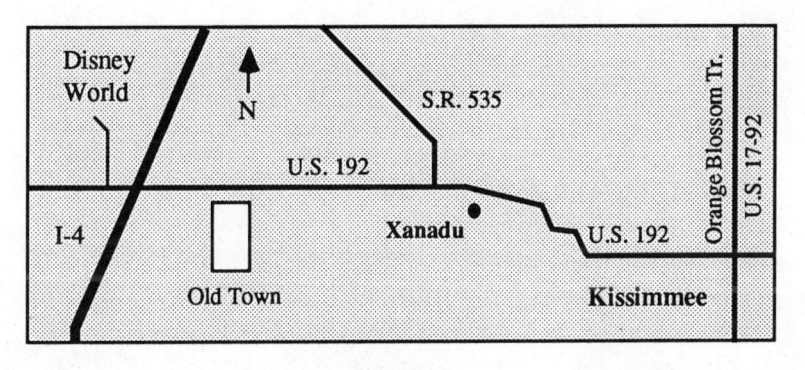

Xanadu

What to expect: according to its proprietors, the home of the future straight out of the 21st century. Xanadu is composed of interconnecting, different-sized domes. The domes are made from polyurethane foam that has been sprayed on the inside of large, inflated balloons. The foam is sprayed on in layers until the walls and roof are rigid, sturdy, and four-to-six inches thick. The balloon is peeled away, and windows and doors are then cut into the walls.

Xanadu contains 15 rooms, including a super-large bathroom that holds a whirlpool bath, a solar sauna, and a saltwater float tank. A tour guide periodically leads groups through the house, but you can also view it on your own. On the tour, the guide fills you in on the home's latest electronic appliances and computer systems.

TravelPlanner: nightlife

Nightlife by location

Disney World
Broadway At The Top 136
Hoop-Dee-Doo Musical Revue 140
Pleasure Island 146
Polynesian Luau Revue 148

International Drive
King Henry's Feast 140
Mardi Gras 143
The Plantation Dinner Theater 145

Kissimmee area
Arabian Nights 135
Fort Liberty Wild West Dinner Show & Trading Post 138
Little Darlin's Rock 'n' Roll Palace 141
Medieval Times 144

Orlando - downtown
Church Street Station 137
Mark Two Dinner Theater 143

Nightlife by type

Dinner attractions
- Arabian Nights 135
- Broadway At The Top 136
- Fort Liberty Wild West Dinner Show & Trading Post 138
- Hoop-Dee-Doo Musical Revue 140
- King Henry's Feast 140
- Mardi Gras 143
- Medieval Times 144
- Polynesian Luau Revue 148

Dinner theaters
- Mark Two Dinner Theater 143
- The Plantation Dinner Theater 145

Music, dancing, and entertainment
- Church Street Station 137
- Little Darlin's Rock 'n' Roll Palace 141
- Pleasure Island 146

Nightlife

Arabian Nights

TravelFacts

Location: 6225 W. Bronson Hwy. (U.S. 192), Kissimmee 34741.
Map: Page 136.
Telephone: (407) 396-7400 (Kissimmee), (407) 239-9223 (Orlando), 800-553-6116.
Hours: Generally one show daily at 7:30 P.M. During high seasons an additional performance may be added. Call to confirm show times.
Price: Dinner and show - $27.95 adults, $16.95 ages 3 to 11, under 3 free.
Reservations: Recommended.
Dress: Casual.

What to expect: a two-hour dinner attraction featuring beautiful horses and exhibitions of fine horsemanship. The Arabian Nights show draws its animals from a stable of 80 horses representing 10 breeds, including Arabians, Andalusians, Lippizzaners, Clydesdales, American quarter horses, and French Percherons. While a fairy-tale story line unfolds, the finely trained horses parade and dance to music ranging from Strauss to a country hoedown. You'll also see stunt riding, comedy acts, and a Roman chariot race.

Dinner, which is served as the show progresses, consists of

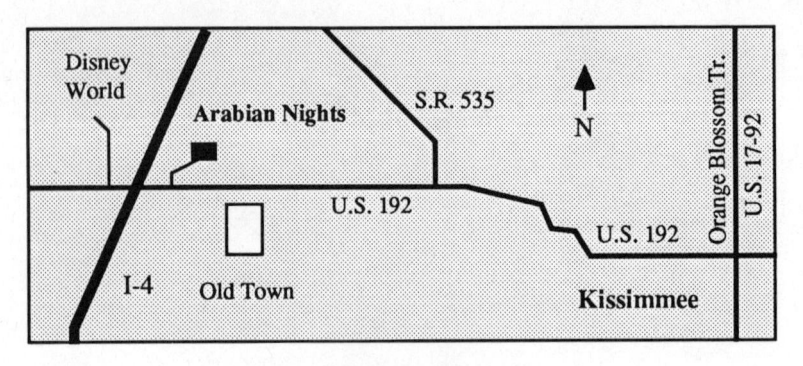

Arabians Nights

soup, salad, chicken or ribs or vegetarian lasagne, rolls, dessert, and beverages (including beer and wine).

TravelVenture tip: Visitors take in the show from tiers of bench-seated tables. Ladies will find getting in and out of the bench seating easier if they wear slacks.

Broadway At The Top

TravelFacts

> *Location:* 4600 N. World Dr., Disney World, in the Contemporary Resort hotel's Top of the World dining room on the 15th floor.
> *Map:* Page 139.
> *Telephone:* (407) 824-3611, (407) 824-1000.
> *Hours:* Seatings at 6 P.M. and 9:15 P.M.
> *Price:* Dinner and show - $40 adults, $18 ages 3 to 11.
> *Reservations:* Required, may be made up to 30 days in advance. Call (407) 934-7639.

What to expect: dinner followed by a musical revue. Two guys and three dolls dance and sing their way through classic hits from Broadway shows. Dinner entrees include prime rib, Cornish game hen, fresh fish, filet mignon and fresh fish, seafood fettucine, and roast duckling.

TravelVenture tip: The Top of the World's 15th-floor location gives patrons a great view of Disney World.

Church Street Station

TravelFacts

Location: 129 W. Church St., Orlando 32801.
Map: Page 137.
Telephone: (407) 422-2434.
Hours: 11 A.M. to 2 A.M. daily.
Price: Admission charged after 5 P.M. — $14.95 adults, $9.95 ages 4 to 12. Ages 3 and under free.

What to expect: a sprawling entertainment, dining, and shopping complex with the emphasis on turn-of-the-century nostalgia.

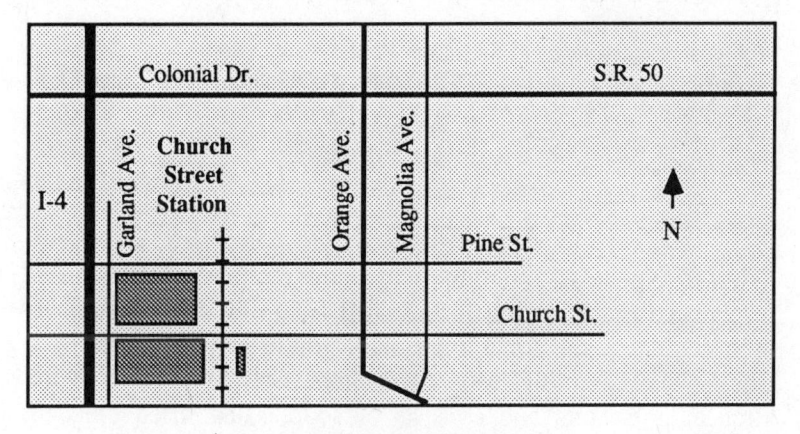

Church Street Station

Church Street Station features: Rosie O'Grady's Good Time Emporium (live Dixieland with the Good Time Jazz Band), Cheyenne Saloon & Opera House (live country and western music), Orchid Garden Ballroom (classics from the '30s through today), Phineas Phogg's Balloon Works (a disco playing today's hits) Apple Annie's Courtyard (live folk and bluegrass), Lili Marlene's Aviator's Pub and Restaurant (full service restaurant serving lunch 11 A.M. to 4 P.M. and dinner 5:30 P.M. to midnight), Bumby Arcade (shops, eateries, and a French bakery), Buffalo Trading Co. (shop selling Western wares), The Church Street Station Historic Depot Renovation (gift and souvenir shops plus an ice cream parlor), Church Street Station Exchange (three-story festival marketplace with 57 shops and eateries).

Fort Liberty Wild West Dinner Show & Trading Post

TravelFacts

Location: 5260 W. Bronson Hwy. (U.S. 192), Kissimmee 34741.
Map: Page 139.
Telephone: (407) 351-5151, 800-347-8181.
Hours: Fort and trading post 10 A.M. to 10 P.M. daily. Dinner shows at 6:30 P.M. and 9 P.M. daily in high season, 8 P.M. in low season. Show times may vary; call to confirm.
Price: Dinner and show - $25.95 adults, $17.95 ages 3 to 11, under 3 free.
Reservations: Required.
Dress: Casual.

What to expect: an entertaining two-hour dinner show held inside a recreated old-West log fort. Seated ten to a table beneath the high ceiling of the fort's mess hall, you're served dinner by a singing and cavorting troop of soldiers. Chow comes from the kitchen in buckets and consists of soup, salad, fried chicken, barbecued pork, baked beans, baked potatoes, corn on the cob,

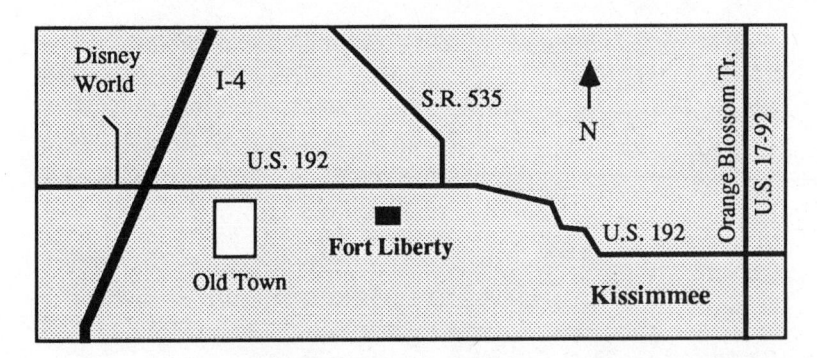

Fort Liberty Wild West Dinner Show & Trading Post

apple pie, and ice cream. The entertainment, which takes the theme of a medicine show, is nonstop and zips right along with sing-alongs, comedians, a magic show, trick roping, audience-participation skits, and an Indian family performing tribal dances.

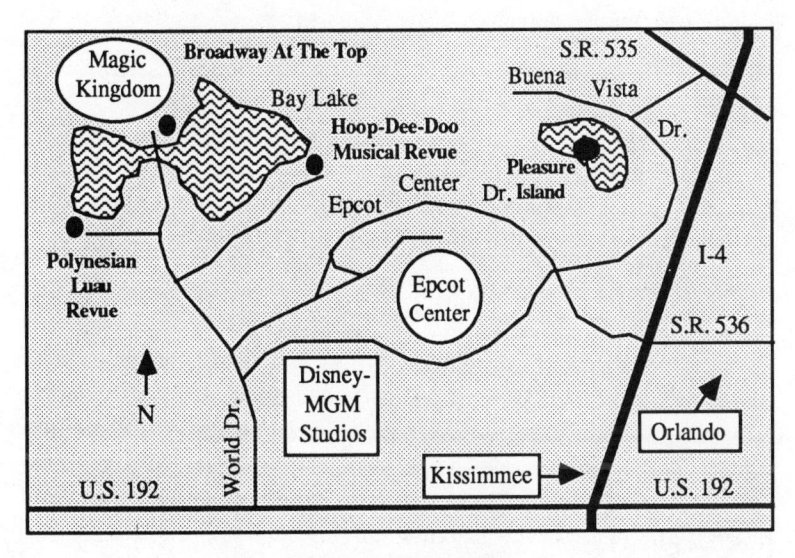

Disney World nightlife

The fort's Trading Post houses an Indian museum and a variety of shops.

TravelVenture tip: In addition to being a fun show for adults, the Fort Liberty dinner attraction is especially appealing to kids.

Hoop-Dee-Doo Musical Revue

TravelFacts

> *Location:* Pioneer Hall, Fort Wilderness, Disney World.
> *Map:* Page 139.
> *Telephone:* (407) 934-7639.
> *Hours:* Dinner show at 5 P.M., 7:30 P.M., and 10 P.M. daily. Show times may vary; call to confirm.
> *Price:* Dinner and show - $30.74 adults, $24.38 ages 12 to 20, $15.90 ages 3 to 11.
> *Reservations:* Required, may be made up to 30 days in advance.
> *Dress:* Casual.
>
> **TravelVenture tip:** This show is popular, make your reservation as far ahead of time as possible.

What to expect: two hours of delightful entertainment. When the singing, dancing, and joking is over, you'll leave the Hoop-Dee-Doo Musical Revue wearing a smile on your face. Dinner consists of barbecued ribs, fried chicken, corn on the cob, and strawberry shortcake.

King Henry's Feast

TravelFacts

> *Location:* 8984 International Dr., Orlando 32819.
> *Map:* Page 142.
> *Telephone:* (407) 351-5151, 800-347-8181.

Hours: Dinner shows at 6 P.M. and 8:30 P.M. daily in high season, 8 P.M. in low season. Show times may vary; call to confirm.
Price: Dinner and show - $25.95 adults, $17.95 ages 3 to 11, under 3 free.
Reservations: Required.
Dress: Casual.

What to expect: a fun dinner attraction hosted by King Henry VIII himself and set in the king's recreated castle-like country home. Guests are seated at 12-person tables in the Grand Hall where "wenches" serve the feast — soup, salad, roast chicken, ribs, boiled potatoes, vegetables, apple pie, and ice cream. The king's Royal Entertainers, occasionally backed up by volunteer guests, provide two hours of continuous singing, dancing, comedy, and specialty acts. Among the acts are a magician, swordfighting knights, and an amazing sword swallower.

Little Darlin's Rock 'n' Roll Palace

TravelFacts

Location: 5770 W. Bronson Hwy. (U.S. 192), Kissimmee 34741, at the Old Town shopping village.
Map: Page 142.
Telephone: (407) 396-6499 (Kissimmee), (407) 827-6169 (Orlando).
Hours: Noon to 2 A.M. daily.
Price: After 5 P.M. - $8.50 adults and children.
Reservations: Not accepted.

What to expect: live evening entertainment provided by '50s rock 'n' rollers. In addition to the oldies stars, Little Darlin's offers a '50s house band and a dance floor. The Nashville Network often tapes these performances for showing on its "Rock 'n' Roll" program. Food is available.

142 ORLANDO AND DISNEY WORLD

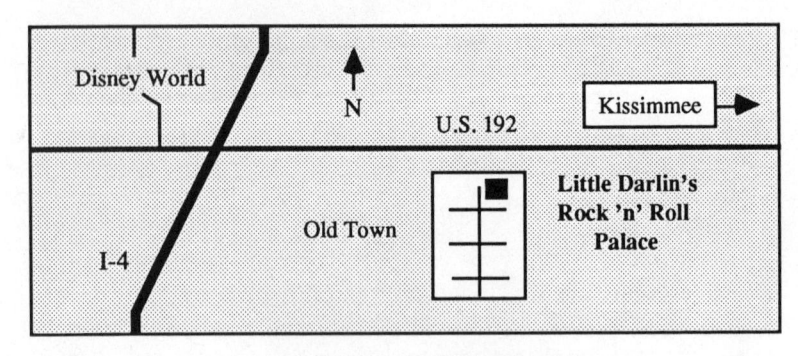

Little Darlin's Rock 'n' Roll Palace

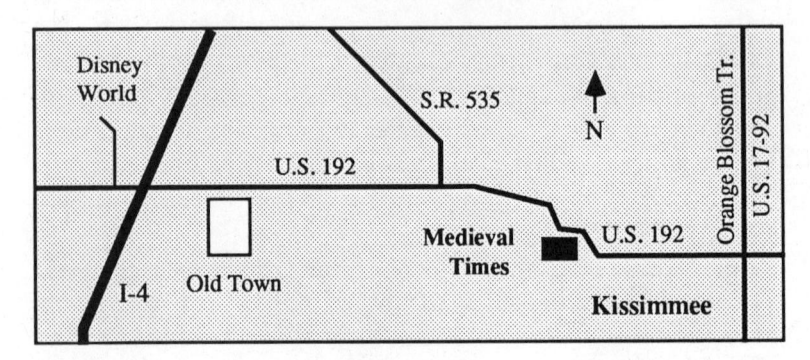

Medieval Times

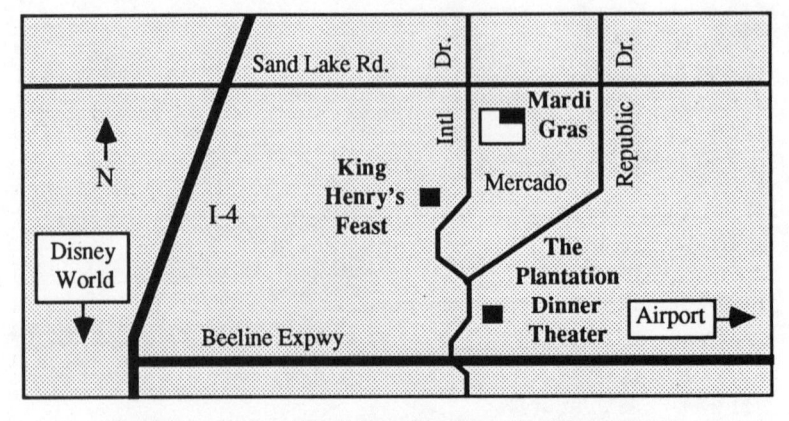

King Henry's Feast, Mardi Gras, The Plantation Dinner Theater

Mardi Gras

TravelFacts

Location: 8445 International Dr., Orlando 32819, in the Mercado shopping center.
Map: Page 142.
Telephone: (407) 351-5151, 800-347-8181.
Hours: Dinner shows at 6:30 P.M. and 9 P.M. daily in high season, 8 P.M. in low season. Show times can vary; call to confirm.
Price: Dinner and show - $27.95 adults, $19.95 ages 3 to 11, under 3 free.
Reservations: Required.
Dress: Casual.

What to expect: a two-hour cabaret-style dinner show. Seated at 12-person tables, guests dine family style on soup, salad, prime rib, potatoes, pie, and ice cream. The songs of an MC-singer and the tunes of a jazz band enhance the meal. Specialty acts add a bit of spice. After dinner, Mardi Gras puts on a stage show that takes you to Carnivals in Rio, Paris, and New Orleans. The performers add to the intimacy of the small theater by not only dancing and singing across the stage, but throughout the aisles as well.

Mark Two Dinner Theater

TravelFacts

Location: 3376 Edgewater Dr., Orlando 32804.
Map: Page 145.
Telephone: (407) 422-3191.
Hours: Tuesday through Saturday: dinner from 6:30 P.M., show at 8 P.M.; Sunday: dinner from 5:15 P.M., show at 6:30 P.M.; Wednesday and Saturday matinees: lunch from 12:15 P.M., show at 1:15 P.M.
Price: Dinner and show: $24 to $28 adults, $19 to $23 ages 12 and under.
Reservations: Required.

What to expect: a dinner theater staging periodically changing plays. Call to determine current production. The pre-show meals, both lunch and dinner, are served buffet style. Entrees include roast beef, chicken, seafood, and Polynesian ham.

Medieval Times

TravelFacts

Location: 4510 W. Vine Street (U.S. 192), P.O. Box 422385, Kissimmee 34742-2385.
Map: Page 142.
Telephone: (407) 396-1518 (Kissimmee), (407) 239-0214 (Orlando), 800-327-4024, 800-432-0768 (in Florida).
Hours: Depending on the season and day of the week, one show at 8 P.M. or two shows at 6 P.M. and 8:30 P.M. Call to confirm show times.
Price: Dinner and show - $26 adults, $18 ages 3 to 12.
Reservations: Required.
Dress: Casual.

What to expect: an entertaining — even thrilling — dinner show held in a recreated 11th-century castle. Tiers of bench-seated tables line both sides of the castle's 1,000-seat, rectangular arena. To help you get in tune with the 11th century, the castle's "wenches" dish out roast chicken and pork ribs which are eaten hands on — without silverware. Hot towels take care of the greasy hands.

During the meal, knights put on exhibitions of horsemanship. Afterwards, the competition begins. The arena's seats are divided by color into six sections. Six mounted knights, each wearing a different section's color, compete in events that include lancing, jousting, and, as the competition heats up, sword fighting. The audience participates by cheering on its knight.

TravelVenture tip: Ladies will find getting in and out of the bench seating easier if they wear slacks.

The Plantation Dinner Theater

TravelFacts

Location: 9861 International Dr., Orlando 32819, in the Orlando Heritage Inn.
Map: Page 142.
Telephone: (407) 352-0008, 800-447-1890, 800-282-1890 (in Florida).
Hours: Dinner from 7 P.M., show at 8:15 P.M. Tuesday through Saturday.
Price: $25.95 adults, $12 ages 12 and under.
Reservations: Suggested.

What to expect: a hotel restaurant turned dinner theater. Following dinner, which is served at your table, a troupe of performers take over the stage rising from one corner to put on periodically changing plays. Dinner entrees include: New York strip steak, chicken breast, grouper, and veal cutlet. Children can choose from a hamburger, pizza, or fried chicken fingers.

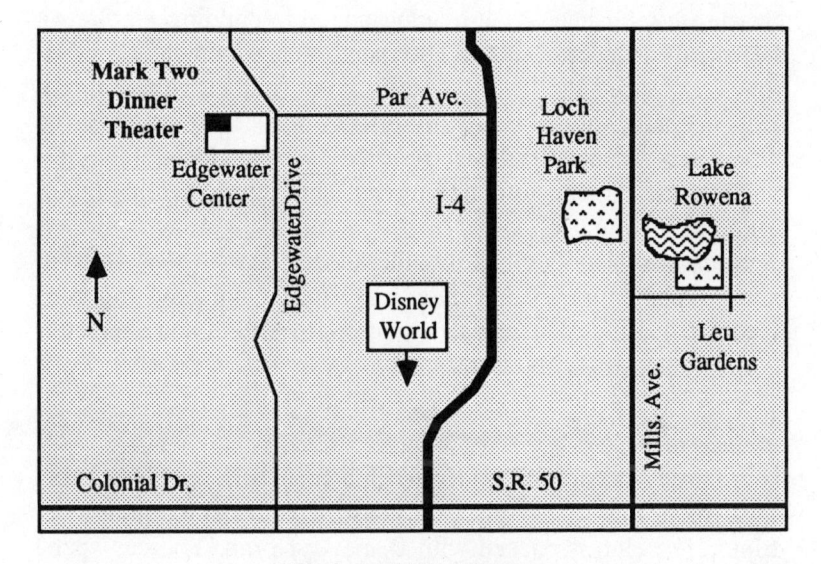

Mark Two Dinner Theater

Pleasure Island

TravelFacts

Location: Walt Disney World Village, adjacent to the Disney Village Marketplace.
Map: Page 139.
Telephone: (407) 934-7781.
Hours: Shops - 10 A.M. to midnight. Clubs - 7 P.M. to 2 A.M.
Price: Free admission between.10 A.M. and 7 P.M. After 7 P.M., $10.55 ages 18 and over. Under 18 not admitted to Pleasure Island after 7 P.M. No age restriction nor admission charge to enter the Portobello Yacht Club, and The Fireworks Factory restaurants, day or night.

What to expect: an entertainment complex boasting shops, restaurants, and nightclubs — six of them. Pleasure Island actually is an island hugging the shoreline of Buena Vista Lagoon. Foot bridges cross narrow waterways to connect the six-acre island to the shore.

According to Disney legend, Pleasure Island has quite a history. A Pittsburgh entrepreneur named Merriweather Adam Pleasure established a sail-making and ship-building empire on the island in the late 1800s. The inept management of his heirs, however, caused the business to go bust. And Pleasure's lavish residence and waterfront factory district fell into disrepair in the 1950s. But Disney has now restored the abandoned factories, warehouses, and sail lofts and turned them into a waterfront entertainment complex.

Pleasure Island's clubs provide variety: classic rock 'n' roll, country, contemporary hits, alternative music, comedy, and even a recreated British-like private club from the 1920s and 30s.

Adventurers Club

This Disney version of a private club for world travelers offers much more than just a place to boast of your explorations over drinks. The club is packed with Disney-type fun. You can spend quite a bit of time browsing the wall-to-wall memorabilia — everything from Ashanti fertility dolls to a stuffed zebra. You can relax and watch the comedic antics of the club's maids and butlers. You can take in a light-hearted tour of the Trophy Room given by Fletcher Hodges, the club's curator. And you can visit the club's bar-equipped library to view a humorous skit.

The Comedy Warehouse

Shows at The Comedy Warehouse are held at set times — check the sign at the entrance. The comedians here frequently target Disney World with their skits and spoofs.

Mannequins Dance Palace

This popular club features recorded contemporary sounds, a rotating dance floor, animated mannequins, and house dancers performing on a stage above the dance floor. (Ages 21 and above only.)

Neon Armadillo Music Saloon

This is no honky tonk saloon. The Neon Armadillo sports an upscale Western decor of oak wood, neon signs, and Georgia O'Keefe prints. The club features live country music.

Cage

The Cage features alternative music, lasers, strobe lights, a high-decibel sound system, and 169 video monitors showing dancers picked up by two video cameras.

XZFR Rock 'n' Roll Beach Club

The XZFR (pronounced Zephyr) features live rock 'n' roll classics and a beach party theme.

Pleasure Island's restaurants include The Fireworks Factory (specializing in barbecue), and an Italian restaurant, the Portobello Yacht Club. See the Dining section for details. You can also get a wide variety of fast food at Merriweather's Market.

Oh, and if you run out of things to do and get bored, you can take in a movie at Pleasure Island's ten-screen theater.

Polynesian Luau Revue

TravelFacts

Location: Luau Cove, Polynesian Village Resort hotel, Disney World.
Map: Page 139.
Telephone: (407) 934-7639.
Hours: Shows at 4:30 P.M., 6:45 P.M., and 9:30 P.M.
Price: Dinner and show - $29 adults ($25 at the 4:30 P.M. show), $23 ages 12 to 20 ($20 at the 4:30 P.M. show), $15 ages 3 to 11 ($11 at the 4:30 P.M. show).
Reservations: Required, may be made up to 30 days in advance.

What to expect: a lagoon-side luau accompanied by a troupe performing the music and dances of Hawaii and the South Seas. The 4:30 show, called Mickey's Tropical Revue, is designed especially for kids with Mickey Mouse and the other Disney characters in attendance.

TravelPlanner: shopping

Shopping by location

Disney World
Crossroads of Lake Buena Vista 153
Disney Village Marketplace 154
Pleasure Island 162

International Drive area
Belz Factory Outlet World 151
Dansk Factory Outlet 154
The Florida Mall 155
Mercado Mediterranean Village 157
Quality Outlet Center 162

Kissimmee
Kissimmee Manufacturer's Mall 157
Old Town 158
Osceola Square Mall 161

Orlando - central
Church Street Market 151
Church Street Station Exchange 152
Colonial Plaza Mall 153

    Ivanhoe Antique Row 156
    Orlando Fashion Square 160

Winter Park

    Park Avenue 161

Shopping by type

Factory outlets

    Belz Factory Outlet World 151
    Dansk Factory Outlet 154
    Kissimmee Manufacturer's Mall 157
    Quality Outlet Center 162

Indoor malls

    Belz Factory Outlet World 151
    Church Street Market 151
    Church Street Station Exchange 152
    Colonial Plaza Mall 153
    The Florida Mall 155
    Orlando Fashion Square 160
    Osceola Square Mall 161

Strip centers

    Crossroads of Lake Buena Vista 153
    Kissimmee Manufacturer's Mall 157
    Quality Center Outlet 162

Specialty

    Church Street Market 151
    Church Street Station Exchange 152
    Disney Village Marketplace 154
    Ivanhoe Antique Row 156
    Mercado Mediterranean Village 157
    Old Town 158
    Park Avenue 161
    Pleasure Island 162

Shopping

Belz Factory Outlet World

TravelFacts

Location: 5401 W. Oakridge Rd., Orlando 32819, at the intersection of International Drive.
Map: Page 159.
Telephone: (407) 352-9611, (407) 352-9600.
Hours: 10 A.M. to 9 P.M. Monday through Saturday, noon to 6 P.M. Sunday.

What to expect: a multi-building complex offering two indoor malls, a strip mall, and some 170 stores. Not all shops in this mall live up to the name factory outlet — a store owned by the company manufacturing the merchandise. Nevertheless, the mall is a good hunting ground for bargain seekers. Among the merchandise you'll find: clothing, shoes, home furnishings, luggage, sports equipment, books, records, cameras, VCRs, and toys.

Church Street Market

TravelFacts

Location: 55 W. Church St., Orlando 33801, between Orange and Garland Avenues, downtown Orlando.

> *Map:* Page 155.
> *Telephone:* (407) 872-3500.
> *Hours:* 10 A.M. to 10 P.M. Monday through Saturday, noon to 6 P.M. Sunday.

What to expect: a collection of specialty shops and eateries. The two-level, red-brick Church Street Market sits on both sides of Church Street. A covered bridge spans the street to connect the two buildings. The market's cupolas and slate roof blend with the adjacent Old Orlando Railroad Depot, an historic landmark dating from 1889. Among the market's wares: clothing, home furnishings, housewares, gifts, and electronics.

Church Street Station Exchange

TravelFacts

> *Location:* 124 W. Pine St., Orlando 33801, between Orange and Garland Avenues, downtown Orlando.
> *Map:* Page 155.
> *Telephone:* (407) 849-0901.
> *Hours:* 11 A.M. to 11 P.M. daily. Commander Ragtime's remains open until 2 A.M.

What to expect: a three-story festival marketplace, done in turn-of-the-century architecture. The Church Street Station Exchange uses white-tile and wood flooring, wrought-iron bannisters with brass handrails, and pressed-tin ceilings to create an old-time atmosphere. The exchange houses some 57 shops, boutiques, and eateries including a second-floor food court. Among the merchandise available: jewelry; clothing, music boxes, collectibles, records and tapes, gifts, and souvenirs. "Commander Ragtime's Midway of Fun, Food and Games" occupies the third floor. The commander's midway is packed with video and arcade games and boasts roller skating waitresses serving food and drink.

TravelVenture tip: Even if you're not interested in video and arcade games, be sure to visit the third floor's Commander Ragtime's Midway of Fun, Food & Games. You can inspect the three full-size bi-planes hanging from the ceiling, the antique vehicles parked about, and a 25-foot replica of the *Queen Elizabeth*.

Colonial Plaza Mall

TravelFacts

Location: 2560 E. Colonial Dr., Orlando 32819.
Map: Page 155.
Telephone: (407) 894-3601.
Hours: 10 A.M. to 9 P.M. Monday through Saturday, noon to 5:30 P.M. Sunday.

What to expect: 100 stores in a sprawling single-level mall. Colonial Plaza's anchor department stores, some of which are multi-level, are: Jordan Marsh, Belk-Lindsey, J Byrons, and Dillard's.

Crossroads of Lake Buena Vista

TravelFacts

Location: State Road 535, Lake Buena Vista, opposite the entrance to Walt Disney World.
Map: Page 158.
Hours: Most stores 10 A.M. to 10 P.M. daily.

What to expect: a strip mall containing 15 shops, 11 eateries, and a 24-hour supermarket. The shops offer: clothing for adults and children, footwear, dry cleaning (same-day service available), eyewear, cards and stationary, souvenirs, electronic items, and books. A bank and a post office are also located at the Crossroads.

Dansk Factory Outlet

TravelFacts

Location: 7000 International Dr., Orlando 32819.
Map: Page 159.
Telephone: (407) 351-2425.
Hours: 9 A.M. to 7 P.M. daily.

What to expect: discontinued and nonconforming tableware at savings up to 60 percent. At this factory outlet you can pick up Scandinavian-design teakwood bowls and cutting boards, stainless steel flatware, enamelware, and glassware.

TravelVenture tip: Dansk will mail your purchases.

Disney Village Marketplace

TravelFacts

Location: Walt Disney World Village, P.O. Box 10,150, Lake Buena Vista 32830-0150.
Map: Page 158.
Telephone: (407) 828-3058.
Hours: 10 A.M. to 10 P.M. daily.

What to expect: cedar-shingled, one-story buildings curving around the 35-acre Buena Vista Lagoon and housing some two dozen upscale shops. The shops offer a wide range of goods including: crafts, souvenirs, toys, clothing, jewelry, housewares,

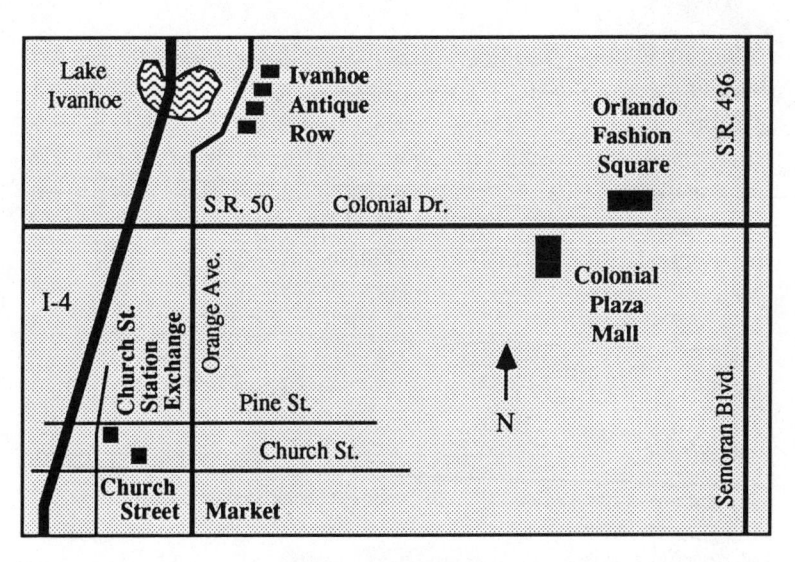

Orlando - central shopping

crystal, and plants. The village also offers full-service restaurants, fast food eateries, and boat rentals (pedal and motor).

TravelVenture tip: Although located at Disney World, there is no admission or parking charge. The Village Marketplace is a superb strolling and browsing spot.

The Florida Mall

TravelFacts

Location: 8001 S. Orange Blossom Trail, Orlando 32809, at the intersection of Sand Lake Road.
Map: Page 159.
Telephone: (407) 851-6255.
Hours: 10 A.M. to 9 P.M. Monday through Saturday, noon to 5:30 P.M. Sunday.

What to expect: a single-level mall with some 175 shops and eateries plus a 12-story hotel, the Sheraton Plaza. The mall is anchored by J C Penny, Sears, Belk-Lindsey, and Maison Blanche. As you make your way along the mall's corridors, notice the change in architectural styles. You can move from Mediterranean-style arches and tile roofs, through a turn-of-the-century Victorian flavor, to sleek and shiny art deco.

Ivanhoe Antique Row

TravelFacts

Location: 1200 section of North Orange Avenue, Orlando, just off Virginia Drive.
Map: Page 155.
Hours: Most shops 10 A.M. to 4:30 P.M. Monday through Saturday. Closed Sunday.

What to expect: a block-long strip of square two-story buildings occupied by more than a dozen antique shops. The shops, which face Lake Ivanhoe, are packed with wares both upstairs and down. Antiques such as baby carriages, milk cans, and wooden chairs also spill out onto the sidewalk.

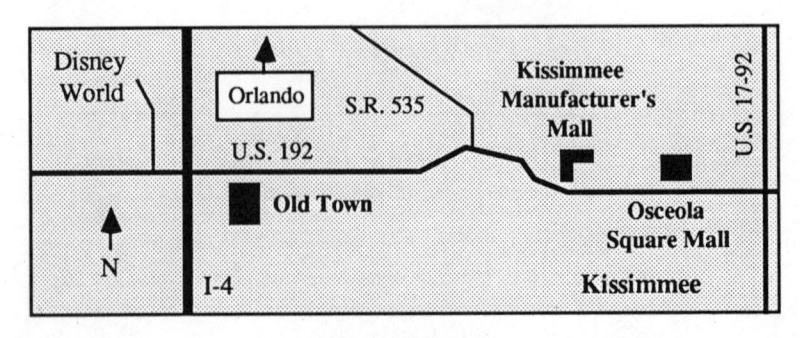

Kissimmee shopping

TravelVenture tip: A must for antique buffs. A scattering of antique shops can also be found farther north along Orange Avenue.

Kissimmee Manufacturer's Mall

TravelFacts

> *Location:* West Bronson Highway (U.S. 192) and Vineland Road, Kissimmee 34741.
> *Map:* Page 156.
> *Hours:* 10 A.M. to 9 P.M. Monday through Saturday, 11 P.M. to 5 P.M. Sunday.

What to expect: 25 outlet and discount stores. Among the merchandise offered: men's, women's, and children's clothing and shoes (including Manhattan, "Just Kids," Aileen, Judy Bond, London Fog, Bass, and Nike) as well as Fenton glass, leather goods, and linens.

Mercado Mediterranean Village

TravelFacts

> *Location:* 8445 International Dr., Orlando 32819, just south of Sand Lake Road.
> *Map:* Page 159.
> *Telephone:* (407) 345-9337.
> *Hours:* 10 A.M. to 10 P.M. daily.

What to expect: an attractive Mediterranean-style shopping, entertainment, and dining complex. Mercado, which means market in Spanish, contains some 50 shops, boutiques, and pushcart vendors; six full-service restaurants; and more than a half-dozen fast

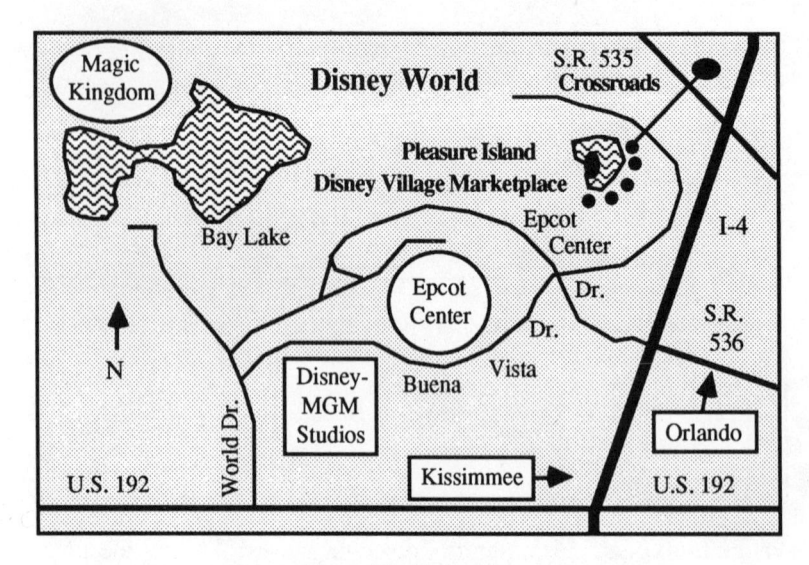

[Map of Disney World area showing Magic Kingdom, Bay Lake, Pleasure Island, Disney Village Marketplace, Epcot Center, Disney-MGM Studios, and surrounding roads including I-4, S.R. 535, S.R. 536, U.S. 192, World Dr., Buena Vista Dr., with Crossroads, Orlando, and Kissimmee labeled]

Disney World shopping

food eateries. Shops are located at street level but housed in one- and two-story buildings lining both sides of a brick sidewalk. In the center of the complex sits a large, flowered courtyard. Throughout the village, wall murals and fountains add to the flavor of the place. Goods in the shops include: Irish woolens, clothing and accessories, crystal, candles, gifts, souvenirs, toys, sundries, crafts, jewelry, and art works.

TravelVenture tip: Lots of atmosphere here, great for browsing.

Old Town

TravelFacts

> **Location:** 5770 W. Bronson Hwy. (U.S. 192), Kissimmee 34741, two miles east of Interstate 4.
> **Map:** Page 156.

Telephone: (407) 396-4888.
Hours: 10 A.M. to 10 P.M. daily.

What to expect: a hundred specialty stores and restaurants in an outdoor shopping center resembling small-town Florida during the 1920s. Old Town's brick-paved main street runs four blocks, with a fountain and a Ferris wheel at one end and a working carousel at the other. Shops occupy the first floors of the boxy one- and two-story buildings that line both the main and side streets. To make your shopping enjoyable, streets are traffic free, sidewalks are shaded with awnings, and benches are plentiful. Among the merchandise you'll find: clothing, jewelry, books,

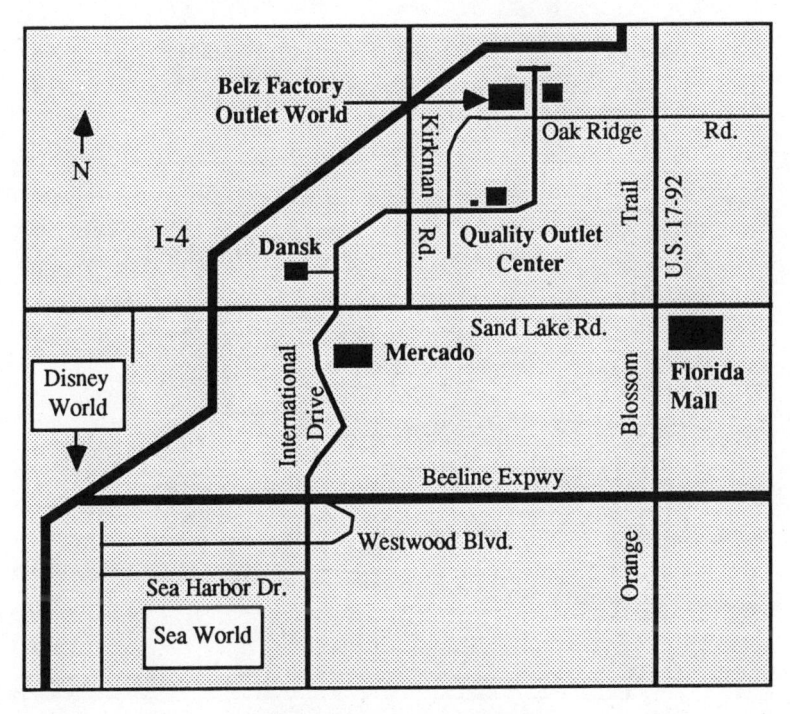

International Drive-area shopping

gifts, souvenirs, sundries, collectibles, pottery, candles, and toys. Restaurants and snack bars are plentiful.

TravelVenture tip: Ideal for strolling the streets and exploring the shops.

Orlando Fashion Square

TravelFacts

Location: 3201 E. Colonial Dr., Orlando 32803.
Map: Page 155.
Telephone: (407) 896-1131.
Hours: 10 A.M. to 9 P.M. Monday through Saturday, noon to 5:30 P.M. Sunday.

What to expect: a 95-store, single-level mall anchored by Sears, Burdines, and Maison Blanche department stores.

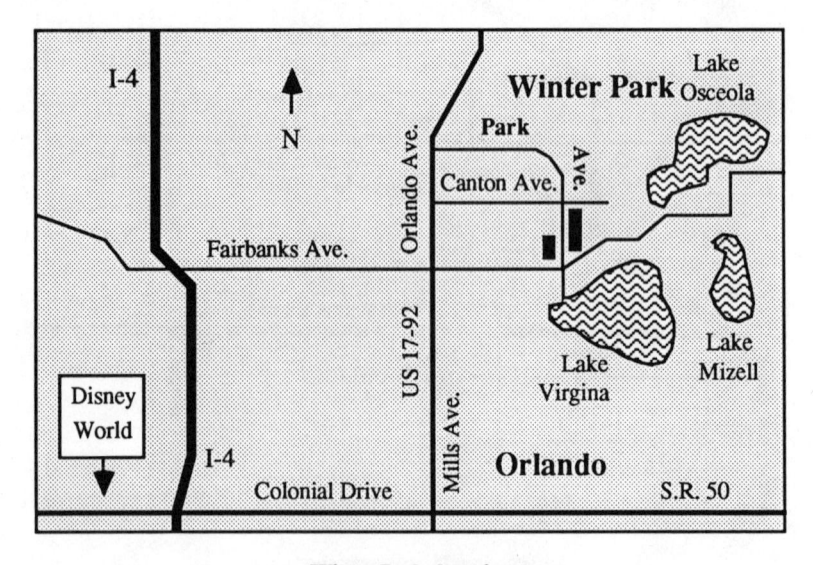

Winter Park shopping

Osceola Square Mall

TravelFacts

Location: 3831 W. Vine St. (U.S. 192), Kissimmee 34741.
Map: Page 156.
Telephone: (407) 847-6941.
Hours: 10 A.M. to 9 P.M. Monday through Saturday, noon to 6 P.M. Sunday.

What to expect: an indoor mall of 61 shops and eateries with J. Byrons, Wal-Mart, and Ross Dress For Less as anchor stores. Adjacent to the mall is a six-theater cinema.

Park Avenue

TravelFacts

Location: Park Avenue, Winter Park, between Fairbanks and Canton Avenues.
Map: Page 160.
Hours: Most stores 10 A.M. to 5:30 P.M. Monday through Saturday.

What to Expect: an upscale shopping strip. Park Avenue has gained popularity as much for its atmosphere as for its elegant shops, boutiques, art galleries, and eateries. The avenue is lined with mostly two-story buildings. Several courtyards and mini malls are tucked away between and inside the buildings. Central Park, home of the Winter Park Art Festival held every March, occupies several blocks on the avenue's west side.

TravelVenture tip: You don't have to be out for serious shopping to enjoy Park Avenue. It's a great street for strolling, window shopping, and, from a shaded bench in Central Park, people watching.

Pleasure Island

TravelFacts

Location: Walt Disney World Village, adjacent to the Disney Village Marketplace.
Map: Page 158.
Telephone: (407) 824-4321.
Hours: 10 A.M. to 1 A.M.

What to expect: a collection of shops sprinkled around Disney World's nighttime entertainment complex. Merchandise includes: Disney T-shirts, souvenirs, and memorabilia; art prints and posters; jewelry; gifts; and Disney's private-label clothing, including travel-safari outfits.

TravelVenture tip: These stores do not warrant a shopping visit on their own. Take them in when visiting the adjacent Disney Village Marketplace or checking out Pleasure Island's nightlife.

Quality Outlet Center

TravelFacts

Location: 5409-5490 International Dr., Orlando 32819.
Map: Page 159.
Telephone: (407) 423-5885.
Hours: Most stores 9:30 A.M. to 9 P.M. Monday through Saturday, 11 A.M. to 7 P.M. Sunday.

What to expect: some 20 stores and factory outlets whose offerings include: clothing, boots, leather goods, linens, Corningware, china and tableware (Mikasa, Villeroy & Boch, Royal Doulton), and American Tourister luggage.

TravelPlanner: dining

Restaurants by location

Disney-MGM Studios Theme Park dining
Backlot Express (fast food) 176
'50s Prime Time Cafe (American) 187
Hollywood and Vine Cafeteria (American) 191
The Hollywood Brown Derby (American) 191
Min and Bill's Dockside Diner (fast food) 199
Soundstage Restaurant (fast food) 209

Disney Village Marketplace dining
Cap'n Jack's Oyster Bar (seafood) 181
Chef Mickey's Village Restaurant (American) 182
Fisherman's Deck (seafood) 189
Steerman's Quarters (steak) 211

Epcot Center dining
Au Petit Cafe (French) 175
Biergarten (German) 177
Le Bistro de Paris (French) 179
Boulangerie Patisserie (fast food) 180
Cantina de San Angel (fast food) 180
Le Cellier (Canadian) 181
Les Chefs de France (French) 183
Coral Reef Restaurant (seafood) 185
Farmer's Market (fast food) 186

Kringla Bakeri og Kafé (fast food) 194
The Land Grille Room (American) 195
Liberty Inn (fast food) 195
Lotus Blossom Cafe (fast food) 198
Mitsukoshi Restaurant (Japanese) 200
Nine Dragons Restaurant (Chinese) 201
Odyssey Restaurant (fast food) 201
L'Originale Alfredo de Roma Ristorante (Italian) 202
Pure and Simple (fast food) 205
Restaurant Akershus (Norwegian) 205
Restaurant Marrakech (Moroccan) 206
The Rose & Crown Pub & Dining Room (British) 207
San Angel Inn Restaurante (Mexican) 208
Sommerfest (fast food) 209
Stargate Restaurant (fast food) 210
Sunrise Terrace (fast food) 212
Yakitori House (fast food) 214

Magic Kingdom dining

Adventureland Veranda (fast food) 174
Aunt Polly's Landing (fast food) 175
Columbia Harbour House (fast food) 184
The Crystal Palace (American) 186
King Stefan's Banquet Hall (American) 193
Liberty Tree Tavern (American) 196
Pinocchio Village Haus (fast food) 203
The Plaza Pavilion (fast food) 203
The Plaza Restaurant (American) 204
Tomorrowland Terrace (fast food) 212
Tony's Town Square Restaurant (Italian) 213

Orlando-area dining

Atlantis (Continental and seafood) 174
Barney's Steak and Seafood House (steak & seafood) 176
Christini's (Italian) 184
Hard Rock Cafe (American) 190
Linda's La Cantina (steak and Italian) 197
Royal Orleans (Cajun-Creole) 208

Pleasure Island dining

The Fireworks Factory (American) 188

Portobello Yacht Club (Italian) 204

Universal Studios Florida dining
Beverly Hills Boulangerie (fast food) 177
Finnegan's Bar & Grill (Irish) 188
Hard Rock Cafe (American) 190
International Food Bazaar (fast food) 192
Lombard's Landing (American) 197
Louie's Italian Restaurant (fast food) 199
Mel's Drive In (fast food) 199
Studio Stars Restaurant (American) 211

Restaurants by cuisine

American
Chef Mickey's Village Restaurant (Disney Village Mrktplce) 182
The Crystal Palace (Magic Kingdom) 186
50's Prime Time Cafe (Disney-MGM Studios) 187
The Fireworks Factory (Pleasure Island) 188
Hard Rock Cafe (Orlando) 190
Hollywood & Vine Cafeteria (Disney-MGM Studios) 191
The Hollywood Brown Derby (Disney-MGM Studios) 191
King Stefan's Banquet Hall (Magic Kingdom) 193
The Land Grille Room (Epcot) 195
Liberty Tree Tavern (Magic Kingdom) 196
Lombard's Landing (Universal Studios) 197
The Plaza Restaurant (Magic Kingdom) 204
Studio Stars Restaurant (Universal Studios) 211

British
The Rose & Crown Pub & Dining Room (Epcot) 207

Cajun-Creole
Royal Orleans (Orlando) 208

Canadian
Le Cellier (Epcot) 181

Chinese
Nine Dragons Restaurant (Epcot) 201

Continental
Atlantis (Orlando) 174

Fast food
Adventureland Veranda (Magic Kingdom) 174
Aunt Polly's Landing (Magic Kingdom) 175
Backlot Express (Disney-MGM Studios) 176
Beverly Hills Boulangerie (Universal Studios) 177
Boulangerie Patisserie (Epcot) 180
Cantina de San Angel (Epcot) 180
Columbia Harbour House (Magic Kingdom) 184
Farmer's Market (Epcot) 186
International Food Bazaar (Universal Studios) 192
Kringla Bakeri og Kafé (Epcot) 194
Liberty Inn (Epcot) 195
Lotus Blossom Cafe (Epcot) 198
Louie's Italian Restaurant (Universal Studios) 199
Mel's Drive In (Universal Studios) 199
Min & Bill's Dockside Diner (Disney-MGM Studios) 199
Odyssey Restaurant (Epcot) 201
Pinocchio Village Haus (Magic Kingdom) 203
The Plaza Pavilion (Magic Kingdom) 203
Pure and Simple (Epcot) 205
Sommerfest (Epcot) 209
Soundstage Restaurant (Disney-MGM Studios) 209
Stargate Restaurant (Epcot) 210
Sunrise Terrace (Epcot) 212
Tomorrowland Terrace (Magic Kingdom) 212
Yakitori House (Epcot) 214

French
Au Petit Cafe (Epcot) 175
Le Bistro de Paris (Epcot) 179
Les Chefs de France (Epcot) 183

German
Biergarten (Epcot) 177

Irish
Finnegan's Bar & Grill (Universal Studios) 188

Italian
Christini's (Orlando) 184
Linda's La Cantina (Orlando) 197
L'Originale Alfredo di Roma Ristorante (Epcot) 202
Portobello Yacht Club (Pleasure Island) 204
Tony's Town Square Restaurant (Magic Kingdom) 213

Japanese
Mitsukoshi Restaurant (Epcot) 200

Mexican
San Angel Inn Restaurante (Epcot) 208

Moroccan
Restaurant Marrakech (Epcot) 206

Norwegian
Restaurant Akershus (Epcot) 205

Seafood
Atlantis (Orlando) 174
Barney's Steak and Seafood House (Orlando) 176
Cap'n Jack's Oyster Bar (Disney Village Mrktplce) 181
Coral Reef Restaurant (Epcot) 185
Fisherman's Deck (Disney Village Mrktplce) 189

Steak
Barney's Steak and Seafood House (Orlando) 176
Linda's La Cantina (Orlando) 197
Steerman's Quarters (Disney Village Mrktplce) 211

Dining

Dining opportunities in Orlando and Disney World offer variety. They'll take you from an Orlando Cajun-Creole restaurant rivaling those in New Orleans to the authentic international cuisine served in Epcot's World Showcase restaurants. And even though Disney's eateries cater to a continually changing clientele, you'll find surprisingly good food. At more than a few the food is excellent.

Disney-MGM Studios Theme Park dining

The studios theme park offers two full-service restaurants (The Hollywood Brown Derby and the '50s Prime Time Cafe), a cafeteria (Hollywood and Vine Cafeteria), and four fast food eateries. The park's showcase restaurant is The Hollywood Brown Derby which is patterned after the famed Hollywood original.

If you want to eat breakfast at the park, head for the Hollywood and Vine Cafeteria, the only Disney-MGM Studios Theme Park restaurant serving a complete breakfast. For a light breakfast — croissants, Danish, rolls, muffins, and beverages — try the **Starring Rolls** bakery adjacent to The Hollywood Brown Derby. Here you can dine outdoors on shaded patio tables. Pies, cookies, and cakes are added to the bakery's menu later in the day.

TravelVenture tip: If you only want to pick up a quick bite for lunch or dinner and keep on touring the studios theme park, stop at one of the food trucks serving such items as sandwiches, corn dogs, hot dogs, and bratwurst. You can usually find one in the area of the Indiana Jones Epic Stunt Spectacular.

Epcot Center dining

How's this for a galloping gourmet — croissants for breakfast in Paris, lunch in Rome on fettucine Alfredo, a chicken and leak pie at tea time in a British pub, sauerbraten for dinner in a Bavarian village, and to round it off, a late evening repast on cous cous in Marrakech, Morocco. If your constitution can take all the food, you don't have to worry about the travel time. Epcot's World Showcase has compressed it for you. In fact, the next day you could start in again by sampling the culinary specialties of Canada, Mexico, China, Japan, and Norway.

In addition to its international restaurants, Epcot has two full service establishments located in Future World — one at the Land pavilion (The Land Grille Room), the other at the Living Seas (Coral Reef Restaurant). Epcot is also well-equipped with fast food eateries. Even in the World Showcase most country pavilions provide a fast food eatery that offers a taste of its national cuisine.

Epcot's full-service restaurants serve lunch from 11 A.M. to 3 P.M. and dinner from 4:30 P.M. until the park's closing. (Serving times can vary; call 407-824-4321 to confirm hours.) These restaurants are exceedingly popular, and most require lunch and dinner reservations. But if you don't get to Epcot early in the morning, you may not get one. In high season, reservations to the more popular French, Italian, and Japanese restaurants, as well as the Coral Reef Restaurant at the Living Seas pavilion, can be completely booked within a few hours after Epcot opens.

To get a reservation, head for the Earth Station located behind Spaceship Earth. As you make your reservation you'll be introduced to some of Epcot's technology. Reservationists appear on the screen of the World Key Information Satellites — a computer system you can also use to obtain information on Epcot and its facilities.

TravelVenture tip: To see exactly what each restaurant offers and charges, step up to one of the Earth Station's counters and ask to see the restaurant menus.

You can also make lunch reservations, but not dinner, at the restaurant itself. All reservations, whether made at the restaurant or at the Earth Station, must be made in person on the day you want to dine. Telephone and advance reservations are not accepted. The exception to that rule: guests at official Disney hotels (those on Disney property) can make dinner reservations up to two days in advance — but not same-day reservations — through their hotel's Guest Services.

TravelVenture tip: Epcot officially opens at 9 A.M., but the main gate will open up to 30 minutes earlier. Although the attractions and pavilions will remain closed until 9 A.M., you can get into the Earth Station to make restaurant reservations. Be there when the gates open, you'll not only assure yourself of getting the restaurant reservation you want, you'll be able to do it before the attractions open so you won't cut into sightseeing time. When the gates open, a few of the waiting crowd will spring from the entrance gate as if at a high school track meet and jog, even run, to the Earth Station. Don't let them stampede you. Even in high season there will be more than enough seats in each restaurant to accommodate the early arrivals. If you arrive later in the day and miss out on a reservation, you still may be able to dine in one of the international restaurants. The Au Petit Cafe in France and Le Cellier in Canada do not accept reservations, operating on a first-come, first- served basis. For reservations-only restaurants, go to the restaurant itself and talk to the host or hostess. Reservations are held only 15 minutes beyond the reservation time, so ask if they are taking any walk-ins to fill tables reserved by no-shows. But this is chancy and may require an extensive wait at the restaurant. If you have your heart set on dining in a particular restaurant, play it safe and get there early to make a reservation.

Magic Kingdom dining

Fast food is the name of the game for most of the 30 odd snack bars and restaurants sprinkled around the Magic Kingdom. But you can also find several full-service establishments. The Magic Kingdom's eateries carry out the theme of the land in which they are located. So choose your restaurant for its atmosphere as much as for its food.

TravelVenture tip: The Magic Kingdom's food emporiums get crowded between 11 A.M. and 2 A.M. To beat the crowds, consider eating lunch at the Liberty Tree Tavern or King Stefan's Banquet Hall. Both require reservations, so you can forget chow lines and table hunts.

Pleasure Island dining

Among Pleasure Island's pleasures are two full-service restaurants: the Portobello Yacht Club and The Fireworks Factory. For light eating, Pleasure Island offers Merriweather's Market, a fast food court. Several of the nightclubs also have fast food and snack bars available.

Disney Village Marketplace dining

The Disney Village Marketplace at Lake Buena Vista offers several full-service restaurants, including Chef Mickey's Village Restaurant and three on board the Empress Lilly riverboat.

Anchored permanently to a dock in Buena Vista Lagoon,. The Empress Lilly is a recreated 19th-century stern-wheel riverboat. The craft is filled with typical Disney detail. Flowered wallpaper, rich mahogany paneling, marble-topped coffee tables, and Victorian chairs and love seats all combine to create a riverboat atmosphere, even down to the ornate, antique-looking faucets in the rest rooms. On board the Empress Lilly — which is named for Walt Disney's wife — are the Fisherman's Deck, the Steerman's Quarters and The Empress Room. Two of these are included below: the Fisherman's Deck and the Steerman's Quarters.

The Village Marketplace also offers a raw bar-seafood eatery (Cap'n Jack's Oyster Bar) and three fast food emporiums: the Lakeside Terrace, Minnie Mia's Pizzeria, and the All American Sandwich Shop.

TravelVenture tip: Seven Disney restaurants hold daily character breakfasts at which costumed characters make the rounds of the tables. You can choose from:

• **Beach Club Resort** Disney characters visit diners at the Cape May Cafe's breakfast buffet. Reservations not available.

• **Contemporary Resort** On the fourth floor, the Contemporary Cafe serves a character breakfast buffet. Reservations not accepted. The cafe also has an Italian-flavored dinner buffet attended by Disney characters.

• **Grand Floridian** The hotel's Grand Floridian Cafe and 1910 Park Fare restaurants offer breakfast with Mary Poppins in attendance. Reservations not accepted.

• **Polynesian Village Resort** Minnie's Menehune Breakfast, a buffet, is held at the hotel's Papeete Bay Verandah. Reservations recommended, call (407) 824-1391.

• **Empress Lilly** Lake Buena Vista's riverboat offers a character breakfast with seatings at 9 A.M. and 10:30 A.M. Reservations required, call (407) 828-3900.

• **Fort Wilderness Campground** Held at Pioneer Hall, this breakfast comes not only with Disney characters Chip and Dale but also Melvin The Moose, cartoons, and a singing-and-dancing show as well. The "Chip and Dale's Country Morning Jamboree Breakfast Show" offers two seatings: 8 A.M. and 9:45 A.M. Reservations required, call (407) 934-7639.

• **Stargate Restaurant** Located in CommuniCore East at

Epcot's Future World, the Stargate is a fast food restaurant. Disney characters are in attendance from 9 A.M. to 10 A.M. daily. Reservations not accepted.

Disney characters also drop in throughout the day at Epcot's Odyssey Restaurant. (Check your Epcot show schedule for times.) And at **Chef Mickey's Village Restaurant** in the Disney Village Marketplace the chef himself — Mickey Mouse — visits the patrons during dinner. Reservations suggested, call (407) 828-3723.

TravelVenture tip: Some Disney World restaurants are keeping vegetarians and the health conscious in mind. Look for such entrees as assorted vegetable platters and vegetarian lasagne. And in fast food eateries you may find menu items prepared with turkey instead of beef or fresh fruit offered as an alternative to French fries.

Universal Studios Florida dining

This theme park offers its visitors dining facilities ranging from fast food to full-service. Universal's major eateries include Studio Stars Restaurant and Lombard's Landing. Reservations are recommended for both and should be made in person at the restaurant. The most popular Universal Studios eatery, though, is its Hard Rock Cafe, which does not accept reservations. The Hard Rock is accessible both from inside the park for those diners who have paid admission to enter Universal Studios and those outside the park who just want to dine at the restaurant without paying the park's admission.

Sea World dining

To feed its visitors, Sea World offers one full-service restaurant and a variety of fast food eateries spread throughout the grounds.

The following selected theme park and Orlando-area restaurants are listed alphabetically. Prices indicate the range of a restaurant's entrees and do not reflect the cost of appetizers, beverages, or deserts. To choose a restaurant, consult the TravelPlanner: dining which lists restaurants both by location and type of cuisine. Then turn to the page indicated in the TravelPlanner for details on those restaurants of interest.

Adventureland Veranda

TravelFacts

Location: Adventureland, Magic Kingdom.
Price: $3.35 to $5.20. Children $2.90 to $2.95.
Menu: Teriyaki steak sandwich or hamburger, fruit salad, marinated pork and noodles, Polynesian chicken sandwich. Children - fried chicken or hot dog.

What to expect: fast food dining indoors or on a veranda. This eatery's decor lets your imagination wander to just about any exotic tropical locale you choose — Manaus in the Amazon, Pago Pago, or along a bank of the Zambezi River.

Atlantis

TravelFacts

Location: 6677 Sea Harbor Dr., Orlando 32821. In the Stouffer Hotel, across from Sea World.
Map: Page 178.
Telephone: (407) 351-5555.
Price: $18 to $33.
Menu: Fresh seafood, chicken, duck, lamb, veal, and beef entrees.
Hours: 6 P.M. to 10 P.M. Tuesday through Saturday. Closed Sunday and Monday.
Dress: Good taste, jackets desirable but not required.
Reservations: Suggested.

Credit cards: All major.

What to expect: a superior hotel restaurant. Beneath a large crystal chandelier and two ceiling murals, you'll enjoy consistently excellent food and service.

Au Petit Cafe

TravelFacts

Location: France, World Showcase, Epcot Center, alongside Les Chefs de France.
Price: $6.95 to $13.75 lunch and dinner. Children - $3.75 to $4.25 lunch and dinner.
Menu: A varied menu that includes tuna and vegetable salad, baked chicken breast, quiche, baked ham and cheese croissant, assorted cheese platter, sautéed strip steak, sausage, prawns, Alaskan crab, snail casserole. Children - chicken and macaroni casserole, breaded fish sticks, ground beef steak.
Reservations: Not accepted.

What to expect: a European tradition — the sidewalk cafe. You'll people watch and dine outdoors at wrought iron tables shaded by an awning.

TravelVenture tip: If you want to eat in France but don't have a reservation, head for the Au Petit Cafe. The cafe does not take reservations, and the food comes out of the kitchen of the French pavilion's popular restaurant Les Chefs de France.

Aunt Polly's Landing

TravelFacts

Location: Tom Sawyer Island, Frontierland, Magic Kingdom.

> *Price:* $1 to $3.10.
> *Menu:* Sandwiches (ham and cheese, peanut butter and jelly) and snacks.

What to expect: back-porch dining that lets you sit alongside the Rivers of America watching keel boats and a paddle wheeler navigate the narrow waters. Aunt Polly's specialty is a rather good peanut butter and jelly sandwich — it's Aunt Polly's remember, not Mamma Leone's.

Backlot Express

TravelFacts

> *Location:* Theme park area, Disney-MGM Studios Theme Park, between Star Tours and the Epic Stunt Spectacular.
> *Price:* $3.30 to $6.25.
> *Menu:* Hamburgers, hot dogs, broiled chicken, chef's salad.

What to expect: fast food in a warehouse-like setting amidst stored film props. In this restaurant it's not hard to fantasize that you've just taken a break from shooting to run inside and grab a bite to eat. It has the decor of a backlot craft shop. Depending on where you choose to sit, you can eat inside among wire-cage prop lockers or on a patio amidst plaster sculptures.

Barney's Steak & Seafood House

TravelFacts

> *Location:* 1615 E. Colonial Dr., Orlando 32803.
> *Map:* Page 178.
> *Telephone:* (407) 896-6864.
> *Price:* Lunch $4.95 to $16.95. Dinner $11.50 to $21.95.

> *Menu:* Steaks, prime rib, chicken, and seafood. The lunch menu also offers hamburgers and sandwiches (steak, smoked turkey breast, barbecue).
> *Hours:* 11:30 A.M. to 11 P.M. Monday; 11:30 A.M. to midnight Tuesday, Wednesday, and Thursday; 11:30 A.M. to 1 A.M. Friday; 5 P.M. to 1 A.M. Saturday; 5 P.M. TO 10 P.M. Sunday.
> *Dress:* Casual.
> *Reservations:* Not accepted.
> *Credit cards:* All major.

What to expect: a popular Orlando eatery serving aged steaks and fresh seafood to the accompaniment of live music. Barney's entrees include unlimited trips to an extensive salad bar — vegetables, fruit, cheese, and slice-your-own light and dark rye bread.

Beverly Hills Boulangerie

TravelFacts

> *Location:* The Front Lot, Universal Studios Florida.
> *Price:* $5.50 to $5.75.
> *Menu:* Sandwiches (ham and cheese, turkey or roast beef on a croissant or a French roll).

What to expect: a counter-service eatery offering dining indoors or at outdoor tables shaded by sycamore trees.

TravelVenture tip: The Boulangerie also sells French pastries.

Biergarten

TravelFacts

> *Location:* Germany, World Showcase, Epcot Center.

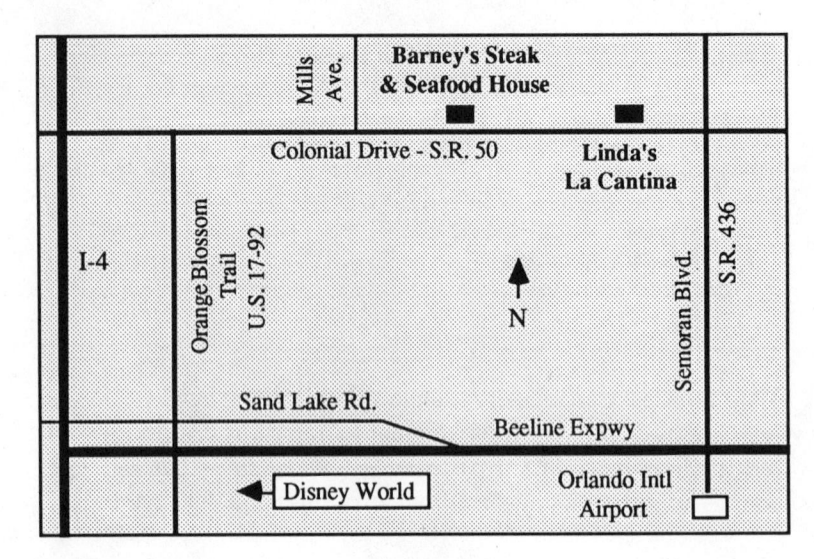

Orlando dining

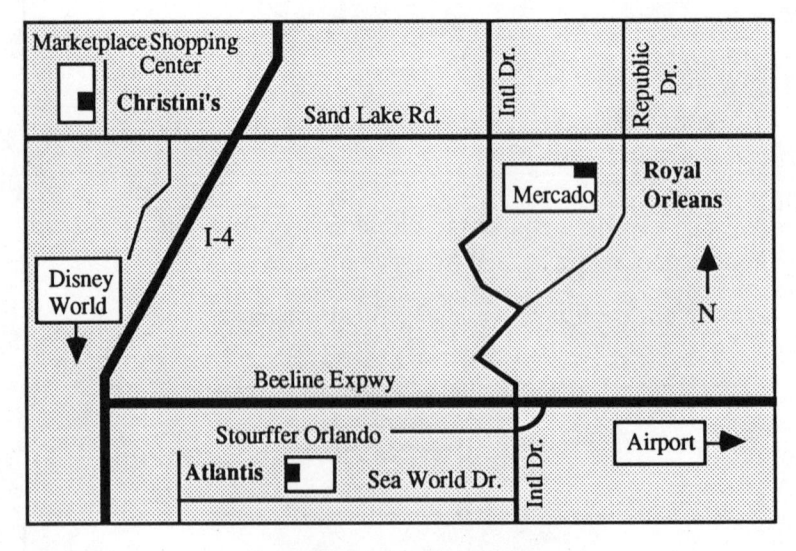

International Drive (south) dining

> ***Price:*** Lunch $7.25 to $9.75. Dinner $10.75 to $17.95. Children $3.25 to $3.95 lunch and dinner.
>
> ***Menu:*** Lunch - pork loin with red cabbage, sauerbraten (a marinated pot roast with red cabbage), roast chicken, grilled bratwurst, sausage plate, meat plate with potato salad, assorted vegetable plate. Dinner - braised veal shank, sauerbraten, roast chicken, sausage plate, beef rolls, breaded veal, seafood stew, roast beef loin, assorted vegetable plate. Most lunch and dinner entrees come with German dumplings. Children - roast chicken, meatballs with egg noodles, or potato pancake for both lunch and dinner.
>
> ***Reservations:*** Required.

What to expect: dining in an outdoor-like evening setting while actually indoors. The Biergarten has recreated the town square of the 16th-century German town of Rothenburg. You'll dine at community tables — eight to a table — amidst an Octoberfest atmosphere of singing, dancing, and oompah band playing.

Le Bistro de Paris

TravelFacts

> ***Location:*** France, World Showcase, Epcot Center. Occupies the second floor of the building housing Les Chefs de France. Entrance on the opposite side of the building.
>
> ***Price:*** Lunch $9.50 to $14.50. Dinner $18.25 to $24.50. Children $3.75 to $4.25 lunch and dinner.
>
> ***Menu:*** Lunch - seafood (scallops, swordfish, blue crabs, poached salmon), strip steak, sautéed veal, and chicken crepes. Dinner - roast veal, grilled lamb, quail, sautéed beef tenderloin, sautéed duck, fresh fish, baked salmon, grilled swordfish, and a seafood platter. Children - fish sticks, chicken breast casserole, or ground beef steak at lunch and dinner.
>
> ***Reservations:*** Required.

What to expect: elegance in both decor and atmosphere, despite the Bistro's name. A carpeted, winding staircase leads to a bright, spacious second-floor dining room with white-painted walls and maroon-cushioned chairs. Tables along the outer walls give a view of the World Showcase Lagoon. Because of the popularity of Les Chefs de France, the French pavilion's original restaurant, Le Bistro was opened to accommodate additional diners.

TravelVenture tip: During off season Le Bistro may not open for lunch.

Boulangerie Patisserie

TravelFacts

Location: France, World Showcase, Epcot Center.
Price: $1.65 to $2.95.
Menu: Quiche Lorraine, croissants (plain, ham and cheese, chocolate), and assorted mousses and pastries including chocolate eclairs and napoleons. Red and white wine available by the glass.

What to expect: a take-out bakery where you can pick up a snack or enough for a meal. After leaving the Boulangerie, carry your food to the tables in the adjacent Galerie des Halles marketplace.

TravelVenture tip: If the goodies you buy are easily portable, consider taking them to the small park on the opposite side of the pavilion. Cut through the "Arcade" between the Plume et Palette and La Signature shops. The park has shaded benches and is generally uncrowded and peaceful.

Cantina de San Angel

TravelFacts

Location: Mexico, World Showcase, Epcot Center, across from the Ma-

> yan pyramid.
> *Price:* $3.35 to $4.50.
> *Menu:* Beef and chicken burritos and tortillas.

What to expect: umbrella-shaded tables on an outdoor patio alongside the World Showcase Lagoon.

TravelVenture tip: A pleasant spot to sit, relax, and enjoy the view.

Cap'n Jack's Oyster Bar

TravelFacts

> *Location:* Disney Village Marketplace, Lake Buena Vista, Disney World.
> *Telephone:* (407) 828-3870.
> *Price:* $4.75 to $9.95. Children $3.75.
> *Menu:* Among the offerings are oysters, clams, crab cakes, fresh seafood, and a cheese and fruit tray. Children - spaghetti with meat sauce.
> *Hours:* 11:30 A.M. to 10 P.M.
> *Dress:* Casual.
> *Reservations:* Not accepted.
> *Credit cards:* American Express, MasterCard, and Visa.

What to expect: dining on both raw and cooked seafood in a building that juts out over Buena Vista Lagoon. Cap'n Jack's offers a good view of the lagoon, the Village Marketplace, and the Empress Lilly.

Le Cellier

TravelFacts

> *Location:* Canada, World Showcase, Epcot Center.

Price: $5.75 to $14.75 lunch. Dinner $6.75 to $14.75. Children $3.25 to $3.50.
Menu: Lunch - sandwiches (pork loin, deli sub, corned beef, turkey club), poached salmon, pork pie, prime rib, fried chicken, fruit and cheese plate. Dinner - chicken and meatball stew, cold meat and cheese plate, fruit and cheese plate, prime rib, chicken and meatball stew, poached salmon, seafood stew over rice, braised cabbage roll with minced pork. Children - chicken and meatball stew or fried chicken for both lunch and dinner.
Reservations: Not accepted.

What to expect: specialties from the various Canadian provinces, served cafeteria style. Le Cellier (The Cellar) offers the atmosphere of an old Quebec wine cellar, with great stone arches and gray stone walls from which hang tapestries of medieval scenes.

Chef Mickey's Village Restaurant

TravelFacts

Location: Disney Village Marketplace, Lake Buena Vista, Disney World, alongside the lagoon opposite the Empress Lilly riverboat.
Telephone: (407) 828-3871.
Price: Breakfast $3.50 to $6.95. Lunch $5.25 to $7.95. Dinner $8.75 to $17.95. Children $2.50 for breakfast, $3.25 to $6.50 for lunch and dinner.
Menu: Breakfast - typical breakfast menu. Lunch - sandwiches (club, turkey, broiled chicken breast), hamburgers, salads, meatloaf, beef stew, fried chicken, fresh seafood. Dinner - broiled pork chops, prime rib, rib-eye steak, steak Oscar, strip steak, broiled chicken, meatloaf, beef stew, salmon lasagne, shrimp scampi, bouillabaisse, seafood casserole. Children at lunch and dinner - hamburger, fried chicken bits, fish, prime rib (dinner only).
Hours: Breakfast 9 A.M. to 11 P.M. Lunch 11:30 P.M. to 2 P.M. Dinner 5:30 P.M. to 10 P.M.
Dress: Casual.
Reservations: Recommended, call (407) 828-3723.
Credit cards: American Express, MasterCard, and Visa.

What to expect: fine dining with a view of Buena Vista Lagoon and the Empress Lilly. Chef Mickey's has two bright, contemporary dining rooms. Tall, narrow glass panes held by thick wooden frames make up the outside walls of one. Two weeping fig trees dominate the room, their branches reaching to the skylights in the peaked ceiling. The second, while less dramatic, also offers a bright atmosphere and fine view. The restaurant's spiral-bound menu resembles a cook book and even includes a few of Chef Mickey's recipes.

Les Chefs de France

TravelFacts

Location: France, World Showcase, Epcot Center.
Price: Lunch $11.50 to $13.75. Dinner $13.95 to $19.95. Children $3.75 to $4.25 lunch and dinner. A vegetable plate priced at $8.75 is available at both lunch and dinner.
Menu: Lunch - prawns, scallops, sautéed fish, sautéed chicken breast, braised beef, sautéed strip steak. Dinner - seafood stew, smoked salmon, prawns, veal, sautéed chicken breast, braised duck, braised beef, sautéed beef tenderloin. Children - chicken and spaghetti, fish sticks, and ground beef steak at lunch and dinner.
Reservations: Required.

What to expect: a restaurant that takes its food seriously. So seriously that not one, but three chefs oversee its operation. And these chefs are three of the biggest names in the French culinary world — Roger Verge, Gaston LeNotre, and Paul Bocuse. Verge runs a restaurant on the French Riviera near Cannes. LeNotre, a renowned pastry chef, operates six bakeries in Paris. Bocuse is no slouch either. He owns a restaurant outside Lyon, has written several cookbooks, and, according to a national newsmagazine, just may be the best chef in the world.

The restaurant's wood paneling, green and white wallpaper, and brass lamps and chandeliers help recreate an atmosphere of the late 1800s. Waitresses at Les Chefs de France wear black dresses with frilly white collars and cuffs. The waiters don black trousers, vests, and bow ties. And both rush between kitchen and table balancing on their finger tips large, circular trays of French delights.

Christini's

TravelFacts

Location: 7600 Dr. Phillips Blvd., Orlando 32819, in the Marketplace shopping center.
Map: Page 178.
Telephone: (407) 345-8770.
Price: $17.50 to $24.95.
Menu: Italian specialties featuring seafood, veal, chicken, lamb, steak and homemade pasta.
Hours: 6 P.M. to midnight Monday through Saturday.
Dress: Casual, although jackets preferred.
Reservations: Recommended.
Credit cards: All major.

What to expect: more than excellent food — you'll also enjoy a warm atmosphere and the harmonies of strolling musicians. Christini's decor blends oak paneling, cushioned oak chairs, frosted glass, and Italian art.

Columbia Harbour House

TravelFacts

Location: Liberty Square, Magic Kingdom.
Price: $3.55 to $4.95. Children $3.20 to $3.55.
Menu: Fruit plate, fried shrimp, fried chicken strips, chicken and fried

> shrimp, shrimp salad, seafood pasta salad, sandwiches (turkey, ham and cheese, tuna salad). Children - hot dog or chicken.

What to expect: fast food with a New England nautical theme. Low, beamed ceilings, hatch covers, ships' wheels, and captain's chairs create the flavor of an old New England sailing vessel. If you're not much on sailing ships, a couple of sections offer the homey, wallpapered decor of an early New England dining room.

Coral Reef Restaurant

TravelFacts

> *Location:* The Living Seas pavilion, Future World, Epcot Center.
> *Price:* Lunch - $8.95 to $22.95. Dinner - $15.25 to $29.95.
> *Menu:* Lunch and dinner - seafood such as tuna, snapper, Maine lobster, shrimp, scallops, seafood fettucine, and grilled swordfish steak. The Coral Reef serves fresh seafood, so menu items will vary with availability and the season. The menu also offers two non-seafood dishes: broiled chicken breast and New York strip steak. Children - fried fish, fettucine, fried chicken strips, grilled hot dog.
> *Reservations:* Required.

What to expect: excellent but pricey seafood. The restaurant also lets you enjoy the pavilion's undersea world. Lighting at the Coral Reef is subdued. Each table is lit only by it's own narrow-beam ceiling spotlight. Consequently, your attention focuses on a wall made up of 8-foot-high acrylic panels that stretch for 50 feet. This is your window into The Living Seas' 5.7 million-gallon aquarium. As you dine you can watch sharks, rays, sea turtles, a variety of fish, and even an occasional diver glide by. To ensure all tables have a good view, the restaurant rises from the aquarium in three levels.

The Crystal Palace

TravelFacts

Location: Just off Main Street, near Adventureland, Magic Kingdom.
Price: Breakfast $4.75 to $5.25. Lunch $5.75 to $9.50. Dinner $6.50 to $13.50. Children $3.25 to $5.50 lunch and dinner.
Menu: Breakfast - scrambled eggs, French toast, hot cakes. Lunch - roast chicken, baked fresh fish, pasta plate, prime rib, beef tenderloin, Mexican club sandwich, fruit platter, salads (seafood and chef's). Dinner - prime rib, baked fresh fish, roast chicken, beef tenderloin, pork roast, pasta plate. Children - roast chicken, pasta and meatballs, or Mexican hot dog at both lunch and dinner.

What to expect: meals served cafeteria style. In keeping with the Magic Kingdom's Main Street tradition, The Crystal Palace has a turn-of-the-century look. An impressive palm-filled atrium greets you at the entrance.

TravelVenture tip: The Crystal Palace and Tony's Town Square Restaurant are the only Magic Kingdom restaurants serving breakfast.

Farmers Market

TravelFacts

Location: The Land, Future World, Epcot Center.
Price: $3.75 to $6.25.
Menu: Soups, salads, sandwiches (beef and cheese, seafood, club, meatball subs, and grilled chicken breast), pastas (tortellini, fettucine, lasagne), baked potatoes topped with varied sauces, baked macaroni with cheese, and barbecue beef, chicken, or pork.

What to expect: a row of fast food stands, each offering a different specialty. You buy your food and then carry it to one of the tables sitting in the center of the pavilion.

TravelVenture tip: The Farmers Market idea works well in theory. But in reality, during peak hours the Farmers Market does not have enough tables and chairs to go around — and not enough room for Disney to add more. Before you buy, look around to see if you'll have a place to sit and eat. Many people reserve a table by leaving a member or two of their party to occupy it. Another drawback — if everyone wants something different and you have small children who can't carry a tray, your food buying becomes a cumbersome, time-consuming operation.

50's Prime Time Cafe

TravelFacts

Location: Theme park area, Disney-MGM Studios Theme Park, on Vine Street across from Echo Lake.
Price: Lunch $6.50 to $14.95. Dinner $9.95 to $16.75.
Menu: Lunch - sandwiches (club, hot roast beef, hamburgers, turkey burgers), salads, meatloaf, shrimp, broiled chicken, chicken pot pie, fresh fish, pot roast, rib-eye steak. Dinner - broiled chicken, Swiss steak, fresh fish, roast lamb, T-bone steak, meatloaf, shrimp, tenderloin filet, grilled salmon sandwich, salads (Caesar and lobster).
Reservations: Required. Make reservations in person at the restaurant starting at 9 A.M.

What to expect: dining in mom's kitchen circa 1955. The 50's Prime Time Cafe is built and furnished like a contemporary home in the 1950s. After a spell in the living room-like waiting area, you are seated in one of more than a dozen kitchenettes. Each comes equipped with a black-and-white television set and a mom-like waitress. The television offers clips of period programs, and the mom-waitress serves such homey favorites as meatloaf, hamburgers, and pot roast.

Finnegan's Bar & Grill

TravelFacts

> **Location:** Production Central area, Universal Studios.
> **Price:** $5.95 to $13.95. Children - $3.95 to $4.95.
> **Menu:** Sandwiches (roast beef, corned beef, ham), hamburgers, bangers & mash (sausage & mashed potatoes), pot pies, Irish stew, salmon, fish and chips, corned beef and potatoes, beef casserole, Shepherd's pie. Children - hamburgers, ham and cheese sandwich, fried fish, chicken fingers.
> **Reservations:** Not required.

What to expect: an excellent recreation of an Irish-flavored New York City bar and grill. A mahogany bar with high-backed chairs runs the length of this large and roomy saloon. Wooden tables and chairs stand on the bar's tile floor. Pressed tin covers the ceiling. And recorded Irish tunes fill the room. It's not hard to imagine a film crew using this backlot eatery for shooting.

TravelVenture tip: If you don't find dining in a bar appealing, Finnegan's also offers tables without the saloon atmosphere in a large adjacent room.

The Fireworks Factory

TravelFacts

> **Location:** Pleasure Island, Disney World.
> **Price:** Lunch $5.50 to $15.95. Dinner $12.95 to $22.95. Children $3.95 to $5.50 for lunch and dinner.
> **Menu:** Lunch - salads (seafood, chicken breast, chef's, fruit), sandwiches (hamburgers, BLT, tuna, barbecue pork, barbecue chicken, smoked turkey, barbecue beef brisket, rib-eye steak), ribs, prime rib, smoked chicken, smoked shrimp, barbecue chicken. Dinner - salads (chicken breast and seafood), baby back ribs, Texas beef ribs, chicken and ribs, shrimp and ribs, shrimp and chicken, filet mignon, barbecue pork chops, rib-eye steak, sirloin strip steak, fried chicken, barbecue shrimp, catfish, barbecue chicken. Children - Southern fried

> chicken, hamburger, barbecue chicken, shrimp dinner, barbecue baby back ribs for lunch and dinner.
> *Hours:* 11:30 A.M. to 2 A.M.

What to expect: dining in a warehouse. Disney's theme for this eatery goes that the restaurant has moved into a former fireworks factory that has suffered an explosion. The dining room's walls are the same pressed-tin panels making up the building's exterior. Ducts and steel girders are exposed at the ceiling. You'll see a couple of brick walls that are only partially standing. And the plain wooden tables are covered with yellow-and-black checkered oilcloth. The warehouse atmosphere works quite well with the restaurant's specialty — barbecue ribs.

TravelVenture tip: While the restaurant's atmosphere and menu make a good blend, its prices seem out of synch. Unless you are a devoted barbecue rib fan, before deciding on The Fireworks Factory check out the atmosphere, prices, and food offerings at Pleasure Island's Portobello Yacht Club just around the corner.

Fisherman's Deck

TravelFacts

> *Location:* Empress Lilly riverboat, Disney Village Marketplace, Walt Disney World.
> *Telephone:* (407) 828-3900.
> *Price:* Lunch $5.50 to $9.95. Dinner $13.95 to $21.75. Children $3.25 to $3.75 at lunch, $3.25 to $6.50 for dinner.
> *Menu:* Lunch - salads (tuna, seafood and chicken, chef's), sandwiches (corned beef, grilled chicken, club), hamburgers, seafood crepes, chicken pot pie, stir-fried seafood with pasta, grilled turkey steak, sirloin steak, fresh fish. Dinner - fresh trout or catfish, Maine lobster, baked shrimp and crab meat or fresh seafood, stir-fried seafood with pasta, fresh seafood, beef filet, beef filet and shrimp, chicken. Children - prime rib (dinner only), macaroni and cheese, hamburger, chicken pot pie, catfish fingers at both lunch and dinner.

> *Hours:* Lunch 11:30 A.M. to 2 P.M. Dinner 5:30 P.M. to 10 P.M.
> *Reservations:* Accepted.
> *Credit cards:* American Express, MasterCard, and Visa.

What to expect: a riverboat atmosphere, seafood, and a nautical view. From its perch on the second deck of the Empress Lilly, the Fisherman's Deck looks out over the bow to give diners a good view of Buena Vista Lagoon.

Hard Rock Cafe

TravelFacts

> *Location:* 1000 Universal Studios Plaza, Orlando 32819.
> *Map:* Page 193.
> *Price:* $5.95 to $12.95.
> *Menu:* Salads, sandwiches (BLT, club, chicken breast, and fish), hamburgers (including a vegetarian burger), barbecue (ribs, pork, and chicken), rib-eye steak.
> *Hours:* 11 A.M. to 2 A.M.
> *Dress:* Casual.
> *Reservations:* Not required.
> *Credit cards:* All major.

What to expect: hamburgers and rock 'n' roll. This restaurant is one of a chain of Hard Rock Cafes with locations spread around the world from London to Tokyo. Like its counterparts, Orlando's cafe features high-decibel recorded music, a bustling atmosphere and an impressive collection of rock memorabilia — posters, photographs, guitars, a stand-up bass, and drums which once belonged to rock musicians. One wall contains three tall stained-glass windows depicting rock 'n' roll pioneers Chuck Berry, Elvis Presley, and Jerry Lee Lewis.

The Orlando Hard Rock Cafe has been built in the shape of an electric guitar lying on its back. A 300-foot bridge — the guitar's neck — leads to the cafe which is housed in a classical-style building rising from the guitar body. The cafe is accessible both to patrons visiting Universal Studios (from the Cinemagic Center area) and those entering from outside the park.

TravelVenture tip: Diners do not have to buy an admission to Universal Studios Florida to eat at the Hard Rock Cafe.

Hollywood and Vine Cafeteria

TravelFacts

> *Location:* Theme park area, Disney-MGM Studios Theme Park, on Vine Street across from Echo Lake.
> *Price:* Breakfast $4.50 to $5.25. Lunch $5.95 to $10.95. Dinner $7.50 to $14.75. Children $2.75 to $5.50 lunch and dinner.
> *Menu:* Breakfast - egg dishes, French toast, pancakes. Lunch - salads, baby back ribs, fresh seafood, grilled pork chop, roast chicken, tortellini (cheese-filled pasta with meatless sauce), ground beef steak. Dinner - salads (chicken breast or seafood), grilled sirloin, prime rib, veal shank, fresh seafood, ribs, pork chop, roast chicken, tortellini. Children - peanut butter and jelly with marshmallow sandwich, broiled chicken, pasta, fresh fish, and tortellini for lunch and dinner.
> *Reservations:* Not available.

What to expect: meals served cafeteria style in a restaurant reminiscent of a 1950s diner. The decor is art deco with stainless steel and black marble trim against pink walls. A 42-foot mural stretches along one wall and depicts old Hollywood landmarks, including the early Disney Studios. The cafeteria also offers outdoor dining on a patio at umbrella-shaded tables.

The Hollywood Brown Derby

TravelFacts

> *Location:* Hollywood Boulevard, Disney-MGM Studios Theme Park, ad-

> jacent to the outdoor Theater of the Stars.
>
> *Price:* Lunch $6.95 to $14,75. Dinner $12.95 to $21.50. Children $2.50 to $5.50 at lunch.
>
> *Menu:* Lunch - sandwiches (roast turkey, pastrami, smoked pork, hamburgers), Cobb salad (plain, shrimp, or lobster), fruit and cheese plate, veal, baked grouper, gumbo, New England dinner (corned beef and cabbage), pasta and seafood, roast chicken, plus a changing vegetarian plate. Dinner - baked grouper, pasta and seafood, fettucine, stuffed chicken breast, roast chicken, pork chops, veal, lamb, strip steak, filet mignon, plus a changing vegetarian plate. Children - peanut butter and jelly with marshmallow sandwich, broiled chicken, pasta Parmesan, fried fish for lunch and dinner.
>
> *Reservations:* Required. Starting at 9 A.M. make reservations in person at the restaurant.

What to expect: a California-style two-level restaurant serving excellent food. This 250-seat restaurant is patterned after the original Brown Derby located on Hollywood's Vine Street. In 1930s Hollywood the Brown Derby was the place to see and be seen.

In Disney's Brown Derby ivory-colored stucco walls rise above a band of mahogany paneling. The walls are filled with framed caricatures of stars — reproductions from the original Derby's collection. Three large chandeliers hang above the main, lower-level dining room where large, potted palm tress add to the California feel. Among the specialties the tuxedoed servers can bring to your table is Cobb salad. Bob Cobb, the original Derby's owner, created his salad at the Brown Derby in the 1930s, and it's still a featured favorite there today.

TravelVenture tip: Disney's Hollywood Brown Derby does have a drawback. The restaurant is large and quite open, so it tends to be somewhat noisy. But so probably does the original.

International Food Bazaar

TravelFacts

> *Location:* Cinemagic Center, Universal Studios Florida.

Price: $3.25 to $6.75.
Menu: Pasta, pizza, fried chicken, barbecue pork sandwich, hamburgers, bratwurst, knockwurst, hot dog, Greek salad, tuna salad pita sandwich, lamb pita, quiche, stir-fried beef, sweet and sour chicken or pork, shrimp lo mein.

What to expect: a fast food court with international flavors. This eatery has five counters, each of which serves Italian, American, German, Greek or Chinese food.

TravelVenture tip: The restaurant has TV monitors mounted high on columns to entertain you with movie and TV clips.

King Stefan's Banquet Hall

TravelFacts

Location: Cinderella Castle (second floor), Magic Kingdom.

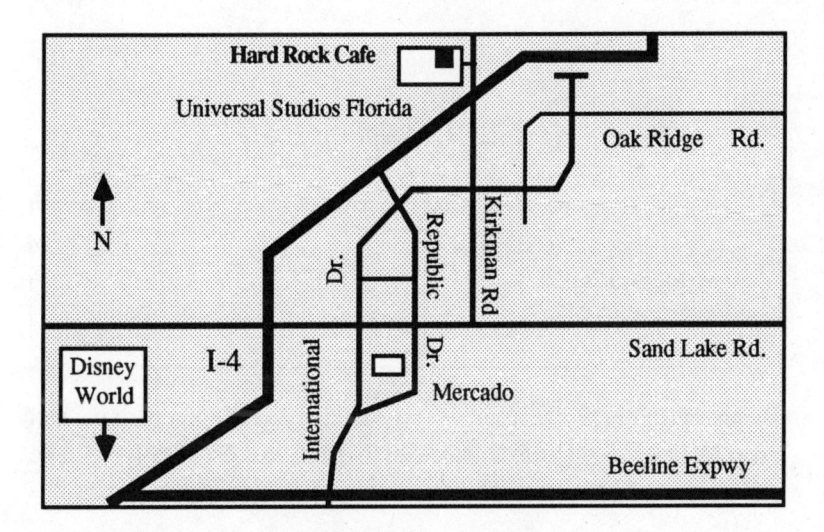

International Drive (north) dining

Price: Lunch $7.25 to $11.25. Dinner $17.50 to $20.75. Children $3.75 to $4.25 at lunch and $4.45 to $6.95 for dinner.
Menu: Lunch - prime rib sandwich, fish sandwich, seafood plate, fruit salad, broiled chicken breast, club sandwich. Dinner - prime rib, filet mignon, fresh fish, and fried chicken breast with fettucine. Children - cheeseburger, fish nuggets, or chicken pot pie at lunch and prime rib, fish nuggets, or chicken pot pie for dinner.
Reservations: Required. Starting at 9 A.M. make reservations in person at the restaurant.

What to expect: dining inside Cinderella Castle, off pewter ware, with service provided by waiters and waitresses clothed in medieval costumes. To reach the banquet hall, which is named for Sleeping Beauty's father, you climb a spiral stairway that winds around a thick, fluted column. Just inside the hall a sword-carrying suit of armor stands vigil. Blocks of stone form Gothic arches and dozens of diamond-shaped panes make up the leaded windows that look out on Fantasyland. Large brass chandeliers hang from wood-lined ceiling vaults. The inside of this restaurant will carry you back half-a-dozen centuries.

Kringla Bakeri og Kafé

TravelFacts

Location: Norway, World Showcase, Epcot Center.
Price: $1.70 to $4.95.
Menu: Open-face sandwiches of beef, turkey, or seafood. Varied pastries.

What to expect: open-air dining on a covered porch. You can drop in here to pick up a snack of Norwegian pastries or to take on a full-fledged meal of typical Scandinavian open-face sandwiches.

The Land Grille Room

TravelFacts

Location: The Land pavilion, Future World, Epcot Center.
Price: Breakfast $4.25 to $9.95. Lunch $5.75 to $17.75. Dinner $11.50 to $24.50. Children $2.95 to $5.50 lunch and dinner.
Menu: Breakfast - the expected specialties. Lunch - sandwiches (club, barbecue Pork, grilled steak), pizza, lasagne, seafood, chicken, and steaks. Dinner - T-bone steak, Oriental chicken breast, lasagne, pizza, prime rib, beef tenderloin, barbecue pork, and seafood (Maine lobster, fresh swordfish, stir-fry shrimp). Children - hamburger, chicken, or pasta for lunch and dinner.
Reservations: Recommended for lunch and dinner.

What to expect: a revolving restaurant that offers a slow spin around the prairie, desert, and prehistoric scenes from The Land's boat ride. The Land Grille Room offers a contemporary decor that combines maroon walls, oak trim, and brass lamps. Tables are arranged on two levels around the restaurant's circular outer edge — a higher, inner ring with standard restaurant booths and a lower, outer ring with tables that face out. The Land Grille Room's turning speed is adjustable, and a complete revolution takes anywhere from 30 minutes to an hour.

TravelVenture tip: If you are as interested in the view as in eating, ask the hostess for a table in the lower, outer ring. Note, though, that if you are a party of two, you may be seated in one of the lower ring sections that contain three very close two-person tables that offer no privacy.

Liberty Inn

TravelFacts

Location: American Adventure, World Showcase, Epcot Center.
Price: Lunch $2.95 to $4.80. Dinner $2.95 to 5.75.

> *Menu:* Lunch - hamburgers, hot dogs, chicken breast sandwich, fried chicken, chicken and pasta salad, shrimp and pasta salad, taco salad. Dinner - the lunch menu plus barbecue beef, roasted half chicken, baked macaroni and cheese with ham.

What to expect: outdoor dining either on a covered patio or alongside a laurel oak tree at umbrella-shaded tables.

TravelVenture tip: The American Adventure is the only place to buy a box of popcorn at Epcot. Two popcorn carts are located at the America Gardens Theater by the Shore, the outdoor theater next to the lagoon.

Liberty Tree Tavern

TravelFacts

> *Location:* Liberty Square, Magic Kingdom.
> *Price:* Lunch $5.95 to $14.95. Dinner $15.75 to $17.95. Children $2.95 to $4.25 lunch and dinner.
> *Menu:* Lunch - sandwiches (including ham, prime rib, broiled chicken breast, and hot seafood) hamburgers, prime rib, fresh fish, chilled seafood plate, seafood salad, scallops. . Dinner - fresh fish, scallops, hot seafood plate, Maine lobster, grilled chicken, filet mignon, prime rib. Children - chicken, cheeseburger, hot dog, or ham and cheese sandwich for lunch and dinner.
> *Reservations:* Required. Starting at 10 A.M. make reservations for lunch or dinner in person at the Liberty Tree Tavern.

What to expect: servers in colonial garb providing table service that starts out with a basket of walnut bread. At the Liberty Tree Tavern you'll step into a large, colonial-style waiting room while your table is prepared. A pair of two-tier candle chandeliers hang from the ceiling above a wood-plank floor. The far wall is filled with a brick fireplace loaded with cooking pots and kettles. On the mantle above it sits a rack of long-stemmed meerschaum pipes. The dining area is broken up into several small to mid-sized dining rooms. Wooden sideboards and brick fireplaces stand here and there. Paintings of colonial scenes hang on the walls. And a tin lantern sits on each wooden table.

Linda's La Cantina

TravelFacts

> *Location:* 4721 E. Colonial Dr., Orlando 32803.
> *Map:* Page 178.
> *Telephone:* (407) 894-4491.
> *Price:* $6.25 to $22.95. Children $2 to $4.
> *Menu:* Steaks, seafood, and Italian dishes — manicotti, veal Parmesan, lasagna, spaghetti, and ravioli. Children - ground sirloin, spaghetti, lasagna.
> *Hours:* Tuesday 5 P.M. to 10:00 P.M. Wednesday through Saturday 5 P.M. to 10:30 P.M. Closed Sunday and Monday.
> *Dress:* Casual.
> *Reservations:* Not accepted.
> *Credit cards:* American Express, MasterCard, Visa.

What to expect: thick, tender, tasty steaks. You don't go to Linda's La Cantina for atmosphere. You go when you're hungry. While this bustling restaurant's menu also offers Italian entrees, it's the superb steaks that have kept Orlandoans coming here for almost 40 years.

Lombard's Landing

TravelFacts

> *Location:* San Francisco Street Set, On Location, Universal Studios.
> *Price:* $6.95 to $12.95. Children $3.50 to $4.95
> *Menu:* Salads (salmon Nicoise, Caesar, shrimp, chicken curry, seafood pasta), sandwiches (Reuben, club, fresh grouper), hamburgers, fish

and chips, grilled chicken, crab cakes, New York strip steak, grilled salmon, chicken fettucine. Children - pasta and meatballs, chicken tenders, hog dog..
Reservations: Recommended. Make reservations in person at the restaurant.

What to expect: a classy looking restaurant with nautical decor and a nautical view. Lombard's sits on the recreated Fisherman's Wharf of Universal's San Francisco Street Set in what the studio describes as an 1800s warehouse. The description is not particularly apt. While the restaurant has red-brick walls, it also sports a carpeted floor, polished brass columns and accents, and sweeping half-moon steel arches that support a polished wood-plank ceiling. Large aquariums inside and the studio's lagoon outside the windows also help to make Lombard's a delightful place in which to dine.

TravelVenture tip: During high seasons, Lombard's may replace its standard menu with an upgraded menu for dinner.

Lotus Blossom Cafe

TravelFacts

Location: China, World Showcase, Epcot Center.
Price: $2.80 to $5.25.
Menu: Stir-fried beef or chicken, sweet and sour chicken, pork-fried rice, egg rolls.

What to expect: dining on a covered patio offering a view of the Chinese pavilion. You can get well-fed here. The "Lotus Blossom Combination," for example, consists of stir-fried beef and vegetables, an egg roll, and fried rice.

Louie's Italian Restaurant

TravelFacts

> *Location:* New York City Street, Production Central, Universal Studios Florida.
> *Price:* $4.25 to $6.50. Whole Pizzas $11.25 to $13.75. Sliced Pizza $2.25 to $2.75
> *Menu:* Pizza, linguini, spaghetti, spinach tortellini, lasagne.

What to expect: a large cafeteria serving Italian specialties. Louie's sits in New York's Little Italy section of Universal's backlot sets.

Mel's Drive In

TravelFacts

> *Location:* Hollywood section, Universal Studios Florida.
> *Price:* $2.60 to $4.75.
> *Menu:* Hamburgers, chicken breast sandwich, chili, chili dog, hog dog.

What to expect: a fast food restaurant done in the decor of a '50s diner — plenty of stainless steel and vinyl-backed booths. Despite its name, Mel's serves only walk ins, but it does have vintage cars from the '50s parked in front.

TravelVenture tip: With recorded rock music and a high noise level, the emphasis at Mel's is on nostalgia not relaxed dining.

Min and Bill's Dockside Diner

TravelFacts

> *Location:* Theme Park area, Disney-MGM Studios Theme Park, at Echo

> Lake adjacent to Hollywood Plaza.
> *Price:* $3.75 to $4.60.
> *Menu:* Sandwiches (submarine, tuna salad, turkey), pasta with crab legs and shrimp, fruit plate.

What to expect: a counter-service restaurant housed in a reproduction of a tramp steamer — the *S.S. Down the Hatch* — anchored in Echo Lake. Food is purchased at the ship, which recreates a zany building style popular in 1930s California, and taken to outdoor wooden tables and benches shaded by umbrellas.

Mitsukoshi Restaurant

TravelFacts

> *Location:* Japan, World Showcase, Epcot Center.
> *Price:* Lunch $7.95 to $9.95. Dinner $12.50 to $26.00. Children $4.75 to $4.95 at lunch and $6.50 to $6.75 at dinner.
> *Menu:* Beef, chicken, and seafood specialties prepared Japanese style: either grilled or batter dipped and fried.
> *Reservations:* Required.

What to expect: communal dining with a ceremonial touch. The Mitsukoshi Restaurant occupies the second floor of a massive two-story building that stretches almost the length of the Japanese pavilion. To dine at the Mitsukoshi requires a decision. You can either eat in the Teppanyaki rooms or the Tempura Kiku.

If you go Teppanyaki, a kimona-clad hostess escorts you to one of a series of rooms off a main corridor. Inside each room are four tables, each with seating for eight around three sides. The fourth side is reserved for the chef who, with artistic slicing, tossing, and chopping, prepares your food on a grill built into the table.

When dining in the Tempura Kiku, you'll sit at one of 25

seats around a horseshoe-shaped counter. Here, too, the chefs prepare the food as you watch. The Tempura Kiku features Japanese specialties that are dipped in a batter and then fried.

Nine Dragons Restaurant

TravelFacts

> *Location:* China, World Showcase, Epcot Center.
> *Price:* Lunch $7.95 to $13.50. Dinner $9.50 to $20.75. Children $4.95 to $5.95 lunch and dinner.
> *Menu:* Lunch - Chinese specialties including duck, beef, pork, chicken, and seafood entrees; plus stir-fried vegetables, beef, or seafood. Dinner - duck, beef, chicken, seafood, and stir-fried entrees. Children - sweet and sour pork, shrimp and pork-fried rice, barbecue pork ribs.
> *Reservations:* Required.

What to expect: waitresses in red tunics and long black skirts serving excellently prepared dishes and providing never-an-empty-water-glass service. Don't expect the same food as in your favorite Chinese eatery. Many Chinese restaurants specialize in a particular cuisine. Epcot's Nine Dragons Restaurant, however, offers specialties from throughout the Chinese culinary world — Szechwan, Hunan, Shanghai, Cantonese, and Mandarin.

The dining room itself is large, to help accommodate demand. But hand-carved rosewood dividers, which match the tables, cut the room into more inviting segments. The rosewood furnishings were made in China especially for the Nine Dragons.

Odyssey Restaurant

TravelFacts

> *Location:* Future World, Epcot Center, near the causeway leading to the

World Showcase.
Price: $4.05 to 4.95. Children $3.30.
Menu: Hamburgers, hot dogs, broiled chicken sandwich, and salads. Children - hot dogs.

What to expect: a comfortable restaurant offering roomy, multi-level dining in a contemporary atmosphere.

TravelVenture tip: Mickey, Minnie and the other Disney characters drop in at the Odyssey Restaurant, usually around mid-day and late afternoon. Check your show schedule for exact times.

L'Originale Alfredo di Roma Ristorante

TravelFacts

Location: Italy, World Showcase, Epcot Center.
Price: Lunch $7.95 to $18.95. Dinner $11.50 to $19.75. Children $4.25 to $4.95 lunch and dinner.
Menu: Both lunch and dinner offer a hefty menu of about 20 veal, chicken, and pasta dishes. Children - spaghetti, manicotti, and fettucine.
Reservations: Required.

What to expect: a realistic taste of Italy, with fine food and a brigade of white-coated waiters filling the aisles and squeezing around the tables and red-cushioned chairs. Three crystal chandeliers hang from the restaurant's cross-beamed ceiling. Life-size murals of Italian scenes cover the walls. And if you want still more atmosphere, at dinner add a strolling accordionist and waiters who occasionally burst into song.

Alfredo's claim to fame is fettucine. Back in Rome, at the original restaurant, Alfredo DiLelio perfected his fettucine using high-quality noodles, butter, and Parmesan cheese. Alfredo's of Epcot also turns out a first-rate product. To make sure, the restaurant makes its own noodles right on the premises. A picture window lets you look in on the operation.

TravelVenture tip: At Alfredo's, one of the most popular World Showcase restaurants, the fettucine is a must.

Pinocchio Village Haus

TravelFacts

> *Location:* Fantasyland, Magic Kingdom, next door to "It's a Small World."
> *Price:* $3.55 to $4.25.
> *Menu:* Turkey or club sandwich, hamburger, hot dog, pasta salad.

What to expect: Alpine decor and American fast food.

TravelVenture tip: One row of tables offers a view of the Small World's boats and loading dock.

The Plaza Pavilion

TravelFacts

> *Location:* Tomorrowland, Magic Kingdom, near Main Street.
> *Price:* $2.75 to $4.95.
> *Menu:* Pizza, Italian hoagie, chicken Parmesan sandwich, meatball sub, pasta salad.

What to expect: Italian fast food and a nice view — a pleasant scene made up of a stream in the foreground, a topiary sea serpent on the far bank, and Cinderella Castle filling the background. While eating and enjoying the view, you can ponder whether the birds that come looking for a handout are real or a Disney audio-animatronic creation.

The Plaza Restaurant

TravelFacts

Location: Just off Main Street, near Tomorrowland, Magic Kingdom.
Price: $5.75 to $8.50. Children $2.75 to $2.95.
Menu: Sandwiches (Reuben, hot pastrami, hot roast beef, ham and provolone cheese, turkey club, fresh vegetable), hamburgers, chicken pot pie, fruit and cheese platter, tuna and chicken salad plate. Children - hamburger, hot dog, peanut butter and jelly sandwich.

What to expect: a plain restaurant offering table service in a turn-of-the-century atmosphere. The restaurant's simple decor is perked up somewhat with large wall mirrors and polished brass wall lamps.

Portobello Yacht Club

TravelFacts

Location: Pleasure Island, Walt Disney World.
Price: Lunch $6.95 to $9.95. Dinner $12.95 to $23.95 (pizza: $6.95 to $7.95). Children $3.95 to $5.50 at lunch and dinner.
Menu: Lunch - Italian specialties including pizza, salads, sandwiches, pasta, fresh fish, grilled Italian sausage, chicken breast, grilled scallops. Dinner - Italian specialties including pizza, salads, seafood pasta, veal chops, chicken breast, grilled half chicken, grilled sirloin steak. Children - pizza, hot dog, spaghetti, hamburger for both lunch and dinner.
Hours: 11:30 A.M. to 11:30 P.M.

What to expect: Italian cooking served in a comfortable indoor dining room or outdoors on an awning-shaded patio overlooking Buena Vista Lagoon and the Empress Lilly riverboat. The Portobello Yacht Club's maroon and green upholstery and light blue walls combine with plenty of windows to make a bright, classy atmosphere. The pizza on the Portobello's menu comes out of a wood-burning brick oven.

Pure and Simple

TravelFacts

> **Location:** Wonders of Life pavilion, Future World, Epcot Center.
> **Price:** $3.25 to $4.50.
> **Menu:** Soups, salads, sandwiches (vegetable and turkey hot dog, low-fat hot dog, turkey sub) and bran waffles.

What to expect: fast food for the health conscious. For dessert you can splurge on a yogurt sundae with fruit toppings.

Restaurant Akershus

TravelFacts

> **Location:** Norway, World Showcase, Epcot Center.
> **Price:** Lunch $9.95. Dinner $14.95. Children $4.25 at lunch, $6.50 at dinner.
> **Menu:** Lunch - a buffet consisting of both cold items (such as salads, hard-boiled eggs, vegetables, poached salmon, smoked mackerel, roast chicken, cheese) and hot dishes made with beef, pork, lamb, and seafood (such as meatballs, pork and macaroni casserole, roast pork, and wolffish and dill sauce). Dinner - a buffet similar to lunch but with additional dishes (such as venison and seafood stew).
> **Reservations:** Required.

What to expect: a typical Norwegian buffet known as a *koldtbord* (cold table). The restaurant is located in the pavilion's Akershus Castle, which is a replica of the original in Oslo, Norway. One of the restaurant's two dining areas is a scaled-down replica of the castle's state banquet room, Olaf's Hall.

Don't confuse Norway's koldtbord with a smorgasbord, that's Swedish. Rather than loading up a plate on a single trip to the koldtbord, Norwegians sample their way through the courses, making several visits. Typically, they would start with herring appetizers, progress to the cold salads, meats, and seafood, move on to the hot dishes, and wind it up with the cheeses. Although the buffet is self-service, servers wearing Norwegian-style red vests and black trousers or skirts are on hand to take beverage orders, dessert orders (not included in the price of the buffet), or to answer questions.

Restaurant Marrakech

TravelFacts

Location: Morocco, World Showcase, Epcot Center, at the far end of the pavilion.
Price: Lunch $7.95 to $12.95. Dinner $9.50 to $18.50. Children $3.95 to $4.75 lunch and dinner.
Menu: Lunch - braised chicken; baked grouper; braised or roast lamb; chicken or shrimp brochette; brochette of Kefta (minced beef grilled on a skewer); and cous cous (steamed grain) containing either vegetables, lamb, or chicken. Dinner - roast lamb; grouper; braised chicken; beef, chicken, lamb, shrimp, or seafood brochettes; and cous cous with either vegetables, lamb, or chicken. Children - chicken or Kefta brochette for lunch and dinner.
Reservations: Required.

What to expect: the exotic and the down to earth. Assign exotic to the atmosphere and down to earth to the excellent food. The restaurant is housed in a large hall-like room. Its ceiling rises some 25 feet above the red-carpeted floor. From the carpet to shoulder height arabesques cover the wall. Near the room's center is a marble dance floor — your meal in Morocco comes complete with belly dancer and music provided by a trio of Moroccan musicians. When the entertainment is not live, piped-in music helps keep the atmosphere alive.

The Moroccan national dish is cous cous (pronounced koos koos). The basic ingredient is a coarse, cereal-like grain. The grain is steamed and covered with a layer of lamb and vegetables, chicken and vegetables, or vegetables alone. When you order this dish you won't leave hungry.

TravelVenture tip: The Restaurant Marrakech does not enjoy the popularity of Epcot's French, Italian, and Japanese restaurants. Perhaps the image of Morocco is a little too foreign, too exotic, to give its restaurant mass appeal. Often you can get in without an advance reservation. If you find yourself without a reservation for an Epcot eatery, check out the Restaurant Marrakech. Until word gets around, we'll keep it our secret that Moroccan food is tasty — not overly spicy — and that the combination of price, entertainment, authentic atmosphere, and fine cuisine makes this one of the top restaurants at Epcot.

The Rose & Crown Pub & Dining Room

TravelFacts

Location: United Kingdom, World Showcase, Epcot Center.
Price: Lunch $6.50 to $9.50. Dinner $8.50 to $18.75. Children $2.95 to $3.50 at lunch, $3.25 to $6.95 at dinner.
Menu: Lunch - steak and kidney pie, chicken and leek pie, broiled fresh fish, hot roast beef on an English muffin, fish and chips, vegetable and cheese plate. Children - meat pie, fish and chips, hot roast beef on and English muffin. Dinner - prime rib, roast lamb, steak and kidney pie, sautéed chicken, chicken and leek pie, mixed grill, fish and chips, and broiled fish. Children - meat pie, fish and chips, prime rib.
Reservations: Required.

What to expect: a typical British local pub providing dependably good food. The Rose & Crown comes complete with a horseshoe-shaped bar, brass foot rails, and cold beer — a concession to

American tastes. In Britain they drink their beer at room temperature.

The small dining room is situated off the pub, but it also spills out onto a patio overlooking the World Showcase Lagoon. Shaded by yellow umbrellas, these tables offer a fine view and a tranquil setting.

Royal Orleans

TravelFacts

> *Location:* 8445 International Drive, Orlando 32819, in the Mercado shopping village.
> *Map:* Page 178.
> *Telephone:* (407) 352-8200.
> *Price:* $13.95 to $24.95.
> *Menu:* An extensive list of entrees including seafood, beef, chicken, rabbit, veal, quail, duckling.
> *Hours:* 5 P.M. to 10 P.M. daily.
> *Dress:* Casual.
> *Reservations:* Recommended.
> *Credit cards:* All major.

What to expect: some of the finest Louisiana cooking this side of New Orleans. Although a relatively young restaurant, the Cajun and Creole specialties served in the Royal Orleans have gained it an excellent reputation.

San Angel Inn Restaurante

TravelFacts

> *Location:* Mexico, World Showcase, Epcot Center, inside the Mayan pyramid.
> *Price:* Lunch $7.25 to $13.75. Dinner $10.25 to $20.95. Children $3.75 to

> $4.95 lunch and dinner.
> ***Menu:*** Lunch - Mexican specialities using pork, seafood, fried beef tenderloin, and chicken. Dinner - Mexican dishes made with lobster, shrimp, red snapper, beef tenderloin, pork, and chicken. Children - Beef or chicken tortilla, beef taco, fried chicken.
> ***Reservations:*** Required.

What to expect: a cozy and romantic atmosphere, among the best at Epcot. It may be daylight outside when you enter the San Angel, but even at lunch you'll dine under a darkened evening sky. The restaurant is located inside the Mexican pavilion's recreated Mayan pyramid. A black-haired hostess in a white dress will seat you at a wooden table lit by a solitary candle. The tables sit on a patio overlooking the River of Time. A jungle overruns the river's far bank. And from its thick growth rises a pyramid and a smoldering volcano that glows against the evening sky.

Sommerfest

TravelFacts

> ***Location:*** Germany, World Showcase, Epcot Center.
> ***Price:*** $1.35 to $3.25.
> ***Menu:*** Bratwurst sandwich with or without wine kraut, varied pastries, soft pretzels.

What to expect: outdoor dining in a shaded courtyard at the German pavilion's castle.

Soundstage Restaurant

TravelFacts

> ***Location:*** Studio tour area, Disney-MGM Studios Theme Park.

> *Price:* $1.95 to $5.25. Children $1.
> *Menu:* Sandwiches (subs, meatball sub, chicken salad), soup and salad combination, bean soup, vegetable soup, chef's salad (meat and cheese or seafood), chicken salad, pasta and vegetable salad, pizza, linguini, spaghetti. Children - peanut butter and jelly sandwich.

What to expect: fast food dining in a recreated sound stage. The set is the white and gold interior of the hotel in *Big Business*. This eatery lets you slide right into the feeling that you've taken a break from shooting to grab a bite to eat. The restaurant offers a small food court with three counters, one serving sandwiches, the second offering soups and salads, and the third selling pizza and pasta.

TravelVenture tip: Despite its 560-seat capacity, tables are in short supply during peak dining hours. You may want to get your table first, and then send one or two members of your party to get your food. But with three counters each offering different specialties, your food buying can be a cumbersome, time-consuming operation.

Stargate Restaurant

TravelFacts

> *Location:* Communicore East, Future World, Epcot Center.
> *Price:* Breakfast - $2.70-$3.95. Lunch and dinner - $2.70 to $4.95.
> *Menu:* Breakfast - scrambled eggs and ham, cheese omelet with Canadian bacon or ham on an English muffin, sausage omelet. Lunch and dinner - cheeseburger, chicken-breast sandwich, fruit salad, chef's salad, pizza.

What to expect: fast food in a sprawling dining room. You can chose to sit indoors or outdoors on a large, shaded patio.

Steerman's Quarters

TravelFacts

Location: Empress Lilly riverboat, Disney Village Marketplace, Walt Disney World.
Telephone: (407) 828-3900.
Price: $13.75 to $28. Children $3.25 to $6.50.
Menu: Prime rib, Porterhouse steak, New York sirloin or beef filet cut to order, broiled lamb rack, sautéed veal chop, grilled turkey steak, fresh fish. Children - prime rib, macaroni and cheese, hamburger, chicken pot pie, catfish fingers.
Hours: 5:30 P.M. to 10 P.M.
Reservations: Accepted.
Credit cards: American Express, MasterCard, and Visa.

What to expect: riverboat dining with the emphasis on beef. Located at the stern on the Empress Lilly's first deck, the Steerman's Quarters can't claim a prize-winning view — it's windows look out at the revolving red paddle wheel. But the restaurant offers a touch of elegance that belies its name: red velvet seat cushions and window curtains, flowered carpeting, and ivory wallpaper.

Studio Stars Restaurant

TravelFacts

Location: Now Shooting section, Universal Studios.
Price: $6.95 to $17.50.
Menu: Salads (seafood and chicken), sandwiches (ham and cheese, tuna melt, chicken salad, corned beef, club, shrimp), hamburgers, pasta, roast chicken, sirloin steak, fresh seafood. Children - hamburgers, ham and cheese sandwich, fried fish, chicken fingers.
Reservations: Recommended. Make reservations in person at the restaurant.

What to expect: a pleasant, California-style restaurant serving good food. The circular dining room wraps around a small atrium holding a palm tree. Hanging from the walls overlooking the wooden tables and chairs are dozens of light boxes displaying transparencies of famous faces.

Universal promotes the restaurant as the eatery of choice for all the stars, directors and producers shooting on its backlot. But not to worry. Since Universal is primarily a theme park, chances are remote that the entry of a film crew will disturb your meal. Your best bet for star gazing will be to check the light boxes.

TravelVenture tip: During high seasons, the Studio Stars Restaurant may upgrade its menu for dinner.

Sunrise Terrace

TravelFacts

Location: Communicore West, Future World, Epcot Center.
Price: $3.90 to $4.65. Children $2.45 to $3.65.
Menu: fried flounder, fried shrimp, fried chicken strips, submarine sandwiches (roast beef, turkey and provolone, ham and provolone cheese), chef's salad. Children - peanut butter and jelly sandwich, fried chicken strips, fried shrimp.

What to expect: A spacious, contemporary-style dining room with seating indoors or out. Many tables offer a view of the fountained plaza separating Communicore East and West.

Tomorrowland Terrace

TravelFacts

Location: Tomorrowland, Magic Kingdom.
Price: $3.25 to $5.25. Children $1.
Menu: Hot sandwiches (grilled or fried chicken, barbecue pork, cheese steak sub), cold sandwiches (tuna salad or club), soup and sandwich

combinations (roast beef, ham, or chicken salad with chicken noodle or minestrone soup), salads (fruit, seafood, chef's), chili, and a fruit and cheese board. Children - peanut butter and jelly sandwich.

What to expect: fast food in a large, spacious, and bright dining room. Two counters serve hot and cold sandwiches. A third offers salads plus a combination of soup and smaller sandwiches.

Tony's Town Square Restaurant

TravelFacts

Location: Town Square, Magic Kingdom, on the right as you face Cinderella Castle.
Price: Breakfast $3.50 to $8.75. Lunch $5.75 to $11.95. Dinner $11.95 to $18.75 (pizza $5.95 to $6.50). Children $2.75 to $5.95 lunch and dinner.
Menu: Breakfast - egg dishes, French toast, waffles. Lunch - salads (Nicoise, pasta, and fruit), sandwiches (club, meatball sub, veal sausage, Italian hoagie), hamburgers, chicken and pasta, spaghetti with meatballs, vegetable lasagne, fettucine, seafood linguini, mussels, omelettes. Dinner - pizza, lasagne, shrimp, seafood grille, grilled chicken, steak and lobster, ravioli, turkey breast filet. Children - grilled chicken sandwich, peanut butter and jelly sandwich, pasta with meatballs, pizza for both lunch and dinner.

What to expect: table service, Italian-style food, and two distinct dining areas. You can eat on the cafe's terrace overlooking the Town Square or inside in a turn-of-the-century atmosphere of stained-glass windows, Victorian furniture, and imitation gas lamps.

TravelVenture tip: Tony's Town Square Restaurant and The Crystal Palace are the only Magic Kingdom restaurants serving breakfast.

Yakitori House

TravelFacts

> *Location:* Japan, World Showcase, Epcot Center.
> *Price:* $2.50 to $4.95, children $2.95.
> *Menu:* Broiled teriyaki chicken, beef teriyaki and rice, seafood salad, beef or chicken teriyaki sandwiches. Children - beef teriyaki.

What to expect: substantial meals dished up in a replica of a Japanese teahouse. This teahouse was patterned after one in Japan's Katsura Imperial Villa, which was built for a prince in the early 17th century.

TravelVenture tip: Sample meals are on display in a showcase inside the Yakitori House, so you can see what you'll get before ordering.

TravelPlanner: lodging

Lodging by location

Disney World lodging-Epcot Resorts
Beach Club Resort 221
Caribbean Beach Resort 222
Walt Disney World Dolphin 245
Walt Disney World Swan 245
Yacht Club Resort 247

Disney World lodging-Disney's Village Resorts
Disney's Village Resort 228

Disney World lodging-Fort Wilderness
Fort Wilderness Resort and Campground 230

Disney World lodging-Hotel Plaza
Guest Quarters Suite Resort 234
Hilton at Walt Disney World Village 235
Travelodge Hotel 244

Disney World lodging-Magic Kingdom Resorts
Contemporary Resort 224

The Disney Inn 227
Grand Floridian Beach Resort 233
Polynesian Village Resort 241

International Drive-area lodging

Days Inn-Civic Center/Sea World 226
Econo Lodge-International Drive 229
Embassy Suites-Plaza International 229
Orlando Heritage Inn 239
The Peabody Orlando 241
Rodeway Inn 242
Sheraton World 243
Stouffer Hotel Orlando Sea World 243
Wynfield Inn-Westwood 247

Kissimmee-area lodging

Famous Host Inn 230
Four Winds Motel 232
Gemini Motel 233
Hyatt Orlando 235
Knights Inn-Main Gate 237
Maple Leaf Motel 237
Park Inn International 239
Red Roof Inn 242
Wilson World Hotel Maingate 246
Wynfield Inn-Main Gate East 247

Lake Buena Vista-area lodging

Comfort Inn at Lake Buena Vista 223
Days Inn-Lake Buena Vista Resort 226
Hyatt Regency Grand Cypress Resort 236
Marriott's Orlando World Center 238

Lodging by cost

An asterisk (*) indicates some rates extend into the next higher price category. Double asterisks (**) indicate some rates extend into the next lower price category.

Over $130

    Beach Club Resort (WDW) 221
    Contemporary Resort (WDW) 224
    The Disney Inn (WDW) 227
    Disney's Village Resort (WDW) 228
    Fort Wilderness (Trailers) (WDW) 230
    Grand Floridian Beach Resort (WDW) 233
    Guest Quarters Suite Resort (WDW-LBV) 234
    Hilton at WDW Village (WDW-LBV) 235
    Hyatt Regency Grand Cypress Resort (LBV) 236
    Marriott's Orlando World Center (LBV) 238
    The Peabody Orlando (Intl Dr.) 241
    Polynesian Village Resort (WDW) 241
    Stouffer Hotel Orlando Sea World (Intl Dr.) 243
    Walt Disney World Dolphin (WDW) 245
    Walt Disney World Swan (WDW) 245
    Yacht Club Resort (WDW) 247

$60 to $130

    Caribbean Beach Resort (WDW) 222
    Days Inn-Civic Center/Sea World (Intl Dr.)** 226
    Days Inn-Lake Buena Vista Resort (LBV) 226
    Embassy Suites-Plaza International (Intl Dr.) 229
    Hyatt Orlando (Kiss.) 235
    Orlando Heritage Inn (Intl Dr.) 239
    Sheraton World (Intl Dr.) 243
    Travelodge Hotel (WDW-LBV)* 244
    Wilson World Hotel Maingate (Kiss.) 246
    Wynfield Inn-Main Gate East (Kiss.) 247
    Wynfield Inn-Westwood (Intl Dr.) 247

Under $60

    Comfort Inn at Lake Buena Vista (LBV)* 223
    Econo Lodge-International Drive* 229
    Famous Host Inn (Kiss.)* 230
    Fort Wilderness (Campsites) (WDW) 230

Four Winds Motel (Kiss.) 232
Gemini Motel (Kiss.) 233
Knights Inn-Main Gate (Kiss.) 237
Maple Leaf Motel (Kiss.) 237
Park Inn International (Kiss.) 239
Red Roof Inn (Kiss.) 242
Rodeway Inn (Intl Dr.)* 242

Lodging

Orlando has experienced a hotel-motel building boom in recent years and now has more hotel rooms than any other city in the United States. Accommodations in the Orlando area tend to be clustered around particular areas, including Disney World, Lake Buena Vista, Kissimmee, and International Drive.

Disney World lodging

Disney hotels are among the most pleasant and attractive in the Orlando area. And Disney accommodations can help keep the Disney magic and excitement alive. Staying on Disney property also offers the most convenience for visiting Disney World. But you pay a price — among the highest in the Orlando area. There are few fast food or chain restaurants. You'll depend mainly on the restaurants at your hotel, which will also add to your expenses.

If you plan not to venture beyond Disney World, you can easily get by without a car. These hotels offer free bus service, a part of Disney's transportation system (buses, watercraft, trams, and a monorail) that will carry you to any point in Disney World.

Not all Disney World accommodations are owned and operated by Disney. Hotels at Disney World's Hotel Plaza near Lake Buena Vista as well as the Walt Disney World Dolphin and Swan are "official" Disney hotels, but they are managed and operated independently. Of the accommodations listed below, the following are Disney operated: Beach Club Resort, Caribbean Beach Resort, Contemporary Resort, The Disney Inn, Fort Wilderness Resort and Campground, Grand Floridian Beach Resort, Polynesian Village Resort, Disney's Village Resort, and the Yacht Club Resort.

Disney has grouped their hotels in particular locations: the Epcot Resorts, the Magic Kingdom Resorts, Disney's Village Resort, Fort Wilderness Resort and Campground, and those independent hotels at the Disney Village Hotel Plaza.

TravelVenture tip: Disney-operated accommodations are extremely popular. You must make your reservation months in advance. Plan on three to six months in advance for an off-season visit, six months to a year for a high season visit, and up to two years ahead of time for an ultra-high-season visit (Christmas and Easter).

Lake Buena Vista-area lodging

Lodging in the vicinity of Lake Buena Vista will put you just outside Disney World, near the Disney Village Marketplace. You'll lose a bit in convenience, but you'll save money. Off-Disney lodgings tend to cost less. You'll also find chain and fast food restaurants in the area.

Kissimmee-area lodging

From Kissimmee to a few miles west of Disney World you'll find good buys in accommodations along U.S. 192 (also known as Vine Street, Irlo Bronson Memorial Highway, and until recently Spacecoast Parkway). The area puts you close to Disney, but at greatly reduced cost. Families on a budget will find the Kissimmee area especially appealing. It offers a large, varied selection of motels — many independently owned and offering some of the lowest rates in the Orlando area. Chain restaurants, fast food eateries, and gift shops are plentiful.

TravelVenture tip: During the fall low season, competition along the eastern section of the U.S. 192 heats up, especially among the motels closer to Kissimmee. Many will then post their rates on signs at the front of their property. If you're bargain hunting, cruise this strip and compare rates.

International Drive-area lodging

Accommodations around International Drive will give you a central location between Disney and the other attractions. The area is packed with hotels and motels offering a wide range of room rates. You'll also find abundant chain restaurants, fast food eateries, and tourist shops.

TravelVenture tip: If you are planning a see-it-all trip that will have you hitting the attractions from early morning until well into the evening, you'll be wasting your money if you spend it on amenity-packed, high-priced accommodations. You won't be spending enough time at your hotel to enjoy the extras. What time you do spend there will be mainly for sleeping, so look for a plain, comfortable, lower-priced room. Conversely, if you plan to do the attractions at a more leisurely pace and spend much rest-and-relaxation time at your hotel, put more luxury into your lodging. Aim for higher-priced accommodations offering the amenities that will help you relax and enjoy your stay.

The accommodations that follow are listed alphabetically. All provide color television and air conditioning.

Beach Club Resort

TravelFacts

Location: Epcot Resorts, Walt Disney World (P.O. Box 10,100, Lake Buena Vista 32830-0100).
Map: Page 224.

> *Telephone:* (407) 934-8000. For reservations (407) 934-7639.
> *Rates:* $185 to $295.
> *Restaurants:* Two, plus three snack bars. Room service available.
> *Amenities:* TV with Disney Channel, lobby shops, child-care center, game room, health club, lighted tennis courts, volleyball, croquet lawn, lakeside beach, boat rentals, snorkeling, 2.5-acre pool with water slides off a shipwreck, unlimited use of Disney World transportation system.

What to expect: an upscale, Disney-operated hotel with the flavor of an 1870s New England hotel by the sea. The 580-room, five-story Beach Club, along with its sister hotel the Yacht Club, sits on the shore of a 50-acre lake near Epcot Center's World Showcase. Watercraft shuttle guests between the hotel and the Disney MGM Studios Theme Park. And Epcot's International Gateway entrance near the French pavilion is just a short walk or a quick tram ride away.

TravelVenture tip: The Beech Club offers its guests a special-request food service that can accommodate practically all diets. Your special diet request is made when you check in and is available both through room service and selected restaurants in the hotel.

Caribbean Beach Resort

TravelFacts

> *Location:* Epcot Resorts, Walt Disney World (P.O. Box 10,100, Lake Buena Vista 32830-0100).
> *Map:* Page 224.
> *Telephone:* (407) 934-3400. For reservations (407) 934-7639.
> *Rates:* $79 to $99.
> *Restaurants:* A six-counter fast food court.
> *Amenities:* TV with Disney Channel, coin laundry, gift shop, game room, children's playground, pools, lakeside beach, boat and bicycle rent-

> als, nearby promenade, unlimited use of Disney World transportation system.

What to expect: a Caribbean-flavored hotel complex of 2,112 rooms surrounding a 42-acre lake. Check in at this Disney-operated hotel is accomplished in a large, old-timey "customs house." Rooms are small but attractive and housed in metal-roofed two-story buildings. The brightly painted buildings are divided into five distinct villages, each with its own name — Trinidad, Martinique, Barbados, Aruba, and Jamaica. The heart of the complex, Old Port Royale, contains a fast food court, swimming pool, and white-sand beach.

A foot bridge from Old Port Royale leads to Parrot Cay, a 1.5-acre island in the resort's lake. Parrot Cay is home to tropical trees, plants, children's play areas, winding walkways, and four species of South American parrots. A 1.4-mile promenade circles the lake itself.

TravelVenture tip: The Caribbean Beach Resort is Disney's first moderately priced hotel. If you're on a budget but want accommodations in Disney World, the Caribbean Beach Resort should be your choice. The Caribbean does have a drawback, though. Its only restaurant is a small six-counter fast food court. If you want anything fancier, you'll have to use transportation (your own or Disney's) to go elsewhere in Disney World.

Comfort Inn at Lake Buena Vista

TravelFacts

Location: 8442 Palm Pkwy., Orlando 32819.
Map: Page 227.
Telephone: (407) 239-7300, 800-221-2222.
Rates: $31 to $65.
Restaurants: One.

224 ORLANDO AND DISNEY WORLD

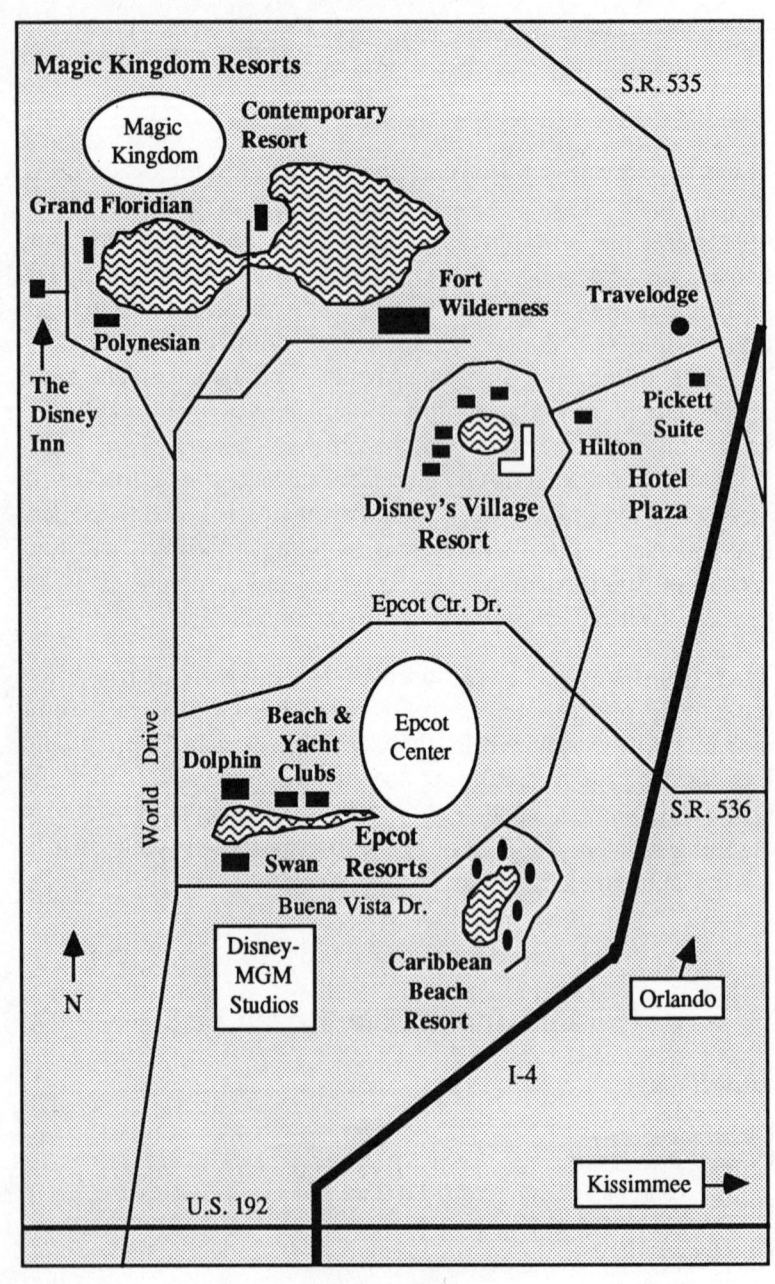

Disney World lodging

Amenities: Non-smoking rooms, game room, coin laundry, heated pool, complimentary transportation to Disney attractions.

What to expect: a pleasant five-story motel with 640 standard double rooms. Although Interstate 4 runs along the back, the palm tree-ringed motel is set well in from both I-4 and Palm Parkway, offering a fairly secluded and tranquil location.

Contemporary Resort

TravelFacts

Location: Magic Kingdom Resorts, Disney World, (P.O. Box 10,100, Lake Buena Vista 32830-0100).
Map: Page 224.
Telephone: (407) 824-1000. For reservations (407) 934-7639.
Rates: $160 to $230.
Restaurants: Three, plus two snack bars. Room service available.
Amenities: TV with Disney Channel, oversize beds available, room balconies (most rooms), concierge-level, lobby shops and boutique, large game room with evening movies, valet parking, two pools, lakeside beach, boat rentals, water skiing, children's playground, shuffleboard, volleyball, tennis courts, health club (with exercise room, sauna, and spa), nearby jogging trail, monorail stop on property, unlimited use of Disney World transportation system.

What to expect: a Disney-operated hotel sitting on the shore of Bay Lake, a short distance from the Magic Kingdom. The Contemporary's 1,046 rooms are split between three-story garden wings and a 15-story concrete A-frame building known as the tower. The Disney monorail train runs through the tower and makes a stop inside the hotel. The Contemporary's recently renovated rooms have oak furniture, paddle fans, and large bathrooms with double black-granite sinks. Rooms on the west side of the tower offer a view of the Magic Kingdom.

TravelVenture tip: The Contemporary Resort has a bustling atmosphere. If relaxation is a high priority, consider Disney's Polynesian Village Resort or The Disney Inn.

Days Inn-Civic Center/Sea World

TravelFacts

Location: 9990 International Dr., Orlando 32819.
Map: Page 240.
Telephone: (407) 352-8700, 800-325-2525.
Rates: $53 to $75.
Restaurants: One.
Amenities: Cable TV with HBO, non-smoking rooms, coin laundry, car rental, pool, playground.

What to expect: a four-story Days Inn with 221 rooms. The inn offers a convenient location near Sea World and close to the Bee Line Expressway and Interstate 4.

Days Inn-Lake Buena Vista Resort

TravelFacts

Location: 12205 Apopka-Vineland Rd., Orlando 32830.
Map: Page 227.
Telephone: (407) 239-0444, 800-325-2525.
Rates: $70 to $90, suites $84 to $130.
Restaurants: One, plus a deli.
Amenities: Cable TV with HBO, oversize beds and kitchenettes available, non-smoking rooms, room balconies, coin laundry, gift shop, game room, car rental, heated pool, complimentary transportation to Disney attractions.

What to expect: a contemporary, five-story hotel with 490 large rooms. This up-scale Days Inn offers a lobby with raised sitting area and rooms reached via interior corridors.

The Disney Inn

TravelFacts

> **Location:** Magic Kingdom Resorts, Walt Disney World (P.O. Box 10,100, Lake Buena Vista 32830-0100).
> **Map:** Page 224.
> **Telephone:** (407) 824-2200. For reservations (407) 934-7639.
> **Rates:** $165 to $195
> **Restaurants:** One, plus two snack bars. Room service available.
> **Amenities:** TV with Disney Channel, oversize beds, room balconies or patios, coin laundry, lobby shops, game room, two golf courses, lighted tennis courts, children's playground, pool, unlimited use of Disney World transportation system.

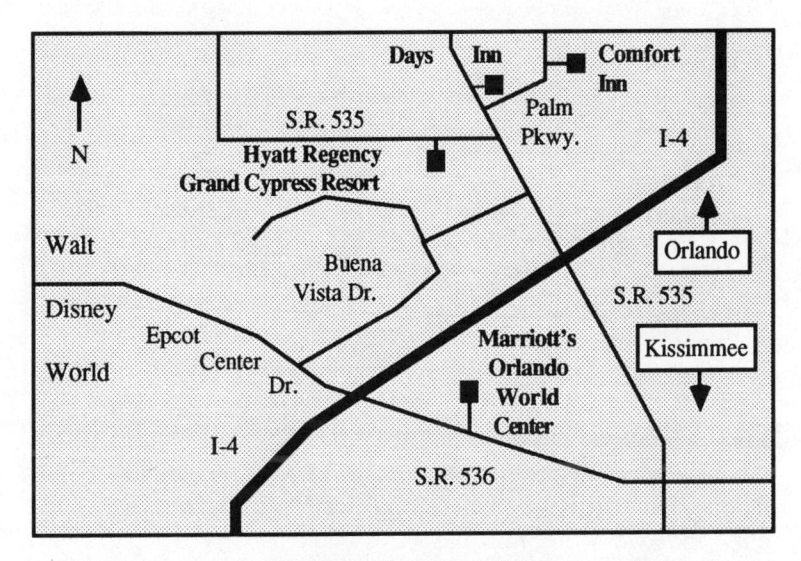

Lake Buena Vista-area lodging

What to expect: a secluded, peaceful, Disney-operated hotel. Should you unwind and get so relaxed that you forget you're at bustling Disney World, you can confirm your location by stepping outside the inn's front door to view topiary sculptures of the Seven Dwarfs. As Disney World hotels go, the inn is on the small side with just 288 rooms in two three-story wings. Its rooms, however, are on the large side with each offering two queen-size beds and a sofa. The hotel is isolated, sitting in a wooded area between two golf courses — the Magnolia and the Palm. Yet your car, or Disney's bus system which serves the inn, will quickly get you to Disney World attractions.

TravelVenture tip: If you want to try to put some get away into a Disney vacation, choose The Disney Inn.

Disney's Village Resort

TravelFacts

Location: Walt Disney World Village. (P. O. Box 10,100, Lake Buena Vista 32830-0100.)
Map: Page 224.
Telephone: (407) 827-1100. For reservations (407) 934-7639.
Rates: One bedroom - $155 to $260, two bedrooms - $270 to $315, three bedrooms - $295 to $335.
Restaurants: None.
Amenities: TV with Disney Channel, oversize beds available, fully-equipped kitchens (most units), daily maid service, coin laundry, game room, four pools, bicycle and electric cart rentals, golf course, lighted tennis courts, unlimited use of Disney World transportation system.

What to expect: almost 600 furnished villas located in woody, secluded areas adjacent to the Disney Village Marketplace. These Disney-operated villas come in a variety of styles. Two-story one- and two-bedroom villas offer contemporary design, plenty of closet space, two or two-and-a-half baths, and a loft-like master bedroom. Some of the two-bedroom villas will house you alongside a golf course in spacious, contemporary quarters with cathedral ceilings. Eight-sided, three-bedroom Treehouse Villas are built on stilts and offer two floors of rustic living quarters. Club Suite villas — smaller one-bedroom accommodations without fully-equipped kitchens — are also available.

Econo Lodge-International Drive

TravelFacts

Location: 8738 International Dr., Orlando 32819.
Map: Page 240.
Telephone: (407) 345-8195, 800-446-6900.
Rates: $52 to $68.
Restaurants: Adjacent.
Amenities: Oversize beds and kitchenettes available, in-room spas available, non-smoking rooms, gift shop, car rental, game room, heated pool.

What to expect: a sprawling, four-story motel with exterior Old English decor. The Econo Lodge has 669 rooms, including suites and efficiencies with kitchenettes.

Embassy Suites-Plaza International

TravelFacts

Location: 8250 Jamaican Ct., Orlando 32819, just off International Drive.
Map: Page 240.
Telephone: (407) 345-8250, 800-362-2779.
Rates: $120 to $130.
Restaurants: Kitchen offering only lunch and dinner room service.

Amenities: Cable TV with movie channel, oversize beds available, non-smoking suites, complimentary buffet breakfast, gift shop, game room, combination indoor-outdoor pool, exercise room, spa, sauna.

What to expect: an all-suite hotel with 246 suites, each offering living area and bedroom. The eight-story lobby is decorated with brick, has a waterfall, and is capped by a skylight.

Famous Host Inn

TravelFacts

Location: 5875 W. Bronson Hwy. (U.S. 192), Kissimmee 34746.
Map: Page 231.
Telephone: (407) 396-8883, 800-441-5477.
Rates: $35 to $62.
Restaurants: Nearby.
Amenities: Heated pool, coin laundry, game room.

What to expect: two-story motel offering 120 rooms. Each room has two double beds and is furnished in oak. The Famous Host has an especially courteous and friendly staff.

Fort Wilderness Resort and Campground

TravelFacts

Location: Walt Disney World (P.O. Box 10,100, Lake Buena Vista 32830-0100).
Map: Page 224.
Telephone: (407) 824-2900. For reservations (407) 934-7639.
Rates: Campsites $37 to $48 with hookups, $30 to $36 without hookups. Trailers $160 to $170.

LODGING 231

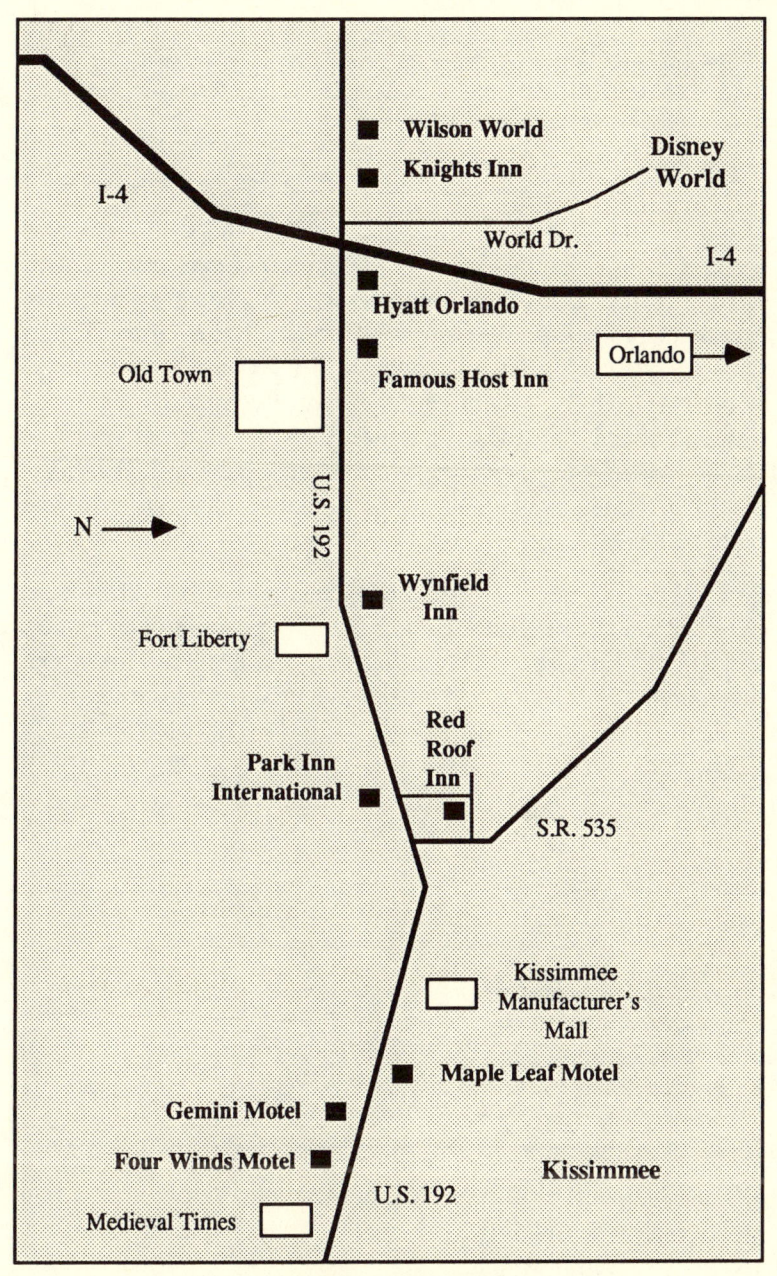

Kissimmee-area lodging

Restaurants: A cafeteria and a snack bar.
Amenities: Coin laundry, shops (groceries and camping supplies), game rooms, pool, lakeside beach, bike paths, bicycle rentals, fishing, boating, jogging trail, tennis courts, riding stable.

What to expect: a large, sprawling campground with 1,190 sites set in a natural setting of Florida cypress and pine trees. If your Disney fantasy leans more toward Davy Crockett than lavish resort hotels, then Fort Wilderness is for you. But even roughing it Disney style can be fairly smooth. While you can pitch a tent — yours or Disney's — you can also rent a completely equipped, air-conditioned, and carpeted trailer. Or you can bring your own trailer. All of Fort Wilderness' campsites have a 110/220-volt electrical outlet, water and waste hookups, charcoal grill, and picnic table.

TravelVenture tip: Lower-numbered campsites tend to be located closer to Bay Lake, River Country, and the campground's shops and activities. Those with higher numbers are deeper in the woods, offering more seclusion and greater potential for relaxation.

Four Winds Motel

TravelFacts

Location: 4596 W. Bronson Hwy. (U.S. 192), Kissimmee 34746.
Map: Page 231.
Telephone: (407) 396-4011, 800-826-5830.
Rates: $25 to $50.
Restaurants: Adjacent.
Amenities: King-size beds available, non-smoking rooms, heated pool.

What to expect: a 50-room independent motel housed in a two-story, red-brick building. The motel offers a friendly staff and rooms furnished in walnut.

Gemini Motel

TravelFacts

Location: 4624 W. Bronson Hwy. (U.S. 192), Kissimmee 34746.
Map: Page 231.
Telephone: (407) 396-2151, 800-648-4841.
Rates: $25 to $50.
Restaurants: Nearby.
Amenities: Cable TV with HBO, non-smoking rooms, coin laundry, pool.

What to expect: a two-story independent motel. The Gemini's 80 rooms each come equipped with two double beds.

Grand Floridian Beach Resort

TravelFacts

Location: Magic Kingdom Resorts, Walt Disney World, near the Magic Kingdom (P.O. Box 10,100, Lake Buena Vista 32830-0100).
Map: Page 224.
Telephone: (407) 824-3000. For reservations (407) 424-2900.
Rates: $205 to $375.
Restaurants: Five, plus two snack bars. Room service available.
Amenities: TV with Disney Channel, oversize beds available, room balconies (most rooms), concierge rooms, lobby shops and boutique, child-care center, game room, pool, lakeside beach, boat rentals, children's playground, health club (with exercise room and sauna), monorail stop on property, unlimited use of Disney World transportation system.

What to expect: a Victorian-style hotel offering the most luxurious of Disney-operated accommodations. The Grand Floridian recalls turn-of-the-century Florida, when high society migrated south for the winter to nest in lodgings such as this hotel. Gabled, red-shingled roofs top the six buildings making up the Grand

Floridian complex. The 901 guest rooms are located in four- and five-story "lodges," while a main building houses the lobby, shops, restaurants, and concierge suites. The flavor of old-time Florida permeates the hotel. A white, antique Cadillac sits out front. Ceiling fans and lattice work are prevalent. And some of the staff even sport knickers. The five-story lobby, crowned with three stained-glass domes, sports a bird cage elevator, two 16-foot chandeliers, and an aviary. The rooms themselves are furnished with ceiling fans, printed wall coverings, armoires, and brass faucets.

Guest Quarters Suite Resort

TravelFacts

> *Location:* 2305 Hotel Plaza Blvd., Lake Buena Vista 32830, at Walt Disney World Village.
> *Map:* Page 224.
> *Telephone:* (407) 934-1000, 800-424-2900.
> *Rates:* $145 to $225.
> *Restaurants:* One, plus snack bars.
> *Amenities:* Cable TV with movies and Disney Channel, three television sets (two remote controlled), in-room coffee service, complimentary breakfast, refrigerator, microwave ovens available (request when you make your reservation), hair dryer, gift shop, car rental, coin laundry, game room, exercise room, children's playground, heated pool, complimentary transportation to Disney attractions.

What to expect: a seven-story hotel housing 229 one- and two-bedroom suites. The Guest Quarters offers an apartment-like atmosphere. Each suite contains one or more bedrooms, a separate living area with dining tables and chairs, and a bathroom equipped with its own small-screen television. The Guest Quarters serves its guests a complimentary buffet breakfast in an attractive restaurant off the lobby.

Hilton at Walt Disney World Village

TravelFacts

Location: 1751 Hotel Plaza Blvd., Lake Buena Vista 32830.
Map: Page 224.
Telephone: (407) 827-4000, 800-728-4414.
Rates: $130 to $225.
Restaurants: Three, plus two snack bars. Room service available.
Amenities: Remote-controlled TV with Disney Channel, radio, oversize beds available, room balconies, suites and kitchenettes available, non-smoking rooms, concierge service, lobby shops and boutiques, car rental, game room, child-care center, coin laundry, health club, two heated pools, lighted tennis courts, valet parking, complimentary transportation to Disney attractions.

What to expect: a contemporary hotel near the Walt Disney World Village Marketplace. At the entrance to the 10-story boomerang-shaped building stands a waterfall and fountain. Shades of maroon and touches of pink decorate the lobby from the carpet through the marble trim to the ceiling tiles. The Hilton's 813 rooms are elegantly furnished in contemporary decor. A high-tech bedside telephone system lets you control the television and air conditioner with just a touch.

Hyatt Orlando

TravelFacts

Location: 6375 W. Bronson Hwy. (U.S. 192), Kissimmee 34746, at the interchange of I-4 and U.S. 192.
Map: Page 231.
Telephone: (407) 396-1234, 800-228-9000.
Rates: $119 to $129.
Restaurants: Three, plus a deli.
Amenities: Cable TV with HBO and Cinemax, radio, in-room movies, hair dryers, non-smoking rooms, boutique-gift shop, beauty salon,

> car rental counter, game room, coin laundry, four heated pools, playground, spa, tennis courts, jogging trail.

What to expect: a sprawling complex of two-story buildings offering 948 rooms and a location close to Disney World. Rooms at the Hyatt are spacious and come with hair dryers and separate vanity areas.

Hyatt Regency Grand Cypress Resort

TravelFacts

> *Location:* One Grand Cypress Blvd, P.O. Box 22156, Orlando 32819.
> *Map:* Page 227.
> *Telephone:* (407) 239-1234, 800-228-9000.
> *Rates:* $140 to $230.
> *Restaurantss:* Five. Room service available.
> *Amenities:* Cable TV with movie channel, in-room movies, oversize beds available, concierge service, lobby shops and boutiques, beauty salon, car rental, game room, child-care center, coin laundry, large pool with water slide and rock grottos, lakeside sand beach, health club (exercise rooms, spas, saunas, massage room), tennis courts, jogging and nature trails, volley ball, shuffleboard, 27-hole Jack Nicklaus golf course, pro shop and golf academy, 40-stable Equestrian Center with riding trails, racquet ball, rental boats and bicycles, valet parking, transportation around resort and to attractions and airport.

What to expect: a 1,500-acre resort with the best hotel in the area. The 750-room Hyatt rises 18 stories and sports the Hyatt Regency trademark — a lobby atrium. The 200-foot atrium boasts tall palm trees, gardens, small pools and waterfalls, and even works of art. The art is part of a $1 million collection of paintings and sculptures on display throughout the building, the grounds, and the guest rooms. The rooms themselves offer luxury living with a Florida feeling — rattan furniture, shutters, and ceiling fans. To get around the Grand Cypress' many acres, the resort runs refurbished Belgian trolley cars. These trolleys were built between 1910 and 1918, and as late as 1975 they were still rolling through the streets of Brussels. The Grand Cypress Resort also offers villas with from one to four bedrooms. Call 800-228-9000 for information.

Knights Inn-Main Gate

TravelFacts

Location: 7475 W. Bronson Hwy. (U.S. 192), Kissimmee 34746.
Map: Page 231.
Telephone: (407) 396-4200, 800-722-7220.
Rates: $39 to $51.
Restaurants: Nearby.
Amenities: Satellite TV with Showtime, non-smoking rooms, kitchenettes and sofas (some rooms), pool.

What to expect: an attractive one-story motel with 120 rooms done in old-English decor — beamed ceilings and plenty of wood trim. Part of the Knights Inn chain, the motel offers a variety of room configurations: one double bed, one double bed plus sofa, two double beds, and one double bed plus sofa and kitchenette. Pets are welcome.

Maple Leaf Motel

TravelFacts

Location: 4647 W. Bronson Hwy. (U.S. 192), Kissimmee 34746.
Map: Page 231.
Telephone: (407) 396-0300.
Rates: $25 to $44.

> *Restaurants:* Nearby.
> *Amenities:* Cable TV with HBO, heated pool, discounted attractions tickets.

What to expect: an independent 44-room motel. The Maple Leaf puts two double beds in each room, except for one — that has a king-size bed.

Marriott's Orlando World Center

TravelFacts

> *Location:* One World Center Drive, Orlando 32821, at I-4 and State Road 536.
> *Map:* Page 227.
> *Telephone:* (407) 239-4200. 800-228-9290.
> *Rates:* $179 to $229.
> *Restaurants:* Three, plus two snack bars; 24-hour room service available.
> *Amenities:* Cable TV, radio, oversize beds available, room balconies, suites and kitchenettes available, non-smoking rooms, concierge service, lobby shops and boutiques, beauty salon, car rental, game room, child-care center, coin laundry, health club, sauna, indoor and outdoor (heated) pools, 12 lighted tennis courts, 18-hole championship Joe Lee golf course, valet parking, transportation to attractions.

What to expect: a 27-story upscale hotel housing 1,503 rooms. A popular convention hotel, the Marriott has an atrium lobby and sprawling public areas filled with trees, plants, fountains, and miniature waterfalls. Outside, around the hotel's huge pool, are more waterfalls, cascading down Central Florida boulders (man-made, that is). Swans, ducks, and goldfish swim in an adjacent canal. The hotel's rooms, decorated in Florida pastels, are bright and attractively furnished in oak.

Orlando Heritage Inn

TravelFacts

Location: 9861 International Dr., Orlando 32819.
Map: Page 240.
Telephone: (407) 352-0008, 800-447-1890, in Florida 800-282-1890.
Rates: $70 to $115.
Restaurants: One, room service available.
Amenities: Cable TV with HBO, in-room movies, radio, oversize beds available, non-smoking rooms, mini refrigerators, in-room safes, guest services desk, heated pool.

What to expect: a two-story hotel offering a turn-of-the-century-Florida feel. The Orlando Heritage Inn has brought back the front porch, furnished it with rocking chairs, and cooled it with paddle fans. The old-Florida flavor also carries over into the inn's 150 rooms. They're furnished with chests of drawers, wood-framed mirrors, and wooden, half-moon headboards.

Park Inn International

TravelFacts

Location: 4960 W. Bronson Hwy. (U.S. 192), Kissimmee 34746.
Map: Page 231.
Telephone: (407) 396-1376, 800-327-0072, in Florida 800-432-0276.
Rates: $39 to $59.
Restaurants: One.
Amenities: Cable TV with HBO, queen-size beds available, gift shop, coin laundry, game room, pool, spa.

What to expect: multiple, two-story buildings housing 200 attractively furnished rooms. The Park Inn also offers nicely landscaped grounds and a lakeside location with sand beach.

TravelVenture tip: A fine choice, good value for your money.

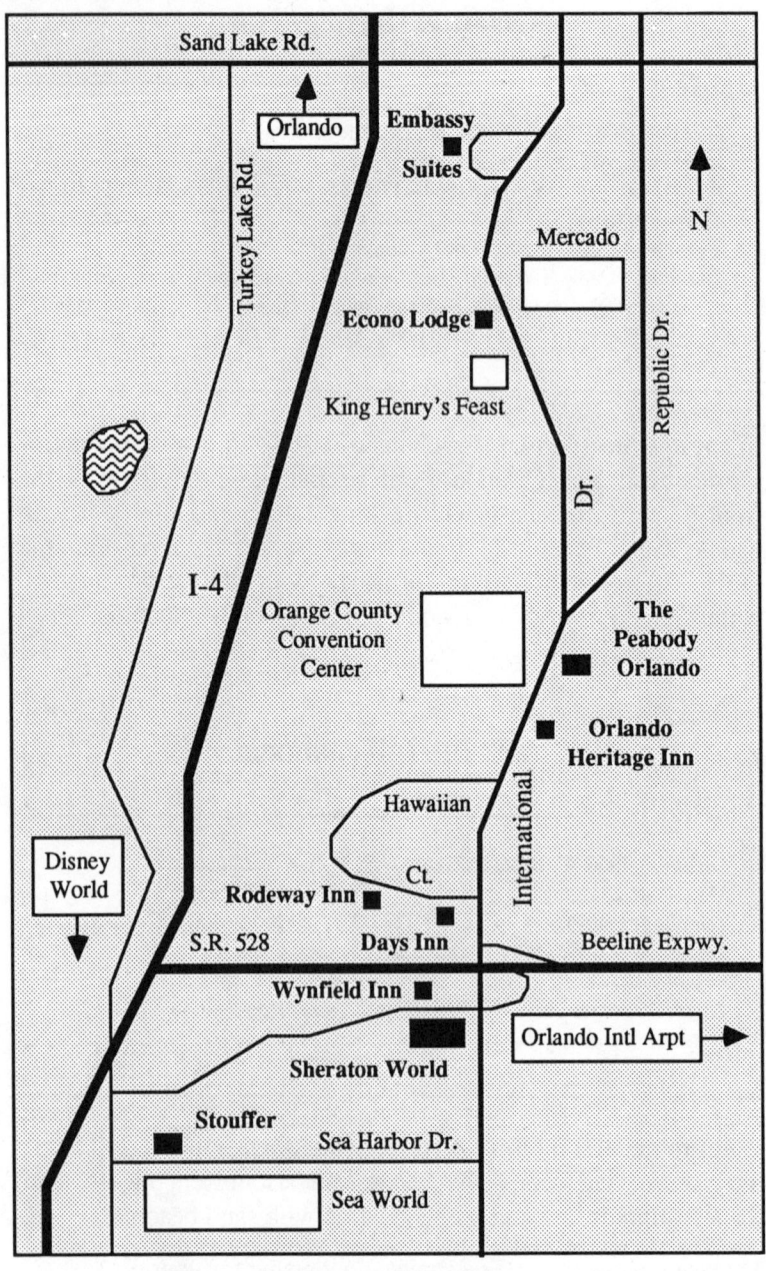

International Drive lodging

The Peabody Orlando

TravelFacts

> *Location:* 9801 International Dr., Orlando 32819.
> *Map:* Page 240.
> *Telephone:* (407) 352-4000, 800-732-2639.
> *Rates:* $170 - $235.
> *Restaurants:* Three. Room service available.
> *Amenities:* Remote-control cable TV, concierge service, daily newspaper, child-care center, business center, valet parking, gift shop and boutique, car rental counter, Delta Air Lines counter, game room, double-size Olympic pool, health club, sauna, spa (indoor and outdoor), lighted tennis courts.

What to expect: one of Orlando's main convention hotels, located directly across International Drive from the Orange County Civic Center. The Peabody, a luxury hotel, boasts 891 elegant rooms decorated in pastels. Large bathrooms have marble counter tops and come equipped with hair dryer and mini-TV. The Peabody features a daily procession of its hallmark ducks, just as they've done at the original Peabody in Memphis for over half a century. The ducks leave their fourth-floor roost daily at 11 A.M. Taking an elevator to the lobby, they march along a red carpet to a fountain where they spend the day. At 5 P.M. the ducks fall in for the return parade.

Polynesian Village Resort

TravelFacts

> *Location:* Magic Kingdom Resorts, Walt Disney World (P.O. Box 10,100, Lake Buena Vista 32830-0100).
> *Map:* Page 224.
> *Telephone:* (407) 824-2000. For reservations (407) 934-7639.
> *Rates:* $180 to $260.
> *Restaurants:* Three, plus two snack bars. Room service available.
> *Amenities:* TV with Disney Channel, oversize beds available, room bal-

conies or patios (most rooms), concierge service, lobby shops and boutiques, valet parking, game room, children's playground, two pools, lakeside beach with swimming, boat rentals, health club, monorail stop on property, unlimited use of Disney World transportation system.

What to expect: a Disney-operated hotel made up of eleven two- and three-story, Polynesian-style longhouses. The impressive, three-story lobby gets you right into a South Seas mood. It features a massive atrium filled with tropical trees and plants surrounding a waterfall. The lush, tropical landscaping continues throughout the grounds, which lead to a white-sand beach at the edge of the Seven Seas Lagoon.

Red Roof Inn

TravelFacts

Location: 4970 Kyng's Heath Rd., Kissimmee 34746.
Map: Page 231.
Telephone: (407) 396-0065, 800-843-7663.
Rates: $27 to $55.
Restaurants: Nearby.
Amenities: In-room movies, king-size beds available, non-smoking rooms, weekday newspaper, coin laundry, pool.

What to expect: a new, three-story motel offering small but comfortable rooms decorated in blues and grays.

Rodeway Inn

TravelFacts

Location: 9956 Hawaiian Ct., Orlando 32819, just off International Drive.
Map: Page 240.

Telephone: (407) 351-5100, 800-826-4847.
Rates: $44 to $69.
Restaurants: Nearby.
Amenities: Oversize beds available, balconies (some rooms), non-smoking rooms, kitchenettes available, in-room spa (some rooms), pool.

What to expect: a two-story beige-brick motel offering 221 rooms. The inn's rooms are furnished with rattan and are reached via inside corridors. Good landscaping, plenty of palm trees.

Sheraton World

TravelFacts

Location: 10100 International Dr., Orlando 32821.
Map: Page 240.
Telephone: (407) 352-1100, 800-327-0363, in Florida 800-341-4292.
Rates: $95 to $128.
Restaurants: One, plus a deli. Room service available.
Amenities: Cable TV, oversize beds available, non-smoking rooms, lobby shops and boutique, beauty salon, car rental counter, coin laundry, game rooms, three heated pools, spa, tennis courts, exercise room, miniature golf course.

What to expect: 788 rooms in two- and three-story buildings occupying 28 acres. The buildings form an enclosing rectangle around the motel's rambling, park-like grounds. Its popularity with British tourists gives Sheraton World an international flavor.

TravelVenture tip: A good choice for relaxing and pool-side sun bathing amidst pleasant, neatly manicured landscaping.

Stouffer Hotel Orlando Sea World

TravelFacts

Location: 6677 Sea Harbor Dr., Orlando 32821, west of International

Drive and across the street from Sea World.
Map: Page 240.
Telephone: (407) 351-5555, 800-327-6677.
Rates: $170 to $239.
Restaurants: Four. Room service available.
Amenities: Cable TV, in-room movies, clock radio, king-size beds available, concierge service, lobby shops including beauty salon, child-care center, game room, pool, children's playground, lighted tennis courts, fitness center (spa, Nautilus equipment, wet and dry saunas), transportation to Disney World.

What to expect: spacious and quiet rooms done in a tropical-Florida decor of rattan with pink, burgundy, and beige pastels. The Stouffer has a rectangular shape with its 782 rooms stacked one deep along its length, two deep on the sides. The rest of the interior is occupied by a football field-size atrium 10 stories high. The atrium-lobby is filled with trees, plants, a goldfish pond with waterfall, and a couple of gazebos — one of which is an aviary.

Travelodge Hotel

TravelFacts

Location: 2000 Hotel Plaza Blvd., Lake Buena Vista 32830, at Walt Disney World Village.
Map: Page 224.
Telephone: (407) 828-2424, 800-348-3765.
Rates: $119 to $149.
Restaurants: One, plus snack bars. Room service available.
Amenities: TV with Disney Channel, radio, in-room movies, in-room coffee service, in-room safe, hair dryer, oversize beds, room balconies, non-smoking rooms, concierge service, gift shop, car rental, coin laundry, game room, children's playground, heated pool, complimentary transportation to Disney attractions.

What to expect: a pleasant hotel with 325 rooms. The Travelodge has recently refurbished its rooms, using plenty of brass trim, pastel colors, and fine furnishings. The rooms, which have separate vanity areas, are located in an 18-story circular tower. Each offers a view and a furnished balcony from which to enjoy it.

Walt Disney World Dolphin

TravelFacts

Location: Epcot Resorts, 1200 Epcot Resort Blvd., Lake Buena Vista, FL 32830.
Map: Page 224.
Telephone: (407).934-4000. For reservations (407) 934-7639.
Rates: $190 to $260.
Restaurants: Five, plus two snack bars. Room service available.
Amenities: TV with Disney Channel, oversize beds available, concierge-level rooms, lobby shops, beauty salon, airline and car rental counters, child-care center, game room, three pools, lakeside beach, health club, lighted tennis courts, unlimited use of Disney World transportation system.

What to expect: a 1,509-room convention-oriented hotel located at Disney World but operated by the Sheraton Corporation. The 27-story Dolphin, along with its sister hotel the Swan, was designed by post-modernist architect Michael Graves. Graves has topped the Dolphin with a pair of 55-foot-high fiberglass and steel dolphin sculptures. At its entrance a 25-foot waterfall cascades down a series of shells and into a seashell pool supported by two dolphins. And a lighted fountain sits on each of the Dolphin's four nine-story wings The dolphin sits alongside a 50-acre lake. Water taxis shuttle guests between the hotel and the Disney MGM Studios Theme Park. And Epcot's International Gateway entrance near the French pavilion is just a short walk or a quick tram ride away.

Walt Disney World Swan

TravelFacts

Location: Epcot Resorts, 1200 Epcot Resort Blvd., Lake Buena Vista, FL

32830.
Map: Page 224.
Telephone: (407).934-3000. For reservations (407) 934-7639.
Rates: $185 to $255.
Restaurants: Two, plus a snack bar. Room service available.
Amenities: TV with Disney Channel, oversize beds available, concierge-level rooms, lobby shops, beauty salon, child-care center, game room, two pools, lakeside beach, health club, lighted tennis courts, unlimited use of Disney World transportation system.

What to expect: a 758-room, convention-oriented hotel operated by Westin Hotels & Resorts. Post-modernist architect Michael Graves designed the 12-story building, giving it a curved roof line and crowning it with a pair of 47-foot-high fiberglass and steel swan sculptures. The Swan sits at the shore of a 50-acre lake. Water taxis shuttle guests between the hotel and the Disney MGM Studios Theme Park. And Epcot's International Gateway entrance near the French pavilion is just a short walk or a quick tram ride away.

Wilson World Hotel Maingate

TravelFacts

Location: 7491 W. Bronson Hwy. (U.S. 192), Kissimmee 34746.
Map: Page 231.
Telephone: (407) 396-6000, 800-669-6753.
Rates: $65 to $80.
Restaurants: One.
Amenities: Oversize beds, non-smoking rooms, lobby boutique, game room, coin laundry, indoor and outdoor pools, spa.

What to expect: a 443-room hotel built by Kemmons Wilson, founder of the Holiday Inn chain. The hotel boasts a massive atrium enclosing a spa, a pool with three-tier waterfall, and the hotel's restaurant.

Wynfield Inn-Main Gate East

TravelFacts

Location: 5335 W. Bronson Hwy. (U.S. 192), Kissimmee 34746.
Map: Page 231.
Telephone: (407) 396-2121, 800-468-8374.
Rates: $60 to $74.
Restaurants: Adjacent.
Amenities: Non-smoking rooms, complimentary coffee and fresh fruit in the lobby, game room, coin laundry, pool.

What to expect: a two-story, 120-room motel with nicely furnished, contemporary rooms. Particularly friendly and helpful staff.

Wynfield Inn-Westwood

TravelFacts

Location: 6263 Westwood Blvd, Orlando 32821, west of International Drive.
Map: Page 240.
Telephone: (407) 345-8000, 800-346-1551.
Rates: $60 to $74.
Restaurants: Adjacent.
Amenities: in-room movies, non-smoking rooms, complimentary coffee and fresh fruit in the lobby, game room, coin laundry, two pools.

What to expect: a pleasant, two-story motel with 300 nicely furnished, contemporary rooms. The Wynfield's staff is especially cheerful and friendly.

Yacht Club Resort

TravelFacts

Location: Epcot Resorts, Walt Disney World (P.O. Box 10,100, Lake

> Buena Vista 32830-0100).
> *Map:* Page 224.
> *Telephone:* (407) 934-7000. For reservations (407) 934-7639.
> *Rates:* $185 to $295.
> *Restaurants:* Two, plus a snack bar. Room service available.
> *Amenities:* TV with Disney Channel, lobby shops, child-care center, game room, health club, croquet lawn, lakeside beach, snorkeling, 2.5-acre pool with water slides off a shipwreck, unlimited use of Disney World transportation system.

What to expect: an upscale Disney-operated hotel recreating the atmosphere of a New England resort in the late 1880s. The 635-room Yacht Club's wooden entrance-bridge, clapboard exterior, lighthouse and anchored yacht add to the New England nautical flavor. The landscape even sprouts evergreen trees instead of Florida palms. The five-story Yacht Club, along with its sister hotel the Beach Club, sits on the shore of a 50-acre lake near Epcot Center's World Showcase. Water taxis shuttle guests between the hotel and the Disney MGM Studios Theme Park. And Epcot's International Gateway entrance near the French pavilion is just a short walk or a quick tram ride away. A lakeside boardwalk leads to the hotel's recreation area.

TravelVenture tip: The Yacht Club offers its guests a special-request food service that can accommodate practically all diets. Your special diet request is made when you check in and is available both through room service and selected restaurants in the hotel.

Index

A

Adventureland, 87-89; map, 85
Adventureland Veranda, 174
Adventurers Club, 146-147
Albin Polasek Galleries, 17-18; map, 20
Airlines, 7-8
Alfred Hitchcock: The Art of Making Movies, 124
Alfredo's, 202-203
American Adventure Pavilion, The, 67
American Journeys, 96
Amtrak, 8
Anacomical Players, 58
Animal Actors Stage, 126
Animation Tour, 30-31
Arabian Nights, 135; map, 136
Atlantis restaurant, 174-175; map, 178
Atlantis Theater Water Ski Show, 108
Au Petit Cafe, 175
Aunt Polly's Landing, 175
Auto Train, 8

B

Back to the Future, 126
Backlot Express, 176
Backstage Magic, 56
Backstage Plaza, 32
Backstage Studio Tour, The, 31-34
Barney's Steak & Seafood House, 176-177; map, 178
Beach Club Resort, 221-222; map, 224
Bed and breakfast, 19, 52
Belz Factory Outlet World, 151; map, 159
Beverly Hills Boulangerie, 177
Biergarten, 177-179
Big Thunder Mountain Railroad, 90
Bijutsu-kan Gallery, 68
Bistro de Paris, Le, 179-180
Body Wars, 57
Boneyard, The, 125
Boulangerie Patisserie, 180
Broadway at the Top, 136-137; map, 139
Buses, 8

C

Cage, 147
Calling Dick Tracy, 29
Canadian Pavilion, 73
Cantina de San Angel, 180-181
Captain Eo, 59
Cap'n Jack's Oyster Bar, 181

Cap'n Kids' World, 108-110
Car rental, 9-10
Caribbean Beach Resort, 222-223; map, 224
Carousel of Progress, 97
Catastrophe Canyon, 32
Cellier, Le, 181-182
Character breakfasts, 172-173
Charles Hosmer Morse Museum of American Art, 18-19; map, 20
Chef Mickey's Village Restaurant, 182-183
Chefs de France, Les, 183-184
Chinese Pavilion, 64-65
Chinese Theater, 30
Chip and Dale's Country Morning Jamboree Breakfast Show, 172
Christini's, 184; map, 178
Church Street Market, 42, 151-152; map, 155
Church Street Station, 39-42, 137-138; maps, 41, 137
Church Street Station Exchange, 40, 47, 152-153; map, 155
Cinderella Castle, 94
Cinderella's Golden Carrousel, 94
Cinemagic Center, 126
Colonial Plaza Mall, 153; map, 155
Columbia Harbour House, 184-185
Comedy Warehouse, The, 147
Comfort Inn at Lake Buena Vista, 223-224; map, 227
CommuniCore, 54-56
Contemporary Resort, 225-226; map, 224
Coral Reef Restaurant, 185
Cornell Fine Arts Center, 20; map, 20
Cosmic Concerts, 102
Country Bear Jamboree, 90
Cranium Command, 57
Crossroads of Lake Buena Vista, 153-154; map, 158
Crossroads of the World, 26

Crystal Palace, The, 186

D

Dansk Factory Outlet, 154; map, 159
Day's Inn-Civic Center/Sea World, 226; map, 240
Days Inn-Lake Buena Vista Resort, 226-227; map, 227
Diamond Horseshoe Jamboree, The, 91
Dining, 168-214
    Disney-MGM Studios Theme Park, 168-169
    Disney Village Marketplace, 171-172
    Epcot Center, 169-171
    Magic Kingdom, 171
    Pleasure Island, 171
    Sea World, 173-174
    Universal Studios Florida, 173
    Vegetarian meals, 173
Discovery Island, 21-22; map, 23
Disney Inn, The, 227-228; map, 224
Disney Learning Adventures, 22-23; map, 23
Disney-MGM Studios Theme Park, 23-38; maps, 23, 27
    Animation Tour, 30-31
    Backstage Studio Tour, The, 31-34
    Dining, 168-169
    Don't miss, 25
    Great Movie Ride, The, 34-35
    Hours, 23
    How to see, 24-25
    Indiana Jones Epic Stunt Spectacular, 35-36
    Monster Sound Show, The, 36-37
    Muppet Theater, 37
    Price, 23-24
    Star Tours, 37
    Superstar Television, 37-38

Disney Village Marketplace, 154-155; map, 224
Disney's Village Resort, 228-229; map, 224
Disney World
    Character breakfasts, 66-67
    Dining, 168-173
    Discovery Island, 21-22; map, 23
    Disney Learning Adventures, 22-23; map, 23
    Disney-MGM Studios Theme Park, 23-38; maps, 23, 27; see also: Disney-MGM Studios Theme Park
    Disney Village Marketplace, 154-155; map 158
    Epcot Center, 49-73; maps 50, 55; see also: Epcot Center
    Epcot Center dining, 169-171
    Hotels, 219-220; map, 224
    Magic Kingdom, 81-97; maps, 82, 85; see also: Magic Kingdom
    Pleasure Island, 146-148, 162; maps, 139, 158
    River Country, 104-105; map, 105
    Typhoon Lagoon, 118-120; map, 116
    Wonders of Walt Disney World, 130-131
Dolphin: see Walt Disney World Dolphin
Downtown Orlando Walking Tour, 38-47; map, 41
Dreamflight, 96
Dumbo, the Flying Elephant, 94

E

E.T. Adventure, 126
Earthquake — The Big One, 125

Econo Lodge-International Drive, 229; map, 240
Electronic Forum, 56
Elvis Presley Museums, 47-49; maps, 48
Embassy Suites-Plaza International, 229; map, 230
Empress Lilly, 171-172
Enchanted Tiki Birds, 89
Epcot Center, 49-73; maps, 50, 55
    American Adventure, The, 67
    Canada, 73
    China, 64-65
    CommuniCore, 54-56
    Dining, 169-171
    Don't miss, 51
    France, 70-72
    Future World, 53, 54-56; map, 55
    Germany, 65
    Horizons, 58
    Hours, 49
    How to see, 50
    Italy, 65-66
    Japan, 67-68
    Journey into Imagination, 59
    Land, The, 59-60
    Living Seas, The, 60-61
    Mexico, 62
    Morocco, 68-70
    Norway, 62-64
    Price, 49
    Spaceship Earth, 54
    United Kingdom, 72-73
    Universe of Energy, 56
    Wonders of Life, 57-58
    World of Motion, 58-59
    World Showcase, 61-73; map, 55
Epcot Outreach, 56-57

F

Famous Host Inn, 230; map, 231

Fantasy Theater, 110
Fantasyland, 93-94; map, 85
Fantasyland Theater, 94
Farmers Market, 186-187
Feeding Pools, 110
Fez House, 69
50's Prime Time Cafe, 187
Finnegan's Bar & Grill, 188
Fireworks Factory, The, 188-189
Fisherman's Deck, 189-190
Florida Mall, The, 155-156; map, 159
Flying Tigers Warbird Air Museum, 73-75; map, 74
Fort Liberty Wild West Dinner Show & Trading Post, 138-140; map, 139
Fort Wilderness Resort and Campground, 230-231; map, 224
Four Winds Motel, 232; map, 231
French Pavilion, 70-72
Front Lot, 124
Frontierland, 90-91; map, 85
Funtastic World of Hanna-Barbera, The, 124
Future World, 53, 54-61; map, 55

G

Gallery of Arts and History, 69
Gemini Motel, 233; map, 231
Gator Jumparoo Show, 76
Gatorland Zoo, 75-77; map, 77
German Pavilion, 65
Gertrude's Walk, 47
Ghostbusters, 125
Goofy About Health, 58
Grand Floridian Beach Resort, 233-234; map, 224
Grand Prix Raceway, 97
Grandma Duck's Farm, 95
Great Movie Ride, The, 34-35
Guest Quarters Suite Resort, 234; map, 224

H

Hall of Prayer for Good Harvest, 64
Hall of Presidents, The, 91
Hard Rock Cafe, 190-191; map, 193
Harvest Theater, 60
Harvest Tour, 60
Haunted Mansion, The, 92
Hawaiian Rhythms, 110
Hilton at Walt Disney World Village, 235; map, 224
Hollywood, 126
Hollywood and Vine Cafeteria, 191
Hollywood Brown Derby, The, 191-192
Hoop-Dee-Doo Musical Revue, 140; map, 139
Horizons, 58
House of the Whispering Willows, 65
Hyatt Orlando, 235-236; map, 231
Hyatt Regency Grand Cypress Resort, 236-237; map, 227

I

Il Teatro di Bologna, 66
Image Works, 59
Impressions de France, 71
Indiana Jones Epic Stunt Spectacular, 35-36
International Food Bazaar, 192-193
Italian Pavilion, 65-66
It's a Small World, 93
Ivanhoe Antique Row, 156-157; map, 155

J

Japanese Pavilion, 67-68
Jaws, 125
John Young Planetarium, 220
Journey into Imagination, 59
Jungle Cruise, 88

INDEX

K

King Henry's Feast, 140-141; map, 142
King Stefan's Banquet Hall, 193-194
Kissimmee Livestock Market, 77-78; map, 79
Kissimmee Manufacturer's Mall, 157; map, 156
Kissimmee-St.Cloud Convention and Visitors Bureau , 10
Kitchen Kabaret, 60
Knights Inn-Main Gate, 237; map, 231
Kongfrontation, 125
Kringla Bakeri og Kafe, 194

L

Land Grille Room, The, 195
Land, The, 59-60
Leu Gardens and Leu House Museum, 78-81; map, 79
Liberty Inn, 195-196
Liberty Square, 91-93; map, 85
Liberty Square Riverboat, 91
Liberty Tree Tavern , 196-197
Linda's La Cantina, 197
Listen to the Land, 59
Little Darlin's Rock 'n' Roll Palace, 141; map, 142
Living Seas, The, 61
Lodging, 219-248
    Disney World, 219-220
    Lake Buena Vista area, 220
    Kissimmee area, 220-221
    International Drive area, 221
Lombard's Landing, 197-198
Louie's Italian Restaurant, 199
Lottery, The, 34
Lotus Blossom Cafe, 198

M

Mad Tea Party, 94
Maelstrom, 63
Magic Eye Theater, 59
Magic Journeys, 94
Magic Kingdom, 81-97; maps, 82, 85
    Adventureland, 87-89; map 85
    Dining, 171
    Don't miss, 83
    Fantasyland, 93-94; map 85
    Frontierland, 90-91; map 85
    Hours, 81
    How to see, 82-83
    Liberty Square, 91-93; map 85
    Main Street, U.S.A., 86-87; map 85
    Mickey's Starland, 94-95; map 85
    Price, 81
    Tomorrowland, 95-97; map 85
Main Street Cinema, 87
Main Street, U.S.A., 86-87; map, 85
Making of Me, The, 58
Mannequins Dance Palace, 147
Maple Leaf Motel, 237-238; map, 231
Mardi Gras, 143; map, 142
Mark Two Dinner Theater, 143-144; map, 145
Marriott's Orlando World Center, 238; map, 227
Medieval Life, 97-98; map, 96
Medieval Times, 144; map, 142
Meet Mickey Mouse, 95
Mel's Drive In, 199
Mercado Mediterranean Village, 157; map, 159
Mexican Pavilion, 62
Mickey's Starland, 94-95; map, 85
Mickey's Hollywood Theater, 95
Mickey's House, 95
Mickey's Tropical Revue, 148
Mike Fink Keelboats, 91
Min and Bill's Dockside Diner, 199-200
Mission to Mars, 96
Mitsukoshi Restaurant, 200-201

Monster Sound Show, The, 36-37
Moroccan Pavilion, 68-70
Morse Museum of American Art, 18-19; map, 20
Mr. Toad's Wild Ride, 94
Muppet Theater, 37
"Murder She Wrote!" Post Production, 124
Mystery Fun House, 98; map, 99

N

Neon Armadillo Music Saloon, 147
New York Street, 32
Nickelodeon Studios Production Tour, 124
Nine Dragons Restaurant, 201
Norseman, The, 64
Norwegian Pavilion, 62-64
Now Shooting, 124-125

O

O Canada, 73
Odyssey Restaurant, 201-202
Old Town, 158-160; map, 156
On Location, 125-126
Orange County Historical Museum, 99-101; map, 100
Originale Alfredo di Roma Ristorante, Le, 202-203
Orlando Fashion Square, 160; map, 155
Orlando Heritage Inn, 239; map, 240
Orlando Museum of Art, 101-102; map, 100
Orlando/Orange County Convention & Visitors Bureau, 10, 11
Orlando Science Center, 102-103; map, 100
Osceola Square Mall, 161; map, 156

P

Park Avenue, 161; map, 160
Park Inn International, 239; map, 231
Peabody Orlando, The, 241; map, 240
Penguin Encounter, 110-111
Penny Arcade, 87
Peter Pan's Flight, 94
Phantom of the Opera Horror Make-Up Show, The, 126
Pinocchio Village Haus, 203
Pirates of the Caribbean, 89
Plantation Dinner Theater, The, 145; map, 142
Plaza Pavilion, The, 203
Plaza Restaurant, The, 204
Pleasure Island, 146-148, 162; maps 139, 158
Polasek Galleries, 17-18; map, 20
Polynesian Luau Revue, 148; map, 139
Polynesian Village Resort, 241-242; map, 224
Portobello Yacht Club, 204-205
Post Production Editing and Audio, 34
Potter Train Museum, The, 103-104; map, 104
Production Central, 125
Production Studio Tour, 124
Pure and Simple, 205

Q

Quality Outlet Center, 162; map, 159

R

Red Roof Inn, 242; map, 231
Renaissance Street Theater, 72
Residential Street, 32
Restaurants, 168-214
    Disney-MGM Studios Theme Park, 168-169

Disney Village Marketplace, 171-172
Epcot Center, 169-171
Magic Kingdom, 171
Pleasure Island, 171
Sea World, 173-174
Universal Studios Florida, 173
Vegetarian meals, 173
Restaurant Akershus, 205-206
Restaurant Marrakech, 206-207
River Country, 104-105; map, 105
River of Time, The, 62
Rodeway Inn, 242-243; map, 240
Rose & Crown Pub & Dining Room, The, 207-208
Rosie O'Grady's Good Time Emporium, 40
Royal Orleans, 208; map, 178

S

San Angel Inn Restaurante, 208-209
Scenic Boat Tour, 105-106; map, 106
Sea Lion and Otter Show, 111
Sea World, 107-114; maps, 109
    Atlantis Theater Water Ski Show, 108
    Cap'n Kids' World, 108-110
    Don't miss, 107
    Fantasy Theater, 110
    Feeding Pools, 110
    Hawaiian Rhythms, 110
    Penguin Encounter, 110-111
    Price, 107
    Sea Lion and Otter Show, 111
    Sea World Theater, 111
    Shamu Stadium, 111-112
    Sharks, 112-113
    Sting Ray Feeding Presentations, 113
    Tropical Reef, 113-114
    Whale and Dolphin Stadium, 114
Sea World Theater, 111

Shamu Stadium, 111-112
Sharks, 112-113
Sheraton World, 243; map, 240
Shopping, 151-162
Sid Cahuenga's One-of-a-Kind, 28
Silver Meteor,The, 8, 41
Silver Star, The, 8, 41
Sinkhole, The, 114-117; map, 116
Skyway, 94
Snow White's Adventures, 94
Sommerfest, 209
Sound Works, 36
Soundations, 36
Soundstage Restaurant, 209-210
Space Mountain, 54
Spaceship Earth, 168-169
Special Effects Workshop and Shooting Stage, 33
Star Conversation, 29
Star Tours, 37
Stargate Restaurant, 210
StarJets, 97
Steerman's Quarters, 211
Sting Ray Feeding Presentations, 113
Stouffer Hotel Orlando Sea World, 243-244; map, 240
Studio Stars Restaurant, 211-212
Sunrise Terrace, 212
Superstar Television, 37-38
Swan: see Walt Disney World Swan
Swiss Family Treehouse, 88
Symbiosis, 60

T

Theater of the Stars, 29
Tide Pool, 114
Tom Sawyer Island, 90
Tomorrowland, 95-97; map, 85
Tomorrowland Terrace, 212-213
Tony's Town Square Restaurant, 213
Top of The World: see Broadway at the Top

Tourist information centers, 10-11
Travelodge Hotel, 244-245; map, 224
TravelPlanners, 4-5
Tropical Reef, 113-114
Tupperware International Headquarters, 117-118; map, 116
20,000 Leagues Under the Sea, 93
Typhoon Lagoon, 118-120; map, 105

U

United Kingdom Pavilion, 72-73
Universal Studios Florida, 120-126; map, 122, 123
   Alfred Hitchcock: The Art of Making Movies, 124
   Animal Actors Stage, 126
   Back to the Future, 126
   Boneyard, The, 125
   Cinemagic Center, 126
   Dining, 173
   Don't miss, 121
   E.T. Adventure, 126
   Earthquake — The Big One, 125
   Front Lot, 124
   Funtastic World of Hanna-Barbera, The, 124
   Ghostbusters, 125
   Hard Rock Cafe, 190-191; map, 193
   Hollywood, 126
   How to see, 120-121
   Jaws, 125
   Kongfrontation, 125
   "Murder She Wrote!" Post Production, 124
   Nickelodeon Studios Production Tour, 124
   Now Shooting, 124-125
   On Location, 125-126
   Phantom of the Opera Horror Make-Up Show, The, 126
   Price, 120
   Production Studio Tour, 124
Universe of Energy, 56

W

Walking Tour, Downtown Orlando, 38-47; map, 41
Walt Disney Story, The, 87
Walt Disney Theater, The, 34
Walt Disney World: see Disney World
Walt Disney World Dolphin, 245; map, 224
Walt Disney World Swan, 245-246; map, 224
Walt Disney World Railroad, 87
Water Effects Tank, 33
Water Mania, 127-128; map, 127
WEDway PeopleMover, 95
Wet 'n Wild, 128-130; map, 129
Whale and Dolphin Stadium, 114
Wilson World Hotel Main Gate, 246; map, 231
Wonders of China, 65
Wonders of Life, 57-58
Wonders of Walt Disney World, 130-131
World of Motion, 58-59
World Showcase, 61-73; map, 55
Wynfield Inn-Main Gate East, 247; map, 231
Wynfield Inn-Westwood, 247; map, 240

X

Xanadu — Home of the Future, 131-132; map, 131
XZFR Rockin' Rollerdome, 147

Y

Yacht Club Resort, 247; map, 224
Yakitori House, 214

"What a great adventure story....this is absolutely never-put-it-down reading, even if you don't particularly care about motorcycling or jungles."
— Clive Thomas, WWNZ-AM

Obsessions Die Hard
Motorcycling the Pan American Highway's Jungle Gap
Ed Culberson

Take the armchair adventure of your life! *Obsessions Die Hard* is a thrilling, true adventure tale. It's also an inspiring story of how courage and perseverance can overcome adversity and failure.

Obsessions Die Hard chronicles retired U.S. Army colonel Ed Culberson's determination to fulfill his dream. Culberson wanted to ride his motorcycle along the Pan American Highway between Alaska and Argentina. But in Panama and Colombia the road is broken by an 80-mile gap filled with jungles, rain forests, rivers and swamps.

The Darien Gap forces travelers between North and South America to detour around it by boat or plane. That gap, known as *el Tapón* in Spanish — The Stopper, didn't stop Ed Culberson's dream. It turned it into an obsession.

Armed with a "don't-shoot-him" letter signed by Panamanian General Noriega, the 56-year-old Culberson motorcycles into the gap to confront its dangers. But he suffers failure before meeting success. And along the way he encounters killer bees, arrest by a corrupt law officer, cycling injuries and back-breaking labor to get himself and "Amigo," his BMW motorcycle, through the torturous jungles and swamps.

He also encounters strangers who become friends, including Cuna Indians who guide him and share his triumphs.

"*Obsessions Die Hard* is a riveting account of Culberson's unusual trek through the Darien jungle. I recommend it, unreservedly, to anyone interested in reading an extremely well-written true adventure story."
— Nancy Grimison, *Panama Canal Record*

Don't miss the best adventure story to come along in years
Get *Obsessions Die Hard* today
$11.95 Softcover

If not available in your bookstore
Call toll-free 800-654-0403

Don't buy another airline ticket until you read this book

Fly There For Less
How to Save Money Flying Worldwide

Bob Martin

Save up to hundreds of dollars on your next airline ticket! Whether frequent or infrequent flyer, this book shows you hundreds of concrete, easily followed techniques to consistently obtain the lowest fares on domestic and international flights.

Fly There For Less reveals how the airlines establish and market their fares — and tells you how to put this information to work cutting the cost of your air travel. You'll discover how to search out the lowest fares so that you can:

• Save up to 25 percent on air fare by simply selecting the right flight to your destination.

• Cut the cost of flying with little-known fare types.

• Dramatically decrease your fare by selecting the right airline. One traveler using this strategy flew from London to Nairobi, Kenya, for just $230!

• Uncover nontraditional ticket sources that save you up to 60 percent off the lowest promotional fares.

• Open up low-fare opportunities with air courier travel, frequent flyer programs, last-minute travel clubs and barter exchanges.

• Reap savings by being alert to circumstances offering air-travel bargains.

• Master creative techniques such as buying two tickets instead of one to save money.

Stop spending more than you need to on air travel

Get *Fly There For Less* today
and put these money-saving techniques to work for you
$14.95 Softcover

If not available in your bookstore
Call toll-free 800-654-0403

The reviewers agree — *Fly There For Less* saves you money

"Here is a coherent guide to ferreting out favorable fares....a handy reference for cost-conscious travelers....fascinating."
— *Travel & Leisure*

"*Fly There For Less* guides the air traveler through a maze of air fares....You can save some mega bucks from Martin's creative techniques and strategies."
— *Los Angeles Times*

"An exciting new travel guide called *Fly There For Less*....can save you a substantial amount of money."
— **Arthur Frommer**

"Author Bob Martin helps air travelers get the lowest fares on domestic and international flights."
— *USA Today*

"An informative new handbook, *Fly There For Less,* can help the harried business traveler who doesn't have unlimited resources."
— *The Philadelphia Inquirer*

"In this easy-to-read book, Martin gives you the details so you can decide which (strategies) will work for you."
— *Seattle Post-Intelligencer*

"Included in this book are more strategies for saving money in the air than anyone ever thought possible. This is a great book for travelers looking for ways to avoid handing the airline industry more than they have to."
— *Going Places*

"This guide, whether you travel for business or pleasure, will give you timeless techniques and tips on how to pay the lowest possible airfare every time you fly."
— *Chattanooga News-Free Press*

"*Fly There For Less* details cost-cutting methods that can be used by any international traveler."
— *Toronto Sun*

If not available in your bookstore
Call toll-free 800-654-0403

Explore the Everglades **not only guides you through this unique wonder of nature, it helps you understand it.**

Explore the Everglades

Miriam Lee Ownby

No other place on earth resembles Florida's Everglades. A wide, shallow river of grass, it flows from Lake Okeechobee south and southwest to Florida Bay and the Gulf of Mexico. It is home to myriad varieties of birds and ruled over by that prehistoric survivor, the American alligator.

Miriam Lee Ownby's *Explore the Everglades* guides you through the "Glades." Along the way she shows you the features that make the Everglades unique. She points out the vegetation and the wildlife. And she explains the significance of what you see. With *Explore the Everglades* you can discover:

• Habitats such as hardwood hammocks, tree islands, sloughs and sawgrass prairies.

• The animals, birds and trees that find a home in the Glades, including the endangered woodstork and Florida panther.

• The human inhabitants of the Glades — the Miccosukee Indians.

• The interrelationships of life, land and water that build the Everglades ecosystem.

• Man's impact on the Everglades, from poachers to developers to polluters.

• Efforts to return the Everglades system to its condition in 1900.

Whether an armchair traveler or planning a visit, this book will give you an appreciation of the Everglades and the problems that threaten its very existence.

Enrich your travels through understanding

Get *Explore the Everglades* today
$9.95 Softcover — Available June 1991

If not available in your bookstore
Call toll-free 800-654-0403